Cognition and Representation

Cognition and Representation

EDITED BY
Stephen Schiffer
and Susan Steele

A Westview Special Study

This Westview softcover edition is printed on acid-free paper and bound in softcovers that carry the highest rating of the National Association of State Textbook Administrators, in consultation with the Association of American Publishers and the Book Manufacturers' Institute.

Published in 1988 in the United States of America by Westview Press, Inc., 5500 Central Avenue, Boulder, Colorado 80301, and in the United Kingdom by Westview Press, Inc., 13 Brunswick Centre, London WC1N 1AF, England

Library of Congress Cataloging-in-Publication Data
Cognition and representation.
Includes bibliographies.
1. Cognition. 2. Mental representation.
3. Cognition in children. 4. Psycholinguistics.
I. Schiffer, Stephen R. II. Steele, Susan.
BF311.C5486 1988 153 88-20901
ISBN 0-8133-7656-4

Printed and bound in the United States of America

∞ The paper used in this publication meets the requirements of the American National Standard for Permanence of Paper for Printed Library Materials Z39.48-1984.

10 9 8 7 6 5 4 3 2 1

Contents

PART 3
COGNITIVE DEVELOPMENT

PART 4
SEMANTIC THEORY

Contributors

Bruce M. Bennett
Department of Mathematics
University of California
Irvine, California

Susan Carey
Department of Psychology
MIT
Cambridge, Massachusetts

Lynn A. Cooper
Department of Psychology
Columbia University
New York, New York

Gilbert Harman
Department of Philosophy
Princeton University
Princeton, New Jersey

Donald D. Hoffman
Department of Social Sciences
University of California
Irvine, California

Henry E. Kyburg, Jr.
Department of Philosophy
University of Rochester
Rochester, New York

Richard T. Oehrle
Department of Linguistics
University of Arizona
Tucson Arizona

Daniel N. Osherson
Department of Psychology
MIT
Cambridge, Massachusetts

Thomas Roeper
Department of Linguistics
University of Massachusetts
Amherst, Massachusetts

Edward E. Smith
Department of Psychology
University of Michigan
Ann Arbor, Michigan

Scott Soames
Department of Philosophy
Princeton University
Princeton, New Jersey

Introduction

Cognitive science is an interdisciplinary study of the nature of human information processing. It seeks to describe the ways in which knowledge and goals are represented and the faculties and algorithms that govern the transitions of mental representations in the acquisition of sensory knowledge, and in theoretical and practical reasoning. Cognitive science, accordingly, draws on the traditional disciplines that are concerned with aspects of mental functions: philosophy, psychology, and linguistics, among others.

In 1984 and 1985, the Cognitive Science program at the University of Arizona, with the assistance of the Arizona Humanities Council, invited a number of the most distinguished researchers in cognitive science to present a series of colloquia on the state-of-the-art in their fields. The goal of these colloquia was to identify some of the leading issues and approaches that currently dominate research in cognitive science. This book is a result of, and shares the goal of, these colloquia.

The papers are divided into four groups, each representing a general area of inquiry within cognitive science: The nature and content of psychological theories, Mental representation, Cognitive development, and Semantic theory.

THE NATURE AND CONTENT OF PSYCHOLOGICAL THEORIES

In "Wide Functionalism," **Gilbert Harman** begins with the assumption that psychological explanation is a kind of functional explanation: the psychological states invoked in psychological explanation are to be individuated not in terms of the physical states that realize them but in terms of the functional roles they play in a creature's psychology. The question he addresses is whether psychological explanations are typically wide as opposed to narrow psychological explanations. Wide functional explanations appeal to the actual or possible environments of the creature whose activity is being explained, whereas narrow functional explanation "appeals only to internal states of the creature and says nothing about how the creature functions in relation to an actual or possible environment." Adherence to "methodological solipsism" and certain "Twin-Earth" considerations have, Harman claims, led Jerry Fodor and others to hold that psychological explanations are always narrow functional explanations. But, Harman argues, this is wrong: psychological explanations are typically wide functional explanations. He argues that we wouldn't know how psychological states worked if we didn't understand their relation to the agent's environment and to his actions, and that this is why actual explanations in psychology do refer to the environmental causes of, and to the activity caused by, the agent's psychological states. He argues further that narrow functionalism isn't even methodologically coherent and that Twin-Earth arguments for it are unsound.

Harman's position has important implications for the nature of semantic theories for languages of thought, that is, for inner systems of mental representations. Conceptual-role semantics holds that the content of a mental representation is partly or wholly determined by its functional role in perceptual belief fixation and practical and theoretical reasoning. Theorists who maintain that functional role should be construed narrowly are forced to adopt a two-level theory of content: one level will ascribe functional roles narrowly construed and the other level will ascribe a referential, truth-theoretic semantics. Harman, on the other hand, argues that the content of mental representation can be identified with its functional role if psychological explanations are typically wide functional explanations.

How important is the notion of causality to cognitive science? Not very, **Henry E. Kyburg, Jr.** answers in "Cognition and Causality." Causality, as a category of understanding, may be thought of in three ways: metaphysically, epistemologically, or psychologically. Kyburg argues that the metaphysical role of causality is a lot less significant than is usually thought, that the epistemological role is nil, and that the psychological role is merely of pathological interest. As regards its metaphysical role, he argues that universal causation, as a relation between individuals, can't be a necessary presupposition of science if quantum mechanics can get along without it. As regards its epistemological role, its role in causal reasoning, he argues that "arguments and inferences concerning causal agencies can be dealt with syntactically by the device of adding and deleting certain sentences in a set of sentences construed as a body of knowledge." If this strategy succeeds, then "an extensional language in which nothing more powerful than mere uniformities can be expressed" will suffice for the representation of all of our factual knowledge.

The psychological role of causality is pathological, Kyburg suggests, in that people employ the notion of causality because they are so strongly oriented toward the manipulation of the world, but this interesting fact provides no special role for causality in rational thought. If we can find no better rationale for the notion of causality than the ones we have, then, he concludes, we should do without it.

MENTAL REPRESENTATION

Edward E. Smith and **Daniel N. Osherson's** paper is a study of the "compositionality problem" in typicality. Typicality is a relation between an instance and a concept. The instances of any simple concept, where a simple concept is taken to be that denoted by a single word, vary in how typical they are judged to be. Instances of complex concepts -- in particular for this paper, those denoted by adjective-noun combinations -- also vary for typicality. The problem is how to compute typicality for complex concepts from the simple concepts which compose it.

Smith and Osherson reject all versions of what they term the "external" approach (e.g. fuzzy set theory) -- so-called because the computation doesn't depend on the mental representation of the simple concepts. In such, typicality of an instance in a complex concept is a function of no more than its typicality with respect to the constituent concepts. To use their example, on this view, a guppie cannot be a better instance of pet fish than it is either pet or fish. But, Smith and Osherson claim, it is.

They argue, rather, for one interpretation of the "internal" approach. This approach turns on interpreting prototype as an abstract summary that applies to all members of a class. For any attribute associated with a concept, the relevant values are listed accompanied by a probability score. For example, say, that one of the attributes of fish is size. Let's say further that most fish are between two and 15 inches, although there are both smaller and larger fish. The values associated with size will represent and indicate the relative strength of all these possibilities. Any instance will, of course, fall into one of the three size classes we have established. Given the probability scores, where it falls will allow the computation of its prototypicality. The model presented allows a resolution of the distinction between typicality and vagueness. An atypical instance reflects a judgement of typicality, while an unclear instance reflects vagueness.

Lynn A. Cooper's paper examines the nature of the mental representations and processing operations that contribute to skill in solving spatial problems. Cooper's analysis of cognitive skill is an argument for the existence of multiple cognitive models addressing a single representational problem. Individuals differ in their ability to judge whether different two-dimensional representations of an object are equivalent, i.e. whether they represent the same object. One account of such differences has been that individuals construct the same kind of cognitive model in solving this representational problem, but vary in their efficiency. Cooper, however, argues that a single model is not adequate. Rather different kinds of cognitive models are available, but individuals may vary in their control of the models. For the specific problem at issue in her research, two strategies appear to exist. One involves the generation of a three-dimensional model consistent with the two-dimensional views; the second involves a number of local comparisons of the two-dimensional views. Individuals vary not only in which strategy they choose, but also in the flexibility of alternating strategies.

An interesting question is raised by the first strategy: "Given that the construction of an internal model corresponding to a three-dimensional object must require time, effort, and processing resources, why should such a construction occur when the problem solving task does not require it?" Cooper suggests that the answer to this question has to do with the unifying character of such a representation: this kind of model encodes information for many tasks of spatial reasoning and thus eliminates the need for additional computations on different pieces of stored information.

Cognitive science seeks to know the information-processing procedures by which we arrive at representations of the external world, and it would like to know the nature of the meaning and truth conditions of those representations. Computational theories of vision assume that vision is a nondemonstrative inferential process whereby a visual system infers representations of the environment from images. In "Perceptual Representations: Meaning and Truth Conditions," **Donald D.Hoffman** and **Bruce M. Bennett** offer an account of the meaning and truth conditions of the visual representations that are the outputs of those inferences.

They first rigorously define the notion of an observer, which notion is itself a formalization of the visual system's nondemonstrative inferences. Their account of the meaning and truth conditions of visual representations is given in terms of the defined notion of an observer. This account is, in ways Hoffman and Bennett elaborate, causal and teleological, but makes no mention of functional role. The reader may therefore be interested to compare their account of mental representation with the conceptual-role theory sketched by Harman.

COGNITIVE DEVELOPMENT

Susan Carey argues for a theory of the child's cognitive development that mirrors the kind of knowledge restructuring familiar in the history of science. Children four to five years old differ systematically from adults and older children in their responses to tasks of basic reasoning. The Piagetian view of this fact was that young children have fundamentally different computational and representational capacities. Thus, the differences on a wide range of tasks devolve to a small number of basic cognitive concepts. More recently, researchers in cognitive development have come to believe that the child's cognitive capacities are not distinct in any important sense. The problem has been, then to explain the different responses in anything other than a piecemeal fashion.

Carey's proposal is an attempt to resolve this dilemma. She accepts the current view of the "competent child", but also maintains "that there are far reaching reorganizations of knowledge that unify the description of what might otherwise seem myriad piecemeal changes". Basically, the young child has a theory about a general domain of knowledge -- say, biology (an example that Carey explores in some detail). As the child's experience grows, she or he comes across new pieces of data which must be incorporated in the theory. Ultimately, the strain of incorporating data into the theory results in a change in the theory.

The critical issue for Carey, of course, as she herself recognizes, is the last one. What is theory change? What kind of evidence or weight of evidence triggers such a change in the organization of knowledge?

The issue concerning **Thomas Roeper** is that articulated by Carey but applied to a particular domain of development: Since the linguistic behavior of young children (even younger than Carey's four-year-olds) is obviously different from that of adults, what accounts for the development from child grammars to adult grammars?

Roeper's position is not obviously compatible with the wholesale theory change suggested by Carey. Rather, Roeper uses the "subset principle" as his touchstone. The "subset principle" (from Berwick 1985) is the idea that each "step of a chid's acquisition of grammar must involve movement from a smaller set to a larger set" and never the reverse. The major value of this principle for Roeper is the existence of situations where it appears not to apply -- forcing exploration for an alternative hypothesis.

Roeper examines three examples of acquisition where the two grammars in question are not in a subset relation. All his examples turn on the notion of parametric variation. Parametric variation is the attempt to incorporate into linguistic theory the fact that grammars differ. For example, some languages have obligatory lexical subjects and some don't; English is an example of the former and Italian, of the latter. Since children have to be able to learn both English and Italian, grammatical theory has to include both possibilities -- as well as offering an explanation of how a child decides on the basis of primary data which kind of language she or he is hearing.

Such situations have been argued to present "retreat" cases of acquisition. For example, the data suggest that a child in an English-speaking environment might make the "Italian" choice, only to revise it later. Roeper's idea is that such cases can be solved by a fully articulated modular theory of grammar.

SEMANTIC THEORY

A semantic theory states the information sentences encode relative to contexts, and semantic competence seems to consist in the ability to pair sentences with what they contextually encode. It is therefore tempting to conclude that a semantic theory is itself a theory of competence, at least in the sense that semantic competence consists in knowing what a correct semantic theory states. **Scott Soames** argues that this is a temptation to be resisted. According to Soames, the theorems of a semantic theory should say what proposition each sentence expresses relative to a context of utterance, where the correct conception of propositions is Russellian. Soames spells out the Russellian theory of propositions (according to which, roughly speaking, the proposition expressed by 'Pluto is a plant' is the ordered pair <Pluto, the property of being a planet>), and then shows that, on the view of semantic theories advocated, knowledge of semantic theorems is not necessary and sufficient for semantic competence.

Having argued that understanding a sentence doesn't coincide with knowing what proposition it expresses, Soames uses this result against the familiar "Augustinian" picture of language competence. According to the Augustinian picture, the first language learner has a prior acquaintance with the objects, properties, and propositions that are, in fact, the semantic contents of expressions in the language he or she hopes to learn, and learning the language consists in learning to correlate expressions with the right contents. But this picture appears inconsistent with the noncoincidence Soames claims to have demonstrated. Besides, Soames argues, there is a more fundamental problem with the Augustinian picture. The picture requires us to grasp propositions prior to understanding sentences that express them. But often it is by virtue of understanding a sentence that one acquires knowledge of what proposition it expresses. The Augustinian picture has semantic competence deriving from semantic knowledge, but in many cases -- as when one's only epistemic contact with a proposition is mediated by sentences that express it -- it is just the reverse.

But what is the point of semantics, if not to account for semantic competence? Soames concludes his article by suggesting that semantic theories explicate the representational character of language and by elaborating on what such an explication would accomplish.

The issue of modularity which Roeper raises directly forms a subtext to **Richard T. Oehrle's** paper on the semantic effect of English stress. The problem is simple to illustrate: Each of the three words in the sequence *Bill shot Phil* can be the location of the nuclear accent, but the three sentences do not occur in identical contexts; how can the relation among syntactic form, stress, and context be characterized?

Oehrle's conclusion is that the full range of facts is "not predictable from properties of order and category alone, nor from discourse context alone." Rather than saying that each of these properties obeys some principle or set of principles and that such principle sets can interact, he argues for a theory that directly relates to the location of nuclear accent in a grammatical structure to its acceptability in some context. This theory is relatively powerful, in the sense that it accommodates a greater range of cases than those which actually occur. Oehrle's claim is that no weaker theory can accommodate the actually attested range. He concludes by showing a correlation between the accentual properties of an expression and its other grammatical properties, thereby introducing an inherent limit on the theoretical possibilities.

Stephen Schiffer
Department of Philosophy
City University of New York
New York, New York

Susan Steele
Department of Linguistics
University of Arizona
Tucson, Arizona

PART ONE

The Nature and Content of Psychological Theories

1

Wide Functionalism

Gilbert Harman

Psychological explanation is a kind of functional explanation[1] in the way that some biological explanation is. We explain the maintenance of bodily functions by appeal to processes involving heart, blood, lungs, arteries, veins, nerves, brain, stomach, and other organs. Organs are defined by their function, not their shape or physical constitution. A heart is an organ that pumps a creature's blood: it need not be any particular shape, nor does it have to be made from any particular material, as long as it serves that function. Similarly, psychological events and states can be physically realized in different ways in different creatures, as long as they play the relevant functional role in those creature's psychology. Pain is not be identified with a particular physical event, such as the stimulation of C-fibers, because other sorts of physical event might function as pain does, for example, as a kind of alarm system indicating that something wrong is going on at a particular place in the organism. (See Place 1956.) Beliefs and desires have distinctive functions, beliefs recording information about the world, desires specifying the goals of the system. Both sorts of states can be physically realized in various ways, perhaps even as states of intelligent machines.

I claim that psychological explanations are typically **wide** functional explanations. That is, I claim that such explanations typically appeal to an actual or possible environmental situation of the creature whose activity is being explained. A **narrow** functional explanation appeals only to internal states of the creature and says nothing about how the creature functions in relation to an actual or possible environment. I claim that there are few (if any) narrowly functional psychological explanations of this latter sort.

In arguing for this, I disagree with Jerry Fodor 1980 and others who hold that the relevant psychological explanations are always narrow functional explanations.

I begin with a short history of the issue. Then I say why most psychological explanations are wide functional explanations. Finally I indicate why twin-earth arguments do not show that all such explanations must be narrowly functional.

HISTORY OF THE ISSUE

Functionalism emerged from a behaviorism which identified psychological states and events with dispositions to respond in an appropriate way to appropriate stimuli, where a stimulus was usually conceived as a perceivable aspect of the environment and a response was usually identified with behavior appropriately affecting the environment. (See e.g. Morris 1946.) Such dispositions were "functionally" defined in the sense that they were compatible with various physical bases for the relevant stimulus/-response relations. Since stimulus and response were usually defined partly in terms of events in the environment, behavioristic theories tended to be instances of wide functionalism.

Nonbehavioristic functionalism allows psychological explanations appealing to internal states and events that mediate perceptual input and behavioral output. Many versions of non-behavioristic behaviorism retained the wide functionalism characteristic of behaviorism by continuing to conceive of the relation between perceptual inputs and behavioral outputs in terms of actual or possible environmental occurrences.

For example, in 1954 Wilfrid Sellars argued that we can think of the relevant intervening states and events as analogous to linguistic acts. He distinguished three sorts of functional "transitions" involving mental states and events -- entry transitions from events outside the system to states and events of the system, exit transitions from states and events in the system to outside events, and purely internal transitions between states and events of the system. The entry transitions represented the influence of perception on the system, the exit transitions represented the influence of the system on action, and the purely internal transitions represented inferences. All transitions were to be governed by rules of a Mentalese language game that a person has been conditioned to follow. Rules for entry into the system and exit from it referred explicitly to the environment. For example, a person might be conditioned to think, "That's red," on seeing something red under standard conditions or a person might be conditioned to interpose a pawn on having the thought, "I shall interpose my pawn now!" (See Sellars 1954 and 1963:321-358.)

Fifteen years later in 1969 Daniel Dennett argued that psychological explanation is explanation within an "Intentional system" and "for any system to be called Intentional it must be capable of discriminating and reacting to fairly complex features of its environment." For example, an animal has thoughts about food only if the perception of food under certain conditions can lead it to act appropriately toward the food, by eating it. (See Dennett 1969:72-73.) In 1973 I endorsed this claim of Dennett's and remarked on the way in which the attribution of psychological states makes implicit reference to a "normal case". (I observed that the point applies also to representational states of artificial devices such as a radar aimer used for shooting at enemy planes). I also argued that animals' mental representations must in part represent the satisfaction of their needs by means of appropriate behavior, so "those representations involve representation of a public world."

In 1976 Jonathan Bennett argued in elegant detail that the only likely strategy for explicating psychological notions like belief and desire takes the following form.[2] We must start with the notion of a teleological system. Such a system has an associated goal. To say that the system has such a goal is to say that the laws or principles of the system are such that it does what it can to ensure that the goal is secured.

Next, we need to observe that a system may or may not "register" certain information in its environment concerning what changes are needed in the environment to achieve its goals. The system will not do what is needed to ensure that its goal is secured unless it registers the information that this is needed to ensure that the goal is secured. To say that the system can register such information is to say that there are states of the system (1) that arise from the environment's being such that a certain action is needed in order to achieve the system's goal and (2) that lead the system to act in the required way.

Finally, we need to consider further complications. For example, a system will make mistakes when a state that normally would register a certain environmental situation is caused in an abnormal way and the system might therefore act in ways that will not satisfy its goals but would if the environment were as the system takes it to be. A system can have more than one goal at a time. And so on. Bennett argues that a system has states that are more and more like beliefs and desires as these and other complications are allowed for.

For our purposes, we can ignore the complications. What concerns us is Bennett's claim that psychological notions ultimately must be understood by appeal to concepts of teleology and registration that make reference to an actual or possible environment.

Robert Stalnaker 1984 has recently defended a similar account using a notion of "indication" that resembles Bennett's "registration". Stalnaker stresses that such an account presupposes a notion of "normal conditions." The perceptual belief that P is a state that occurs under normal conditions only if it true that P.[3] And other writers have advocated similar ideas with varying emphases. For example, Fred Dretske's theory (Dretske 1981) places stress mostly on the input or information side.

On the other hand, several writers have opted for a narrower functionalism. In 1960 W.V. Quine advocated a narrow behaviorism that identified a stimulus with a pattern of stimulation of sensory nerves. In a series of papers shortly afterward, Hilary Putnam 1960, 1964, 1967a, and 1967b argued for a nonbehavioristic narrow functionalism, which identified systems of mental states first with something like Turing machines possessing paper tape input and output and then, more realistically, with probabilistic automata possessing "motor outputs and sensory inputs."

Putnam soon abandoned this narrow functionalism because of its commitment to what he called "methodological solipsism." According to Putnam 1975:220, "When traditional philosophers talked about psychological states or 'mental' states), they made an assumption which we may call the assumption of methodological solipsism. This assumption is the assumption that no psychological state, properly so called, presupposes the existence of any individual other than the subject to whom that state is ascribed... This assumption is pretty explicit in Descartes, but it is implicit in just about the whole of traditional philosophical psychology." Putnam then rejected methodological solipsism with the enigmatic remark that "the three centuries of failure of mentalistic psychology is tremendous evidence against this procedure in my opinion."

Jerry Fodor 1981 commented, "I suppose this is intended to include everybody from Locke and Kant to Freud and Chomsky. I should have such failures." Fodor suggested that Putnam himself had provided an argument for methodological solipsism, roughly, the notorious twin-earth argument to be considered below. For that and other reasons Fodor claimed that mental states and processes are "computational", where computational operations are both **symbolic** and **formal**, "symbolic because they are defined over representations and ... formal because they apply to representation in virtue of (roughly) the **syntax** of the representations... Formal operations are the ones that are specified without reference to such semantic properties of representations as, for example, truth, reference, and meaning" (1981:226-227). The upshot is a narrowly functionalistic psychology.

Acceptance of methodological solipsism has led several writers to advocate so called "two-level" theories of meaning. These theories attempt to give an account of meaning by combining "conceptual role semantics" with a specification of conditions of truth and reference. Conceptual role semantics holds that the content of mental representations is partly or wholly determined by the functional role the representations play in the perception-inference-action language game of thought. The theory takes different forms depending on whether functional role is conceived widely or narrowly. Those who conceive functional role widely (Sellars 1954, Harman 1973 and 1987) argue that meaning can be identified with functional role. Other writers suppose that functional role must be conceived narrowly and therefore cannot account for all of the content of mental states. These writers include Hartry Field 1977, Brian Loar 1981, Stephen Schiffer 1981, and William G. Lycan 1984.

CONSIDERATIONS FAVORING WIDE FUNCTIONALISM

Wide functionalism is more plausible on its face than narrow functionalism. Ordinary psychological explanations are not confined to reports of inner states and processes. They often refer to what people perceive of the world and what changes they make to the world. Although some ordinary explanations refer to sensory input and some refer to motor output -- a hallucination, an attempt to move that fails -- even in these cases there is normally implicit reference to a possible environment. A hallucination of a pink elephant is a hallucination of something in the environment. An unsuccessful attempt to pick up the telephone is an attempt to move something in the environment. Furthermore, the explanation of someone's reaction to a hallucination is normally parasitic on explanations of how people react to veridical perception. And, explaining why someone made an unsuccessful attempt to do something is normally parasitic on explanations of successful action.[4]

Consider the hand-eye coordination involved in drawing a picture. This involves a complex interplay between perception and action. What is done next depends on the perception of what has been done so far as well as the perception of hand and pencil. No explanation of what the agent is doing can avoid reference to the effects the agent's act has on the world and the agent's perception of these effects.

Functional explanations in perceptual psychology often appeal to relations between sense organs and the environment, for example, when certain systems of neurons in the eye are identified as "edge detectors." The relevant explanation appeals to facts about edges in the external world, in particular, facts about the way light is differentially reflected to the eye from differently oriented surfaces that meet in an edge.

In Psychological Explanation Jerry Fodor (pp. 111-119) compares psychological explanation to automotive explanation. If we explain how an automobile works by appealing to valve-lifter, carburator, throttle, brakes, speedometer, and so forth, we appeal to parts of the automobile that are functionally defined. For present purposes it is useful to notice that some of these parts have a relatively internal function within the system, for example, the valve lifter and the carburator, whereas others have a function in relation to things outside the system, for example, the brakes are used to stop the automobile, and the speedometer functions to indicate to the driver what the speed is. This parallels the psychological case, in which edge detectors have a function in relation to external things and pain has a more internal function.

Functional explanations of automobiles and of people require the wide view. You do not understand what an automobile is and how it functions if you know only its internal operation independently of the fact that automobiles are vehicles that travel on roads to get people from one place to another, that the accelerator is pressed in order to make the car move, that the brake pedal is pressed in order to stop the car, that the gearshift is moved to a certain position in order to put the car "into reverse" so that it goes "backwards", and so forth. Similarly, you do not understand how people operate psychologically unless you see how their mental states are related to perception of the environment and to action. You do not understand what is going on in the eye unless you understand that the eye is an organ of perception, that certain systems of neurons in the eye function as edge detectors, and so on. If you understand only the uninterpreted program indicating the flow of information or energy in the system without saying what information is flowing, then you do not understand what is going on in the eye or in the brain.

Consider the following uninterpreted program: there are three possible input states, **A**, **B**, and **C**. **A** leads to output **X** and **C** leads to output **Y**; **B** has no effect. Do you understand what is going on? No. You need to know how this system is functioning. In fact, the system is a thermostatically controlled airconditioner. **A** is normally the result of a temperature greater than 72 degrees Farenheit. **B** is normally the result of a temperature between 68 and 72 degrees. **C** is normally the result of a temperature below 68 degrees. The output signal **X** turns on the airconditioner, if it is not already on. Otherwise it leaves it on. The output of **Y** turns off the airconditioner if it is on. Otherwise it leaves the airconditioner turned off. In order to understand this system you need to know the wide functional story. The narrow functional story is insufficient. This is not to deny that there is a narrow story. It is merely to observe that story is insufficient for understanding how the system functions.

Psychology is concerned to provide a functional understanding of people and other animals. Such an understanding requires the wider view. Otherwise, the relevant function of various aspects of the system is not sufficiently specified. This is not to deny the existence of a corresponding narrow story, an uninterpreted program. It is merely to observe that the narrow story is insufficient for psychology.

If you want to understand how a radio receiver works, you need to know that the receiver is designed to pick up signals sent by a transmitter and to convert them into audible sounds that can be heard by listeners. Just knowing how electrical currents flow through the system is not enough. You need to know that certain parts of the system are there in order to tune into signals transmitted at a certain frequency, part of the system functions to retrieve the frequency of the message from signal as it is encoded in a carrier frequency, part functions to screen out competing signals of nearby carrier frequencies, a different part functions to screen out interference from airplanes, and so forth.[5]

Furthermore, a purely narrow functionalism is **methodologically** incoherent. All sorts of currents flow in a radio receiver, only some of which are relevant to its functioning. Others are from that point of view merely leaks, of no importance. If something goes wrong, there may be short circuits. This classification into proper flow of current, leaks, and misfunctions such as short circuits depends on taking the wide functional view of the radio receiver. Nothing about its internal operation, narrowly conceived, dictates these distinctions. Narrow functionalism is not really **functionalism**, since it has no way to capture the relevant functions.

Methodological solipsism is similarly incoherent in psychology. There is no hope of isolating the relevant psychological components of a creature without considering how these components function in enabling the creature to deal with its environment. For example, it is necessary to identify certain parts of the creature as organs of perception. Without the wide view, there is no way to think of internal workings of the creature as a functional system, because there is no way to distinguish functional parts of the system from irrelevant parts and no way to distinguish cases in which something is functioning properly from cases of misfunction. Hallucination involves some sort of misfunction, but there is no way to capture this point within a narrow functionalism. Narrow functionalism is not an intelligible option in the philosophy of mind.

TWIN EARTH

Consider an agent Albert whose actions we wish to explain. Consider also all possible duplicates of Albert from the surface in who are in various possible environments. Some of these duplicates would be on Putnam's "Twin Earth" (Putnam 1975:220), which would resemble earth except that their "water" would not be H_2O but would have a complex chemical structure that Putnam abbreviates as XYZ. These duplicates would not be in the same wide functional states as Albert. For example, Albert believes that water is wet; his duplicate on Twin Earth would not. The Twin Earth duplicate would believe that what he called "water" was wet, but what he called "water" would not be water, since it would be XYZ rather than H_2O. Similarly, Albert sees a tree; one possible duplicate would hallucinate a tree; another would see a tree illusion.

Although Albert's duplicate on Twin Earth would not believe that water is wet, he would have a corresponding belief. His belief would function internally in exactly the say way that Albert's belief does. So we can say that Albert's duplicate on Twin Earth would be in the same belief-state as Albert; it would have the same narrow belief. Indeed, each of Albert's possible duplicates would be in a state corresponding to Albert's belief that water is wet. Each would be in the same narrow belief-state; they would all have the same narrow belief. Similarly, for each of Albert's other psychological states there would be a corresponding psychological state in every possible duplicate. Albert's duplicates would share narrow belief states with Albert.

Furthermore, whatever Albert does in response to sensory input will be exactly the same as what his various duplicates would do in response to the same sensory input. In whatever way that Albert's reaction is to be explained in terms of his psychological states, there would be analogous explanations of the reactions of his duplicates in terms of their corresponding psychological states.

Some writers (e.g. Lycan 1984:234-235) see this as an argument for methodological solipsism. They infer that only Albert's narrow psychological states are responsible for his reaction. His wide states are irrelevant, so his narrow psychological states rather than his wide psychological states are the relevant states for psychological explanation.

This is like saying that Charles' pushing Bob out of the boat was not the cause of Bob's drowning, since Bob would have drowned no matter who had pushed him out of the boat. In an official investigation of the cause of Bob's death, it is more relevant that Charles pushed him out of the boat than simply that **someone** pushed him out of the boar or that his body was subject to a force that pushed him out of the boat. The narrowest explanation is not always the relevant explanation. This is as true for psychology as it is for a court of inquiry into the cause of Bob's drowning. As I have already argued, psychological explanation is functional explanation and that specification of functions typically makes reference to an actual or possible environment.

This is not to say that every aspect of the environment is psychologically relevant. It may be relevant to psychological explanation that Albert is perceiving a transparent fluid but not relevant that what Albert is perceiving is water rather than, say, XYZ, if Albert cannot distinguish water from XYZ.

Many possible duplicates of Albert would think they were seeing water when they were not. Some would be hallucinating. Others would be brains in vats receiving the same sensory stimulation that Albert is receiving. But I claim that an understanding of what happens in such a case is parasitic on an understanding of what happens in veridical perception.

Although we can test the functioning of automobiles and radio receivers in the laboratory even though they are not functioning to drive people from one place to another or to receive broadcasts from radio transmitters, our understanding of the functioning of the tested automobiles and receivers depends on our envisioning them in the relevant context, namely, the context in which they are used to transport people or to receive broadcasts. Similarly, we understand the functioning of a brain in a vat by envisioning it as part of a person in the relevant environment.

CONCLUSION

Psychological explanation is wide functional explanation, because only a wide functionalism gives the understanding sought for in psychological explanations. It is possible to introduce a notion of narrow psychological function by abstraction from the notion of wide psychological function. But an autonomous narrow psychological functionalism would be incoherent, because only a wide psychological functionalism can motivate appropriate distinctions between aspects of a system, irrelevant side effects, and misfunctions.

NOTES

1. See especially Fodor 1968:xvi-xxi, 111-119 and Putnam 1967.

2. Bennett's 1976 analysis builds on an earlier account of teleological explanation by Taylor 1964.

3. Stalnaker 1984, especially p. 64, derives his account from Stampe 1977:42-43.

4. It is true that a person can have a hallucination without being taken in by it and a person can try to do something that he knows he will not succeed in doing. But these are special cases that require a certain amount of sophistication.

5. Smart 1968:91-120 suggests that understanding how people work is like understanding how a radio receiver works and that biology and psychology are therefore more like applied engineering than physical science.

2

Cognition and Causality

Henry E. Kyburg, Jr.

There are three ways in which considerations of causality may be regarded as appearing importantly in cognitive science. First there is the general claim that all science is the search for causes (and perhaps even that it presupposes universal causation), and therefore that **cognitive** science is the search for the causes of cognitive phenomena, and presupposes the doctrine of universal causation. Second there is the peculiarly intimate relation between reasons and causes in cognitive science. We might refer, for example, to "causal reasoning," and claim that much that goes on in the case of inference can be construed as causal reasoning, and should be regarded as subject to, or guided by, a logic appropriate to that kind of reasoning. Finally, it might be claimed that causal relations are of great **psychological** importance, whatever be their role metaphysically or scientifically. That is, whereas in the first place we might say that we are looking for the causes of certain mental phenomena, some of which may be the inferrings of causes among events in the non-mental world, in this last case we are asking for the role that the idea (or concept) of causation plays in our mental economy.

Causality, as a category of the understanding, may be thought of in three ways: metaphysically, as a concept that is presupposed by the pursuit of scientific understanding in general, or that is required for the justifiction of scientific laws in general; epistemoloically, as a central concept in rational inference not only in science but in other areas, as an ingredient of the grounds for the rational acceptance of statements; and psychologically as a purely descriptive concept, as in "Person A attributes the causal power to warm to his kitchen stove." I shall argue that the metaphysical role is both smaller in scope and different in character than is usually thought; that the epistemological role is nil; and that the psychological role is of mainly pathological interest.

CAUSE AND EFFECT

The relation between cause and effect has certainly been regarded as essential to scientific thinking for many years. Hume devotes many pages of the Treatise to discussing causality, and appears to take it as of central importance, despite the fact that he can find nothing to the notion, in the final analysis, but constant conjunction. One senses, in Hume's prose, both disappointment and heroic resignation.

But where and when did this notion of causality that Hume seeks to understand enter philosophy? I am not sure. Hume's notion of cause may be the same as Aristotle's notion of efficient cause, but I am not even sure of that. What is clear is that with Kant causality becomes both conceptually capitalized and elevated into a fundamental category, and that from that time on it has played a large role in the analysis of scientific inquiry. Mill, for example, regards science as the seeking of causes, and his methods are intended as codifications of the procedures for doing so. Some philosophers regard causality -- sometimes even **universal** causality -- as an assumption, or basic "presupposition" of science. Nor is this merely an historical attitude. In the flyer for a recent conference on causality,[2] it is remarked that science has been taken as the search for causes.

La Place, in the preface to his Theorie analytique des probabilites, popularized an image that captures the sense of universal causal determinism. If some intelligence of infinite calculational capacity knew the location and velocity of every particle in the universe and the forces acting on it at some time, then the whole history of the universe and the whole future course of the universe would be fully revealed to him.

In the twentieth century, this view has had some difficult going. Quantum mechanics is irremediably tychistic in its present formulation. Efforts have been made all along, and are still being made, to find a "hidden variable" theory to replace quantum mechanics, so that the tradition of universal causation can still be honored. So far, these efforts have been frustrated.

One response -- a response made, for example, by Russell in Human Knowledge -- is to allow that some features of the universe are irreducibly stochastic in character, but to defend a principle of causality nevertheless by allowing that some causal relations are merely statistical or probabilistic. Thus, although we cannot predict when a particular atom of radium will emit a particle, we can give an exact deterministic formula specifying the time rate of decay of radium. It appears that we have merely replaced a law of the form A always follows **B**, by a law of the form A follows **B** exactly 100p percent of the time.

It is not easy to work out the details of such a view in a plausible way. For the moment let it be observed that this is at any rate not the view of causation that has been prevalent for many years, that derives from Kant or earlier writers, and that found its expression in La Place's image. According to that notion, there is indeed something very much like a power in the world itself or in the events of the world that produces effects from causes. The intuition is that of one billiard ball smashing into another, and thereby **forcing** it to move in a determinate way. From a Kantian point of view, we cannot know these powers, but we can only **understand** the world if we see it in such terms. In neither case, though, does the relation of causality obtain between **classes** of events -- it is individual events that stand (perhaps as individuals of certain types) in the causal relation. And if this is the case, it is hard to see how a statistical law can express a causal relation.[3]

Causality requires a **connection** of some sort between the earlier and later states. Not, as Hume argued so convincingly, a logical connection, but some sort of connection in virtue of which an antecedent individual (event) "brings about" a consequent individual. While a deterministic uniformity may be captured by a relation between classes or properties ("crows are black", "combustion is accompanied by heat"), a causal connection requires relations between individuals: this fire is the cause of that heat; that heat is produced by this fire. That fire (in general) causes heat (in general), may also be true; but it is surely most naturally construed as asserting something about **instances** of fire and of heat.

If this is so, we can see that universal causation plays none of the roles we need to have played. It can hardly be a necessary presupposition of any sort of science if quantum mechanics can get along without it. While some inferences may be causal in character, universal causation seems to play no role in them. And while it is true that some people find it hard to believe in quantum mechanics precisely because it is inconsistent with universal instance-by-instance causation, they may be construed as just another example of the psychopathology of everyday life.

AGENCY AND CAUSALITY

One context in which the notion of causality seems perfectly clear and uncontroversial is that in which it serves to point to responsibilty. "It was the driver of car A that caused the crash," clearly pins responsibility on that person. What is conveyed is that, had he acted in some other way, the crash would have been avoided. The same is true, of course, of the driver of the other car: had he acted in some other way -- that is, had he left the house ten minutes earlier, or had he followed another route, the crash would have been avoided. So the claim that had the first driver done something different, the crash would have been avoided is not **all** that is conveyed by the assertion that he caused the crash.

What is conveyed in addition is responsibility **as an agent**: blame (or praise) for bringing something about. To build a fire or a bridge, to chop down a tree or to plant a field of corn, is to intervene causally -- that is, to manipulate -- the world. And to know in individual cases that someone has built a fire or bridge, is to understand those cases. I take this to be the paradigmatic case of both causal relation and explanation. Note that the intent to produce a certain result is not essential -- the driver of car A need not have intended to produce an accident in order to have caused it. But he must at some point in the antecedent history have been conscious and have acted voluntarily. This homely and familiar world, I suggest, is the source of both our conceptions of causality and of explanation.

The example of the automobile accident has more to offer us. The driver of car A, we say, caused the accident. But the chances are that he did not intend the accident. So we say, for example, that he caused the accident by driving too fast -- it was his excessive speed that was the immediate cause of the accident, and he who is responsible for (the causal agent of) his excessive speed. Or perhaps he didn't even intend to drive so fast. It was just a matter of leaving the car under the command of the cruise control when he started down the exit ramp.

What we see from this is that even in the homely example, we can trace a causal sequence, only one link of which need be intended by the agent. The driver intends to drive fast; by so doing, he causes, is responsible for, an accident. The woodsman intends to warm himself; in order to achieve this end, he finds wood, rubs two sticks together, builds a fire, causing himself to become warm. He is responsible for all the events in the sequence, and for the forest fire that results when his campfire gets out of control. The fundamental locution appears to be **X** caused **Y** by doing **Z**, or, more generally, **X** caused **Y1**, **Y2**, ..., **Yn**, by doing **Z**, where the **Y**'s are a sequence of things for which **X** is responsible.

The notion of responsibility, in turn, is psychologically easy to generalize. If it isn't your fault, and isn't his fault, and it certainly isn't **my** fault, it must nevertheless be somebody's fault. Someone must take responsibility. If not us, and not someone in our clan, then someone in another clan; if not any person, then some non-person -- some non-natural agent. God did it.

Observe that this extension fits in with both the engineering and legal uses of causality. By establishing the cause of the crash, we have fixed responsibility. If no person, then an act of God. We have still fixed responsibility. And just as an ordinary human agent may cause a forest fire by his carelessness, and just as the forest fire is explained by the story of the careless camper, so God may cause a forest fire in His anger, and His anger may explain the forest fire.[4] Finally, just as knowing the cause of fire may enable us to build one when we want one, so knowing the cause of drought may enable us to bring it to an end, with prayers and offerings.

This seems a far cry from the scientific search for causes, and in a cultural sense, no doubt it is. But the spirit seems much the same: it embodies the conviction that there is an explanation for everything (the buck always stops, someone is responsible) and the hope that dedication (to finding the buck's resting place) may give us a way of controlling the future. Understanding causal relations gives us power, both to change our world directly, through our own actions, and indirectly through the actions of others. That is because the corresponding causal chains end in a link that is a voluntary action. It is I who rub the sticks together; **you** who dump water on my baby fire; God who smites you with indigestion for interfering with my project.

To return to the fire in the forest, the causal agents of certain things that I understand are unknown to me. (I find the fire, but I don't find the person who built it.) Furthermore, there are certain things I now understand how to build a fire that I did not understand at an earlier time. Putting such facts together leads naturally (but perhaps not inevitably) to the superstitious postulation of the initiators of causal chains whose effects I experience. And, of course, the obsequious solicitation of more desirable effects.

This same conception of causality as tied up with agency carries over, I suggest, into science and engineering. It is true that not all "causes" are agents (drivers of cars), but often things that we, as agents, can control, or at least can imagine controlling. To know the cause is to see the possibility of manipulation. To know that the gods of the hunt have sent the elk away from our hunting grounds is to be in a position to ask them to bring them back; to know that sympathetic vibration was the cause of the failure of a bridge is not to know how to avoid them in the next bridge, but it is the first step; to know that a certain organism causes the disease that concerns us is to know that if we could destroy that organism we could prevent or cure that disease.

Uniformities are very handy in bringing things about; we can use the fact that combustion of charcoal is uniformly accompanied by heat to cause our steak to become done just right. But not **all** uniformities: to put a penny in my pocket does not cause it to become silver, even though all the coins in my pocket are silver.

We can give an exact translation of the hypotheticals reflecting "causal connections" in a metalinguistic framework. Given a corpus of statements reflecting what we believe to be true about the extensional uniformities of the world, as well as what we believe to be the factual state of the world, we can add and delete statements that are under our control, or that might be under our control, or that might have been under our control, in order to see what follows, or probably follows. Whether or not "the coin is in my pocket" is part of my body of knowledge is under my control -- I can put it in my pocket or take it out-- but whether or not "the coin is silver" is part of my body of knowledge is not under my control. Thus we replace what is essentially a counterfactual speculation by an actual conditional that we can (in principle) implement, because it is just (!) a matter of constructing the appropriate syntactical objects.

Note that this allows us to speak of statistical causality in a certain sense; we can say that Tom's addiction to the lottery caused his family's poverty. That is, knowing how the lottery is run, we can infer from the fact that someone is addicted to it that he will lose a lot of money with high enough probability for us to say that it is "predictable". With the right conception of probability, this fits into the preceding analysis.

CAUSAL REASONING

We have claimed -- it would be another matter to have demonstrated -- that arguments and inferences concerning causal agencies can be dealt with syntactically by the device of adding and deleting certain sentences in a set of sentences construed as a body of knowledge. To put just a bit more flesh on these bones, suppose, as is not implausible, that a body of knowledge can be represented by means of a finite basis, where a basis is a finite set of logically independent statements from which the contents of the body of knowledge can be derived. A body of knowledge may have a number of bases; we assume that some basis provides the means for the appropriate syntactical manipulation.

To support a causal conditional we add to the basis of our body of knowledge a statement that we **can** make true, corresponding to the antecedent of the conditional, and show that then the consequent of the conditional becomes well supported. To support a counterfactual, we find the basis element or elements that imply the denial of the antecedent, and replace them with new basis elements that embody the antecedent. In some cases there may be more than one way to do this -- but some counterfactuals are ambiguous.

Does this take care of all our problems of counterfactual and conditional reasoning? That would be a large claim, and in all probability it would be false. But it is not clear that this approach will not provide for the representation of any ordinary, garden variety, counterfactual reasoning, and in particular causal reasoning. What this means is that, in the corpus itself an extensional language in which nothing more powerful that mere uniformities can be expressed will suffice for the expression of our factual knowledge. This is controversial, of course.

But let us look at a few useful kinds of conditionals. One useful kind is the conditional observation: If I were to observe X, then [statement]. (To observe whether or not X is another matter -- it is to perform an action whose outcome might be (for example) either observing X or observing not-X, or, more likely, observing Y, where Y entails X or entails not-X.) The metalinguistic version merely requires that X be expressible in a sentence of the object language suitable for observation, and then that it be added to the corpus of my knowledge. The conditional is true just in case [statement] is then also a number of the corpus. Note that this depends on the principles according to which statements become members of the corpus: deduction from individual statements already in the corpus; deduction from sets of statements already in the corpus; induction according to inductive principles; high probability; etc. For our present purposes we will just leave all these options open.

1) If I were to observe an elephant outside my window, it would be grey. True.

2) If I were to observe an elephant outside my window, it would be pink. False.

3) If I were to observe an elephant outside my window, 2 + 2 would be 4. True.

4) If I were to observe an elephant outside my window, 2 + 2 would be 5. False.

5) If I were to observe that **A** and **B**, then 2 + 2 would be 4.

(5) fails to conform to the pattern in question, since as Hume carefully pointed out, "**A** causes **B**" is not the sort of thing that can be "observed".

Somewhat more difficult than hypothetical conditionals are counterfactual conditionals of observation: If I **had** observed **X** [instead of some **Y** such that **Y** entails the negation of **X**] then [statement]. The difficulty is that we cannot merely add a sentence representing **X** to the corpus, since the corpus already implies the negation of **X**. We must change the corpus -- delete **Y** -- and it is not always clear how to do that. But if **Y** is mentioned explicitly, and if **Y** picks out a particular sentence of the basis of the corpus, then it may be straightforward to replace that sentence with one containing **X** rather than **Y** -- even though in this case there may be some judgments of similarity to be made.

In the simplest case, **Y** is simply an observation that entered the corpus at a time t earlier than now. (E.g., "the fluid in the test tube turned red".) We replace this sentence by a sentence representing **X**: "the fluid in the test tube turned blue", and then continue the history of the corpus. Then we ask whether [statement] belongs to the newly constructed corpus. If so, the conditional is true; if not it is false.

A second variety of conditional that is of particular interest -- especially in view of our earlier analysis of causality -- is the action conditional, both hypothetical and counterfactual. If I were to perform A, then [statement]; if I had performed A, then [statement]. For the former, we add a statement to the corpus, reflecting the fact that I perform A. But suppose that isn't possible? Suppose I **can't** do A? (If I were to jump from here to the next town, I would land so hard that both my legs would break.) In evaluating the conditional of action, I must grant myself the ability to do the action in question.

The antecedent of the conditional should therefore be unpacked as: If I were to will myself to perform behavior A, and were capable of behavior A, then [statement], and correspondingly for the counterfactual. "Willing" is a strange, old-fashioned sounding notion, but (at least in the sense of "choosing" or "deciding") it does seem to correspond to something phenomenologically identifiable. Willing or choosing to do something is not to do it; there are lots of things that might interfere. But in general we have no reason to anticipate such difficulties. Thus (in the straight hypothetical case) we may add to the corpus a statement to the effect that the agent wills, chooses, or whatever, to do A; and, without inconsistency or difficulty, also add the statement that the agent exhibits behavior A. (Should there be something in the agent's corpus that is inconsistent with the agent's willing to do A and exhibiting behavior A, we are in the more complex counterfactual case discussed below.)

6) If I go swimming this afternoon I won't have time to finish my paper. True, despite the fact that with the best (worst?) intentions in the world, I might find myself unable to go swimming (flat tire) and therefore condemned to finish my paper anyway.

7) If I go swimming this afternoon, 2 + 2 will be 4. True; add the appropriate stuff to my corpus, and the world's most famous arithmetical truth will still be there.

8) If I go swimming this afternoon, I'll drown. False, because I am a respectable swimmer, and have every reason to believe that I will not drown -- though of course it is possible.

9) If I go swimming this afternoon, 2 + 2 will be 5. False, since adding the required statements to my corpus will not yield an inconsistency.

But of course the suggestion (should such a sentence be uttered) is that there is an inconsistency -- i.e., that what appears to be stated as a hypothetical is really a counterfactual, and further, attention is directed to the falsity of the antecedent, rather than to any connection between the antecedent and the consequent.

The counterfactual form of the action conditional, like that of the observation conditional, may be ambiguous as to what needs to be deleted to render the formal antecedent consistent with the corpus of knowledge in question. In the simplest case, when I "might perfectly well have" chosen **A** rather than **C**, we need merely back up in time: organize the elements of a basis of the corpus of knowledge according to time, and eliminate those elements dated later than t; and then add the appropriate antecedent. In other cases it may be trickier, and it may be that the context must determine which elements of the basis are to be deleted. Or it may be that there is no determining which elements must be deleted.

This is also often a problem for the general counterfactual. While "If **X** is the case, then [statement]" merely calls for the addition of **X** to the corpus, and an investigation of whether or not [statement] is warranted to an adequate degree, the counterfactual, "If **X** were the case, which it is not, then [statement]" requires some judgment in constructing an appropriate corpus relative to which to judge the truth of the conditional. It is quite clear that the corpus must contain a sentence representing the antecedent **X**, but in general there will be a number of different (minimal) ways of deleting enough material from our actual corpus so that **X** may be consistently added.

CAUSAL THINKING

Even if it be granted that one important conception of causality derives from the idea of a responsible causal agent and can be represented as we have just suggested, we may still ask what other functions the notion of causality performs. What may be more interesting from the point of view of cognitive science is Kant's view of causation as a category of the understanding.

What is the connection between causality and rational thought and inference?

There are a number of reasons to be concerned about causes. One concerns explanation: we feel that we have explained something -- come to understand it -- when we have uncovered its causes. But we have also discovered (at least in principle) how to manipulate it -- how to prevent it, or to bring it about. It has been noted many times that explanation involves a pragmatic element. In the case of theoretical physical explanations (of black holes, for example) we need not be in a position to bring about or prevent the phenomenon in question. But it can still be maintained that the explanation is pragmatic and anthropocentric, if not anthropomorphic: the explanation gives us a handle on **something**, gives us a means of manipulating something or other; and there may also be a superstitious element -- to have a physical explanation of a phenomenon is to know how God could bring it about or prevent it.

That people think in this way -- that they are so strongly oriented toward the manipulation of the world -- is natural and interesting. But it does not provide a special role for causality in rational thought. In fact one can find many of the same aspects of the human psyche in traditional superstitions concerning good luck and bad luck. The difference between the two explanations (a) the accident was caused by driver **A**'s excessive speed and (b) the accident was caused by driver **B**'s walking under a ladder, is not that one is rational and the other superstitious. It is that given what I know about manipulating things in the world, the corpus I would obtain by deleting the assertion of A's excessive speed would not contain knowledge of the accident, while the corpus obtained by deleting B's walking under a ladder would. At least, so I claim, with appropriate provisos and limitations and implicit conditions.

Another context is that of decision theory. In decision theory we are concerned to maximize the value -- usually the expected value in the sense of probability theory -- of our acts. To do this requires that we take account of the causal consequences of the acts open to us. But that requires that we distinguish between what we can manipulate and what we cannot. My choice of an act may be evidence for a bad state of affairs without my having been able to alter that state of affairs by performing a different act.[5] This brings up an important and interesting distinction, having to do with perspective -- the difference between the first person and the third person. When I consider hypothetically what ensues if I perform act A, I consider a corpus like my actual one except that it contains both the assertion that I will to do act A, and that I am capable of doing act A. When I consider hypothetically what ensues if person **P** performs act A, I consider a corpus like my actual one except that it contains the assertion that person **P** performs act A. These are different sorts of additions. The latter, but not the former, provides me with evidence about the state of the agent. That I choose to do A precludes my using A as evidence about my state, except, perhaps in reflection, where I may treat myself in the third person.

Admittedly, this is a strange and inadequately analysed situation. But it is certainly phenomenologically familiar. When I choose, I choose freely; when you choose, your choice provides me with evidence as to your nature. Of course from your point of view the situation is reversed. And, more interesting yet, **after** I have chosen, you and I are in the same boat: we may both look on my choice as casting light on my character. Given all this oddness, it is hardly likely that our propensity, if such there be, to think in causal terms is going to prove enlightening. In fact one might suspect that it is that propensity that makes the situation difficult to comprehend.

There is a third context, in which the importance of causality is so pervasive and central as to be almost unnoticeable, and that is engineering. In order to achieve a certain goal, we devise a system of causally interacting entities: When the operator pushes the button, that causes a circuit to be closed, which allows electricity to charge the grid under the rabbit, which causes the rabbit to jump, which causes the see-saw on which the rabbit is sitting to rise, which causes ... This is quite plain in Rube Goldberg's cartoons, in which we can trace the casual chain ensuing from an agent's action, but it is quite plain also in the case of more complex and realistic machines, including those that contain a random element.

Here it is patent that manipulation and not mysterious causal power is what concern us. If touching wood or thinking pure thoughts enables us to produce a certain desirable effect every time, what more can we possibly ask, from an engineering point of view? It is quite true that it would be useful if the causal chain that leads from touching wood to filling an inside straight could be broken down into smaller links, since a lot of those links might be useful components of other chains. But again, it is an article of faith, a psychological impulse, that suggests there are smaller links, rather than anything in the structure of thought or the structure of reality.

In short, it seems that many of the circumstances in which causal relations are alleged to form the heart of rational thought are circumstances in which, so far as rational argument or rational behavior are concerned, we can get along perfectly well with the notion of manipulation. Uniformities are interesting metaphysically, and enormously important from the point of view of engineering, but to attribute them to the operation of causal powers seems utterly gratuitous. We need no notion of causality to distinguish between uniformities we can falsify by our choices and those that resist such treatment. Psychologically, belief in causal connections may be scientifically useful in leading us to find small links in causal chains, because such small links may be handy for building other chains. But to argue on this basis for the reality of causal connections is a bit like arguing that people will behave themselves only if they believe in eternal damnation, so God must exist.

If we can't do better, we should do without.

NOTES

1. The research on which this paper is based has been partly supported by the U.S. Army Signals Warfare Laboratory.

2. As witness an announcement of a conference on probability and causation held at Irvine, July 15-19. The organizers remark that "The search for causes is so central to science that it has sometimes been taken as the defining attribute of the scientific enterprise.

3. This has been forcefully argued by David Papineau 1985.

4. And be explained, in turn, by the (presumably sinful and sinfully presumptuous) actions of some other agent or agents.

5. There is a whole literature devoted to the debate between (or the reconciliation of) causal and evidential decision theory. This literature has spawned new conditionals, new notions of probability, and new kinds of utility. All of this is beside the point here.

PART TWO

Mental Representation

3

Compositionality and Typicality

Edward E. Smith and Daniel N. Osherson

"Typicality" is a relation between an instance and a concept. The relation is that of exemplification, and it is critical for concept use. In this paper, we are concerned with the "compositionality problem" in typicality, which is roughly the following: If you know something about the typicality of an object in two simple concepts -- say, the typicalities of guppie in pet and fish-- how can you determine the object's typicality in the conjunction of these simple concepts, i.e., guppie's typicality in pet fish?

To appreciate why this problem is important, we need some background about typicality and simple concepts (let us take the "simple" concepts to be those denoted by single words). For any simple concept, its instances vary in how typical they are judged to be. This gradient of typicality is important because it predicts performance in a variety of psychological domains. Thus, the more typical an instance is of a concept, the faster it can be categorized, the earlier it can be accessed when retrieving concept members, the earlier its name will enter a child's lexicon, the more support it can lend to an inductive inference, and so forth (see Mervis and Rosch 1981; Smith and Medin 1981). What holds for simple concepts may well hold for "complex" ones (concepts denoted by multiple words), so an instance's typicality in a complex concept may be a good predictor of performance in a variety of tasks. We therefore want to determine typicality gradients in complex concepts. But, since many complex concepts are novel (e.g., smiling Canadian mounty), we can only determine an instance's typicality in such concepts by computing it from what is known about the instance's typicalities in the simple constituent concepts. And this is the compositionality problem in typicality judgements.

Thus far there have been two general approaches to the compositionality problem, "external" and "internal". In the "external" approach, one attempts to exhibit the typicality of an instance in a complex concept as a function of no more than the typicalities of objects with respect to the constituent concepts. For example, the typicality of a particular guppie in pet fish might be some function of the typicalities of that guppy (and perhaps of other objects) in pet and in fish. What is critical is that the computations do not invoke the mental representations of the constituent concepts. In the "internal" approach, one attempts to exhibit the typicality of an instance in a complex concept as a function of the internal representations of the constituent concepts. The typicality of guppie in pet fish, for example, is computed from the representations of pet and fish.

With the above as background, we can now provide an agenda for the rest of this paper. In the next section, we take up the external approach to our compositionality problem. We focus mainly on some simple versions of this approach (they are the most influential), and demonstrate that they are incompatible with certain empirical phenomena. After this, we move on to the internal approach. First, we consider a version of the approach in which concepts are represented by their exemplars, and then we take up a version in which concepts are represented by abstract summaries. Finally, we discuss the distinction between typicality and vagueness. Throughout the paper, we confine discussion to only one kind of complex concept, adjective-noun conjunctions.

THE EXTERNAL APPROACH

Fuzzy-Set Theory

Perhaps the best known instance of the external approach is fuzzy-set theory, particularly as developed by Zadeh in his early papers (e.g. 1965). A key notion in the theory is that of a characteristic function, c_A:D --> [0,1]; it maps entities in domain D (the domain of discourse) into the real numbers 0 through 1 in a way that indicates the degree to which the entity is a member of concept A. For example, the characteristic function c_{fish}, measures the degree of membership in the concept fish, and when applied to any relevant creature, x, $c_{fish}(x)$ yields a number that reflects the degree to which x is a member of fish. According to the theory announced in Zadeh 1965, the characteristic function of a conjunction, such as pet fish, is related to the characteristic functions of its constituents pet and fish, by (1):

1) $c_{P\&F}(x)=\min[c_P(x), c_F(x)]$

That is, the characteristic function value of the conjunction is the minimum of the characteristic function values of the constituents; e.g. a guppie cannot be a better member of pet fish than it is of pet or fish. To relate these proposals to our concerns, we assume that characteristic function values can be estimated by judgements of typicality. Now (1) can be recast as:

2) $Typ_{P\&F}(x)=\min[Typ_P(x), Typ_F(x)]$,

which is a clear case of the external approach.

The min rule appears to be unequivocally wrong. In the preceding example, (2) says that a particular guppie is no more typical of pet fish than of pet or fish, yet intuition strongly suggests that a guppie is more typical of pet fish than of either constituent (Osherson and Smith 1981). This example demonstrates the "conjunction effect", namely, that if an object is an instance of an adjective-noun conjunction then it is more typical of the conjunction than the noun constituent.

In previous work (Smith and Osherson 1984) we have demonstrated that the conjunction effect is substantial and holds for different kinds of conjunction. We investigated "negatively-diagnostic" conjunctions like brown apple, where the adjective denotes an unlikely value of the object denoted by the noun, and "positively-diagnostic" conjunctions like red apple, where the adjective denotes a likely value of the object denoted by the noun. We found substantial conjunction effects for both kinds of conjunction; in every case, a pictured object that was an instance of a conjunction was rated as more typical of the conjunction than of its noun constituent. Furthermore, in most cases the typicality rating of an instance in a conjunction exceeded the average or maximum rating of that instance in the constituents. These results argue against not only the min rule, but average and max rules as well. We also found that the conjunction effect is greater for negatively-diagnostic than positively-diagnostic conjunctions; e.g., the extent to which a brown apple is judged more typical of brown apple than of apple is greater than the extent to which a red apple is judged more typical of red apple than apple. This finding will later prove useful in evaluating variants of the internal approach.

The Simple Functional Hypothesis

The min, average, and max rules are special cases of the "simple functional hypothesis", or SFH for short (Osherson and Smith 1982). The SFH states that there is a function, f, such that for all conjunctive concepts, A & B, and for any object, x, in the domain of discourse:

3) $Typ_{A\&B}(x)=f[Typ_A(x), Typ_B(x)]$

In Osherson and Smith 1982, we advanced a general argument against the SFH. The argument we proposed goes as follows. Imagine an object -- call it "ballblock", or BB -- that is equally typical of ball and block:

4) $Typ_{block}(BB) = Typ_{ball}(BB)$

Let f be a candidate for the function satisfying the SFH. Since functions of equals are equal,

5) $f[Typ_{round}(BB), Typ_{block}(BB)] = f[Typ_{round}(BB), Typ_{ball}(BB)]$

Now, according to the SFH, the left side of (5) is equal to $Typ_{round\ block}(BB)$, and the right side of (5) is equal to $Typ_{round\ ball}(BB)$. Substituting these equalities into (5) gives:

6) $Typ_{round\ block}(BB) = Typ_{round\ ball}(BB)$

But (6) seems wrong. Intuition suggests that our BB is a better round block than a round ball, because BB seems quite round for a block but not for a ball. Apparently there is no such function as that specified by the SFH.

The preceding argument does not depend on our particular choice of concepts and object. It works just as well, say, with a member of the cat family that is equally typical of housecat and tiger. According to the SFH, such a cat should be equally typical of ferocious housecat and ferocious tiger, but intuition suggests that it will be more typical of ferocious housecat. We have here another empirical phenomenon about typicality and conjunctions: if an object is equally typical of two concepts (tiger and housecat), and each concept is combined with the same adjective to form a positively-diagnostic conjunction (ferocious tiger) and a negatively-diagnostic one (ferocious housecat), then the object will be more typical of the negatively-diagnostic conjunction.

More Complex Versions of the External Approach

Our argument against the SFH indicates that the extent to which a conjunctive concept, A & B, applies to an object, o, depends on more than the extents to which the constituent A applies to o and the constituent B applies to o. Perhaps the relation of A and B to entities other than o need to be considered in determining $Typ_{A\&B}$ (o). This is the approach taken by Zadeh 1982 in his attempt to make fuzzy-set theory compatible with the empirical phenomena we have discussed. Zadeh proposes a normalized min rule. Specifically, for a given conjunctive concept, A & B, and domain D.

7) $(\forall x \in D)\ \ Typ_{A\&B}(x) = \dfrac{\min[Typ_A(x),\ Typ_B(x)]}{\max \min[Typ_A(i),\ Typ_B(i)]}$

The denominator in (7) is the largest value that the min rule can achieve when applied to concepts A and B; for example, in determining the typicality of a particular guppie in pet fish, we now consider how typical a member of pet fish an animal can be given that typicality is computed by the min rule.

Note that (7) is compatible with the external approach as we are still exhibiting the typicality of an instance in a conjunction as a function of the typicalities of that instance and others in the constituents. Note further that (7) is compatible with the conjunction effect; as long as the denominator is less than 1, the typicality for the conjunction will exceed the minimum typicality of the constituents. Also, (7) is immune from our argument against the SFH, since $Typ_{A\&B}(o)$ is no longer a function of just $Typ_A(o)$ and $Typ_B(o)$.

But (7) will not work as an account of conjunctive concepts. It suffers from a problem shared by all min rules, articulated by Jones 1982, namely that it predicts incorrectly that two objects will be judged equally typical of a conjunction if the values of their minimium constituents are equal, even if the values of their maximum constituents differ greatly. To see this, consider two plane figures, o_1 and o_2, both the same imperfect shade of red, but different degrees of squareness. As long as $Typ_{red}(o_i) < Typ_{square}(o_i)$ $(i \in \{1,2\})$, (7) deems both objects to be equally typical of red square. But this seems at odds with the intuition that whichever figure is squarer will be judged more typical of red square.

More generally, in evaluating the typicality of an object in a conjunction, people usually consider both constituents. This claim receives support in some of our recent experiments. In these studies, one group of subjects rated the typicality of various instances in noun concepts (e.g., fruit), a second group rated the typicality of the same instances in adjective concepts (e.g., red), and a third group rated the typicality of the instances in conjunctions (e.g., red fruit). Typicality ratings for the conjunction were found to be substantially correlated with the ratings for both constituents.

While the above indicates there is something wrong with a normalized min rule, it remains possible that the normalization idea will work in the context of some other specific function. However, we know of no support for this idea, and we have demonstrated that certain other plausible normalization schemes also do not work for conjunctions (Osherson and Smith 1982).

THE INTERNAL APPROACH

Some Ground Rules

In discussing the internal approach, we will be talking about mental representations of classes; but these representations make up only part of the mental representation of a concept, namely that part which is called a "prototype". Roughly, a prototype consists of a description of a class of objects, where the properties in the description are characteristic rather than defining of the class (e.g., Smith, Shoben, and Rips 1974) and fit typical instances better than atypical ones.

Prototype representations come in two kinds: (1) "exemplars", where the representation consists of different descriptions for different instances of the concept, and (2) "abstract summaries", where the representation consists of a single description that applies to all members of a class (Smith and Medin 1981). In what follows, we first briefly consider an exemplar-based case of the internal approach and then take up in detail a case that uses abstract summaries.

One more ground rule. In evaluating these proposals, we will use the phenomena that surfaced in our discussion of the internal approach. Recall that these phenomena included the conjunction effect (greater typicality in a conjunction than a noun constituent) and the finding that the conjunction effect is greater for negatively-diagnostic than for positively-diagnostic conjunctions. In addition, we will also consider the "reverse conjunction" effect: when an item is a poor member of a conjunction (e.g., a brown apple paired with the conjunction red apple), it is judged less typical of the conjunction than of the noun constituent (Smith and Osherson 1984).

An Examplar Model

The following proposal is based on the work of Medin and Shaffer 1978, and on the discussion of that work in Smith and Medin 1981. As illustrated on the left-hand side of Figure 3-I, assume that a prototype for a concept like apple consists of property descriptions of some of its exemplars. (To keep things manageable, we consider only three exemplars). Assume further that the exemplars involved are typical apple instances. Figure 3-I also includes the representations of two particular objects (or instances), I_1 and I_2, a typical red apple and a brown apple. The basic idea is that the typicality of an instance in a concept is equal to the instance's similarity to the prototype exemplars. For virtually any reasonable means of computing similarity, I_1 will be more similar to the prototype exemplars than will I_2, because only I_1 matches the color of some of the prototype exemplars. The model therefore correctly predicts that the red apple will be judged to be more typical of apple than is the brown apple.

To extend this account to adjective-noun conjunctions, we assume that adding the adjective restricts the exemplars comprising a prototype to those that are typical of the conjunction. This is illustrated by the representation for red apple on the right-hand side of Figure 3-I. The only difference between this representation and that of apple is that now all exemplars are red apples. For virtually any reasonable means of computing similarity, I_1 will be more similar to the exemplars of red apple than it is to the exemplars of apple, because I_1 will match the color of all of red apple's exemplars compared to only two of apple's exemplars. Thus the model correctly predicts that the red apple will be judged more typical of red apple than apple, i.e., the model reconstructs the conjunction effect for positively-diagnostic conjunctions. A similar analysis suggests that the model can also reconstruct the conjunction effect for negatively-diagnostic conjunctions.

Apple		I_1	I_2	**Red Apple**	
Exemplar 1	red round smooth small	red round smooth medium	brown round smooth medium	**Exemplar 1**	red round smooth small
Exemplar 2	red round smooth medium			**Exemplar 2**	red round smooth medium
Exemplar 3	green round smooth large			**Exemplar 3**	red round smooth large

FIGURE 3-I

Illustration of exemplar representations for the prototypes of apple (left-most side) and red apple (right-most side), alone with representations of relevant instances, I_1, a red apple, and I_2, a brown apple.

We have not bothered to develop this model further because we think it suffers from two problems. First, the model incorrectly predicts that there should be no conjunction effect when virtually all instances of the noun concept have the value denoted by the adjective (e.g., green pea, yellow corn, red blood). In these cases, presumably there is no difference between the exemplars that constitute the prototype for the noun concept and those comprising the prototype for the conjunction, and consequently there is no basis for a conjunction effect. In fact, such cases show a conjunction effect (Smith and Osherson 1984). A second, more serious problem concerns the model's critical assumption that the prototype exemplars are all typical instances. This assumption appears to beg the question of how we decide (in the first place) what instances are typical of complex concepts, which is the fundamental question that we started with. Without a resolution to this problem, the examplar model is not a reasonable account of compositionality and typicality.

Apple(A)		I_1		I_2	
	red 25		red 30		red
1 color	green 5	color	green	color	green
	brown		brown		brown 30
	—		—		—
	—		—		—
	round 15		round 20		round 20
0.50 shape	square	shape	square	shape	square
	cylindrical 5		cylindrical		cylindrical
	—		—		—
	—		—		—
	smooth 25		smooth 30		smooth 30
0.25 texture	rough 5	texture	rough	texture	rough
	bumpy		bumpy		bumpy
	—		—		—
	—		—		—

Sim (A, I_1)	Sim(A, I_2)
=1(25-5-5)	=1(0-30-30)
+0.50(15-5-5)	+0.50(15-5-5)
+0.25(25-5-5)	+0.25(25-5-5)
=15+2.50+3.75	=60+2.50+3.75
≃21	≃ -54

FIGURE 3-II

Illustration of a summary representation for a prototype of apple along with representation of relevant instances (I_1, a red apple, and I_2, a brown apple); beneath each instance representation is the similarity between the instance and the prototype.

A Modification Model

We have recently proposed a "modification" model of conjunctions (Smith and Osherson 1984; Smith, Osherson, Rips, and Keane 1988). In this model, a prototype is an abstract summary that applies to all members of a class. A representation for the prototype of apple is illustrated in the left-most panel of Figure 3-II. The representation specifies: (a) a set of relevant attributes (color, shape, texture, etc.); (b) for each attribute, a set of possible values that instances of the concept can assume (e.g., for color, the values include red, green and brown); (c) the salience of each value of an attribute (which presumably reflects the value's intensity and subjective likelihood), as indicated by the number to the value's right (we refer to these numbers as "votes" for the value); and (d) the diagnosticity of each attribute for the concept, as indicated by the number to the attribute's left. The remaining panels of Figure 3-II illustrate representations for the instances I_1 and I_2. For simplicity, we have assumed that for I_1 and I_2 all votes for an attribute are on one value.

Again, the key idea is that the typicality of an instance in a concept is equal to the instance's simiilarity to the prototype. To measure similarity, we use Tversky's 1977 "contrast" rule, which holds that similarity is assessed by a contrast between common and distinctive features. In our application of the rule, each vote counts as a feature. The similarity between the features of an instance (I) and the features of the apple prototype (A) is given by:

8) $Sim(I,A)=f(I \cap A)-f(A-I)-f(I-A)$

where $I \cap A$ designates the set of votes or features common to the instance and prototype, A-I designates the set of features distinct to the prototype, and I-A designates the set of features distinct to the instance. In addition, f is a function that measures the importance of each set of features -- specifically f multiplies each feature in a set by its diagnosticity. Thus similarity is an increasing function of the features common to an instance and prototype, and a decreasing function of the features distinct to the prototype and distinct to the instance.[2]

For purposes of making computations, it is convenient to use a version of Equation (8) that specifies the common and distinctive features on an attribute-by-attribute basis. This is given by:

9) $Sim(I,A)=\Sigma_i[f_i(I \cap A)-f_i(A-I)-f_i(I-A)]$,

where _i_ indexes the relevant attributes, $I \cap A$ designates the set of features or votes on attibute _i_ common to the instance and prototype, A-I designates the set of features of attribute _i_ distinct to the prototype, and I-A designates the set of features of attribute _i_ distinct to the instance. Beneath each object representation in Figure 3-II, we have used Equation (9) to calculate the object's similarity to the _apple_ prototype. To illustrate, to determine the similarity between the typical red apple (I_1) and the _apple_ prototype on the color attribute, we note that _apple_ and the red apple share 25 red votes, that _apple_ has 5 distinct green votes, that the red apple has 5 distinct red votes, and that each component of the contrast is multiplied by a diagnositicity of 1.0 (See Figure 3-II). The computations are similar for the other attributes. For the examples provided in Figure 3-II, the contrast rule correctly predicts that the red apple, I_1, should be judged to be more typical of _apple_ than is the brown apple, I_2.

We now want to extend this account to adjective-noun conjunctions. To keep things simple, we consider only adjectives that presumably contain a single attribute, for example, _red_ or _brown_. We assume that the adjective does three things: (1) it selects the relevant attribute in the noun (e.g., color); (2) it shifts all votes on that attribute into the value named by the adjective; and (3) it boosts the diagnosticity of the attribute. These assumptions are illustrated by the representation for _red apple_ on the left-hand side of Figure 3-III. The only differences between this representation and that of _apple_ involve the color attribute: now, all votes are on red, and the diagnosticity of color has increased by a factor of two (_two_ being an arbitrary choice on our part). The effects of these differences for typicality are illustrated in the remaining panels of Figure 3-III. Here we have repeated the representations for our red and brown apples, and computed the similarity for each of these objects in the conjunction. When these similarity scores are compared to those in Figure 3-II, the results are that (1) the red apple is more similar to the prototype for _red apple_ than it is to the prototype for _apple_, while (2) the brown apple is less similar to the prototype for _red apple_ than it is to the prototype for _apple_. Result (1) reconstructs the conjunction effect, while result (2) reconstructs the reverse conjunction effect.

Positively Diagostic Cases

Red Apple(RA)		I_1		I_2	
	red 30		red 30		red
1 color	green 5	color	green	color	green
	brown		brown		brown 30
	—		—		—
	—		—		—
	round 15		round 20		round 20
0.50 shape	square	shape	square	shape	square
	cylindrical 5		cylindrical		cylindrical
	—		—		—
	—		—		—
	smooth 25		smooth 30		smooth 30
0.25 texture	rough 5	texture	rough	texture	rough
	bumpy		bumpy		bumpy
	—		—		—
	—		—		—

$Sim(RA, I_1)$	$Sim(RA, I_2)$
=1(30-0-0)	=1(0-30-30)
+0.50(15-5-5)	+0.50(15-5-5)
+0.25(25-5-5)	+0.25(25-5-5)
=60+2.50+3.75	=120+2.50+3.75
≈66	≈ -114

FIGURE 3-III

Illustration of a summary representation of red apple along with representation of relevant instances, beneath each instance representation is the similarity between the instance and the prototype.

Figure 3-IV illustrates a comparable analysis for negatively-diagnostic conjunctions. The prototype for brown apple differs from that of apple only in that now all color votes are on brown and color has doubled in diagnosticity. The effect of these changes for typicality are shown in the remaining panels. Now, in comparison to our original computations in Figure 3-II, we find that the brown apple is more similar to brown apple than it is to apple, while the red apple is less similar to brown apple than it is to apple. We have again reconstructed the conjunction effect and its reverse. Note further that the conjunction effect predicted in this case exceeds that in the previous case, which reconstructs the third effect described earlier.

The modification model is therefore compatible with all conjunction effects. Furthermore, unlike the exemplar model, the current model correctly predicts a conjunction effect even in cases where virtually all instances of the noun concept have the value denoted by the adjective. While all color votes may be on green for both pea and green pea, the diagnosticity of color is greater for the conjunction and this will eventuate in conjunction effects.

Conjunction effects were not the only empirical findings that we used in evaluating the external approach. One other phenomenon was that people consider both constituents in assessing the typicality of an object in a conjunction. The modification model incorporates this phenomenon by positing a representation for a conjunction that is a joint function of the adjective and noun constituents. Another finding of interest is the one demonstrated by our example of an object that is equally typical of ball and block being judged more typical of round block than round ball. Here, the modification model runs into a problem. The most plausible way to account for this phenomenon in terms of the model is to assume that ball and block differ appreciably in their number of shape votes (to the extent these numbers are the same, the ballblock should be equally typical of round block and round ball). But this assumption seems very dubious.

However, a slight revision of the model makes it compatible with the ball-block phenomenon. When an adjective is applied to a noun, instead of all votes on the relevant attribute being shifted to the value denoted by the adjective, perhaps some votes are left in their original position. Thus, in forming round block, while most of the shape votes are shifted to round, some are left on square. Consequently, the ballblock, which also has shape votes on both round and square, will find more matching shape features in round block than in round ball (in the latter, all shape votes are on round). While this revision of the model introduces another free parameter (the proportion of votes shifted), it leads to an interesting prediction. Typicality in a negatively-diagnostic conjunction should be less for objects that maximally exemplify the adjective than for those that moderately exemplify the adjective. The most typical round block is not perfectly round, nor is the most typical ferocious housecat all that scary, and the quintessential square cantelope is probably a bit round. This prediction remains to be tested.[3]

Negatively Diagostic Cases

Brown Apple(BA)			I_1		I_2
	red		red 30		red
1 color	green 5	**color**	green	**color**	green
	brown 30		brown		brown 30
	—		—		—
	—		—		—
	round 15		round 20		round 20
0.50 shape	square	**shape**	square	**shape**	square
	cylindrical 5		cylindrical		cylindrical
	—		—		—
	—		—		—
	smooth 25		smooth 30		smooth 30
0.25 texture	rough 5	**texture**	rough	**texture**	rough
	bumpy		bumpy		bumpy
	—		—		—
	—		—		—

$Sim(BA, I_1)$	$Sim(BA, I_2)$
=2(0-30-30)	=2(30-0-30)
+0.50(15-5-5)	+0.50(15-5-5)
+0.25(25-5-5)	+0.25(25-5-5)
=-120+2.50+3.75	=60+2.50+3.75
≃-114	≃ 66

FIGURE 3-IV

Illustration of a summary representation of brown apple along with representation of relevant instances, beneath each instance representation is the similarity between the instance and the prototype.

TYPICALITY VERSUS VAGUENESS

The compositionality problem that we have been concerned with involves typicality not concept membership. We have distinguished between typicality and concept membership from the outset, and we are not alone in seeing the need for this distinction. Armstrong, Gleitman, and Gleitman 1983 found that while subjects had no trouble rating instances of the concept even number for typicality, they maintained that it made no sense to rate these items for degree of membership in the concept. Even more convincing is a recent demonstration of Rips 1988 that factors that increase typicality may have no influence on concept membership, and vice versa. To illustrate, subjects were told a story whose first part concerned a bird-like animal, and whose second part dealt with an accidental change of the creature into a reptile-like animal. Subjects rated how likely the creature was to be a bird versus a reptile, as well as how typical the creature was of a bird versus reptile, separately for parts 1 and 2 of the story. There was a substantial difference in typicality ratings between parts 1 and 2 (the creature becoming more typical of reptile), but little difference in ratings of how likely the creature was to be a bird or reptile. Evidently, changes in appearances affect typicality (via similarity) but not concept membership.

Given this wedge between typicality and concept membership, it seems plausible that while typicality is graded, concept membership is binary. And if concept membership is binary, then the "compositional problem for concept membership" may be solvable by classical proposals (e.g., an object is a pet fish if and only if it has the essential properties of both pet and fish). This is the position we argued for in earlier papers (Osherson and Smith 1981 and 1982).

A problem with the position just outlined is that unclear cases of concept membership abound, giving rise to an apparent membership-gradient. Take the case of a biologist trying to determine whether a particular creature is a bird or not; the question comes down to whether or not the creature has bird chromosomes, but this question admits of a gradient of answers because the creature's chromosomes may resemble idealized bird-chromosomes to various degrees.

We think that the preceding problem can be overcome by recognizing that such unclear cases reflect vagueness, not typicality. To appreciate the distinction between typicality and vagueness, note that our biologists are not interested in the degree to which the creature exemplifies a bird, but rather in whether it is a bird. As a contrasting case, consider the lay-person's knowledge about penguins. While most of us believe that penguins are atypical of birds, few of us doubt that they are in fact birds; typicality is at play here, not vagueness. Thus, unclear cases (as in the biologist example) reflect vagueness, while atypical cases reflect typicality.

This distinction prompts us to reformulate claims that we have previously made. In earlier papers we explicitly conflated typicality and vagueness (Osherson and Smith 1981), and argued that there was a level of mental representation at which one could draw a sharp distinction between the objects to which a concept applies and those to which it does not apply (Osherson and Smith 1982). We must now introduce a caveat, as the above claim holds only modulo vagueness. Thus, we claim that there is a level of mental representation such that, except for considerations of vagueness, objects may be classified binarily. Or to put it differently, the function describing judgements of concept membership is indeed binarily valued, but it is a partial function which is not defined for unclear cases.

NOTES

1. This research was supported by the U.S. Public Health Service Grant MH37208 and by the National Institute of Education under Contract No. US-HEW-C-400-82-0030.

2. Equation (8) keeps the two sets of distinctive features separate because they can be differentially weighted (Tversky 1977). We do not consider such complications here.

3. The exemplar-based and modification models do not exhaust current instantiations of the internal approach; for other instantiations see Cohen and Murphy 1984 and Thagard 1984.

4

The Role of Spatial Representations in Complex Problem Solving

Lynn A. Cooper

There is considerable evidence, both anecdotal and experimental, for the use of visual/spatial representations in the process of solving problems. Anecdotal evidence frequently takes the form of first-person accounts of the significant and creative use of vivid mental images in certain kinds of scientific discoveries, e.g., Kekule's account of using dream imagery in the discovery of the molecular conformation of benzene. (See Shepard 1978 for a summary of a number of first-person reports of the role of imagery in discoveries.) Experimental evidence relies on the inferred use of spatial representations in laboratory tasks involving mental operations such as rotation (Shepard and Cooper 1982), scanning, and size scaling (Kosslyn 1980).

The research summarized in this paper is an attempt to explore the ways in which spatial representations are used in solving problems requiring the mental representation, assembly, and manipulation of complex visual structures. There are several specific ideas guiding the program of research. The first is the notion that a number of alternative strategies might exist for solving complex problems. These strategies could differ in the form of spatial information used to solve problems and in the operations performed on the represented information in the course of problem solution. A second central idea is that skill or aptitude for solving spatial problems might depend on the particular strategy or set of strategies adopted. More specificially, the research program evaluates the notion that high levels of skill in spatial problem solving are characterized by the flexible use of strategies that are appropriate to the structure of the problem solving situation. Thus, while the primary focus of the research effort is directed toward understanding how spatial representations are used in problem solving, the experimental findings also have implications for more general conceptions of the nature of cognitive skill.

This interest in skill in spatial problem solving is motivated by both theoretical and practical concerns. At a theoretical level, despite a long and rich history of the study of skill, aptitude, or ability in psychology -- dating back to the beginning of the development of systematic testing of mental ability (e.g., Spearman 1923; Thurstone 1938) -- and despite the much more recent resurgence of activity among cognitive psychologists toward the end of providing an information processing account of human intelligence (e.g., Sternberg 1977), there as yet exists no substantial agreement among psychologists on such matters as the nature and number of human abilities that underlie skilled performance in many cognitive domains. A second theoretical motivation comes from the window that the study of skill may provide into the workings of the acquisition or learning process. Much research that currently falls under the general label of "expert-novice" studies is based implicitly on the idea that a characterization of the initial (novice) and final (expert) stages of skilled performance might illuminate the nature of the process by which skill itself is acquired, or at least, that such a description constitutes a necessary first step in any analysis of learning (see, for example, Chi, Glaser and Rees 1982). A third and related theoretical issue centers around a currect debate in cognitive science as to whether human mental functioning is best viewed as a set of relatively independent, modular, or task-specific principles that apply to individual cognitive domains (e.g., Fodor 1983), or whether general, domain-independent mechanisms and principles can be developed. Explorations of the principles underlying skill in particular cognitive domains may inform this question by evaluating their adequacy when applied to related activities.

At a practical level, while psychologists may not agree on the nature, number, or relationships among various aptitudes or skills, intuition and practical experience afford us some compelling observations that any analysis of skill must explain systematically. First, aptitude, ability, or skill is something on which people can differ -- sometimes dramatically -- and on which a given individual can change appreciably at different moments in time. Second, skill in general, and spatial skill in particular, is hardly a unidimensional concept or an index of a single aptitude or ability. Even within the same individual, it is often the case that different aspects of skill in dealing with spatial concepts are dissociable. Consider, for example, the difference between competence at solving "small space" problems -- like those requiring the performance of mental rotation or those involving imagining the results of more complex sequences of spatial transformations on a single object --and competence at solving "large space" problems like reading a map or finding a location in space, in which overall coordinate systems must be represented and manipulated.

And, there are other forms of spatial skill that are familiar to us all, but that do not fall naturally into either of the broad categories above, including understanding the form of a functional relationship between two variables from a graphic representation, or the ability underlying success in occupations like electronics, dentistry, or air traffic control. Even the task of an oufielder, who must mentally extrapolate the probable end state of the trajectory of a ball in order to catch it, requires some form of mental calculation about the behavior of objects transforming in space.

Attempts by psychologists to analyze cognitive skill fall into three sorts of categories. The first is the familiar psychometric approach, used in the development of standardized tests of aptitude. The goal of this approach is to characterize, at a descriptive level and for purposes of a prediction, differences in performance on items and on tests as a whole. A second approach, which might be called the "traditional" information processing approach, differs from the psychometric approach in that the goal is to develop a cognitive model of the component mental operations underlying performance.

This second way of studying aptitude or skill may take any of several forms. In one form, termed the "cognitive correlates" approach (Pellegrino and Glaser 1979), relationships between level of aptitude scores and values of parameters in information processing analyses of cognitive tasks are sought, and some theoretical interpretation of the relevant process parameters is used as an explanation of the source of the aptitude differences (see, e.g., Hunt, Luneburg and Lewis 1975, and see Cooper and Regan 1983, for a discussion of this approach). In another form, termed the "cognitive components" approach, information processing models are developed to describe performance on tasks which are often similar to items on aptitude tests, but recast into a laboratory format (see, for example, Sternberg 1977). An assumption common to both versions of this approach is that sources of differences--between people or within an individual as a result of learning or instruction -- are quantitative in nature. That is, such differences are conceptualized as differences in the values of the parameters associated with one or more of the component underlying operations. Crucial to interpreting the research generated by this approach is the idea that a single model can adequately characterize the performance of all individuals at all points in time, and that variations result from differences in the efficiency (in terms of speed and/or accuracy) with which one or more of the operations in the model is carried out.

A third approach, which motivates the work described here, postulates qualitative or strategic variation -- as well as quantitative variation -- as a potent determinant of differences in skill. The basic idea is that identifiably different and even multiple underlying models or concatenations of basic processes might best explain performance differences between people or within an individual at varying levels of skill or aptitude.

Based on this analysis of skill as deriving from qualitative or strategic factors, four ways can be distinguished by which the adoption of alternative information processing strategies could lead to differences in performance reflecting level of skill. First, differences between people (or within a person at different times) could exist in the basic composition of the strategy repertoire. That is, some people may simply have more strategies available than others. Second, the same essential set of strategies might be available for different people, but one type of strategy could have a heightened level of availability for a given individual because of practice or recency of use. Third, people could differ in their strategy flexibility, or in their ability to select a strategy most appropriate to the demands or the structure of the currect problem solving situation. Finally, differences may arise from efficiency considerations, as promoted by a traditional information processing approach. That is, people differ in the efficiency, in terms of speed and/or accuracy of performance, with which the operations in a particular strategy, once selected, are actually carried out.

The view that emerges from this framework analyzes skill as a relative superiority in any or all of these four categories and allows for interactions among the categories as well. The highly skilled individual is one who possesses a large repertoire of available strategies, who selects an adaptive strategy, who is able to fine-tune strategy selection to problem solving demands, and who can execute a selected strategy quickly and accurately. Further, an individual can appear to be unskilled or low in ability for any of a variety of reasons. The individual may not have many appropriate strategies available, may not tend to select very useful strategies from the repertoire, may not be adept at switching strategy selection in the face of changing problem requirements, and may not be very efficient at carrying out a strategy that has been selected.

In the remaining sections of this paper, an extensive program of experimental work directed toward evaluating the above analysis of the nature of spatial skill, interactions between the use of strategies and spatial skill, and the role of spatial representations and processing operations in the execution of these strategies is summarized. The program of research was conducted in collaboration with Debra Evans, Randy Mumaw, Charles Muchow, and Linda Greenberg, all of the University of Pittsburgh. In the section immediately following, our work on strategies and mental representations in complex spatial problem solving is described. In the next section, some initial research on spatial representations used in object recognition -- which derives from the problem solving work -- is summarized briefly.

EXPERIMENTS ON STRATEGIES IN COMPLEX SPATIAL PROBLEM SOLVING

The primary experimental task with which we have evaluated the analysis of spatial skill outlined above is one in which subjects must comprehend different types of two-dimensional projections of three-dimensional objects. This problem solving situation was chosen because it affords the opportunity for the use of multiple information processing strategies, it requires some degree of technical skill but that skill can readily be increased by learning, and at face value it seems to require the use of spatial representations and manipulations.

The problem solving task that we have studied most extensively involves judging the equivalence of different forms of representing three-dimensional objects in two dimensions. The problems are similar to the sort typically encountered in beginning courses in mechanical engineering in that two forms of projection are used -- isometric projection, in which an object is shown in approximate perspective such that three sides are visible, and orthographic projection, in which each of the three sides of the object is displayed (by dropping perpendiculars to the plane of projection) as an observer would see that surface if looking directly at it. Figure 4-I shows isometric and orthographic projections of the same three-dimensional objects. Various drawing conventions are used in illustrating objects thus projected, the most important of which is the dashed lines in the orthographic views which represent hidden edges of the depicted objects.

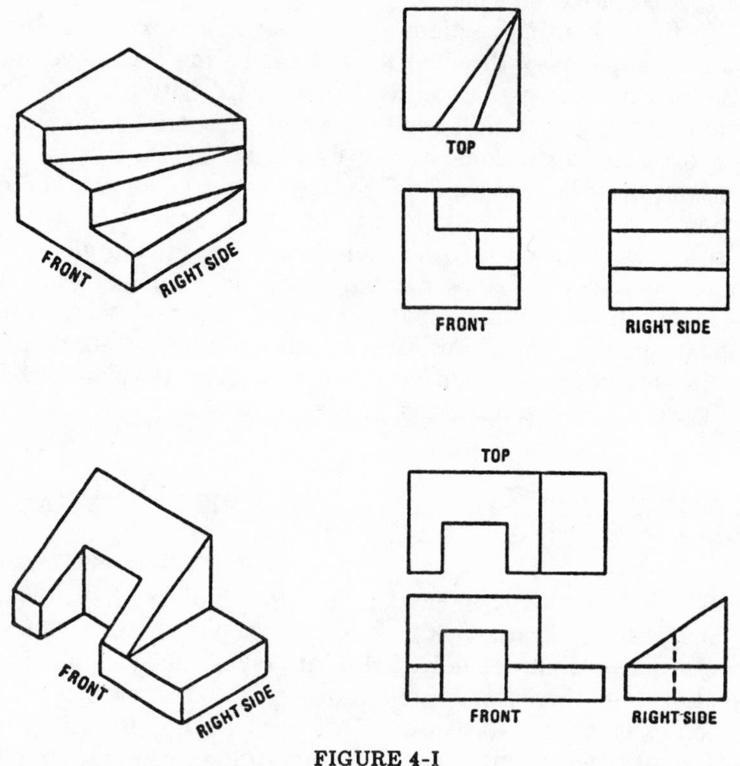

FIGURE 4-I

Isometric (left) and orthographic (right) views of two visual structures

The participants in our experiments have typically been undergraduate students who have completed or were currently enrolled in beginning mechanical engineering courses at the University of Pittsburgh, Carnegie-Mellon University, and the University of Arizona. The initial set of test problems was designed in collaboration with a professional engineer, Dr. William Conturo of the University of Pittsburgh. The actual problem solving task posed to the students was somewhat more difficult than comparison of isometric and othorgraphic projections like those shown above. Rather, we asked them to determine the compatibility of two sets of orthographic views of potentially realizable three-dimensional objects. That is, given two orthographic views and an empty "placeholder" indicating the location of a missing third view, a judgment of "possibility," "correctness," or "compatibility" of that third view, shown in another picture, had to be made.

THE ORTHOGRAPHIC COMPATIBILITY TASK
(Schematic Display)

Question: Will the three views combine to form a possible three-dimensional structure?

Slide 1--Two orthographic views and an empty "placeholder"

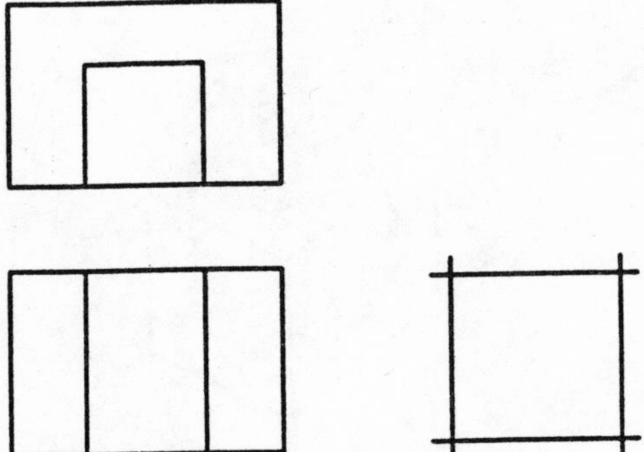

Slide 2--Possible third orthographic view

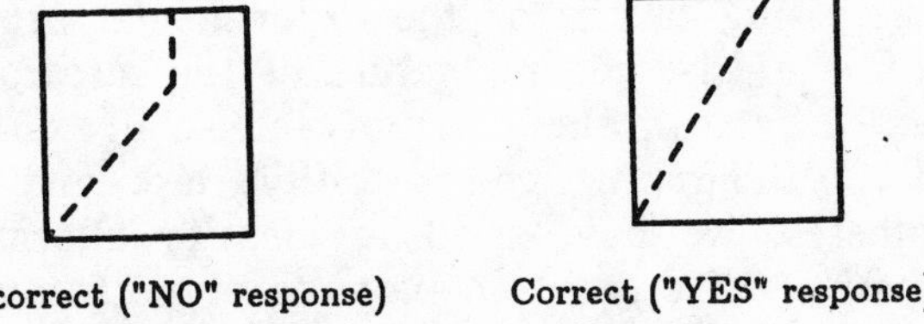

Incorrect ("NO" response) Correct ("YES" response)

FIGURE 4-II

A schematic illustration of the orthographic compatibility task.

Figure 4-II provides a schematic illustration of this "orthographic compatibility" task, and Figure 4-III shows the isometric projection that corresponds to the same three-dimensional object as the correct set of three orthographic projections shown in the previous figure. (It is important to note that the isometric view, while provided for the reader's convenience and comparison, was not shown to the subjects in these experiments. They were simply provided with two orthographic views, followed by a third, and were asked to make the compatibility judgment.) Other tasks involving comparison of various modes of depicting three-dimensional objects have been used in some of our experiments, but pilot work indicated that the orthographic compatibility task produced the most interpretable patterns of performance. Thus, further discussion will be confined to results obtained with this task and with modifications of it.

FIGURE 4-III

Isometric view corresponding to the orthographic compatibility problem illustrated in Figure 4-II.

Before discussing details of the experimental procedure and results, an outline of the general nature of the research approach is appropriate. First, on the basis of intensive examination of data from the "orthographic compatibility" task and guided by working hypotheses, we have tried to identify alternative strategies by qualitative differences in patterns of performance. This initial step in the research program is an important and difficult one. Strategies cannot be manipulated in advance of the actual experimental situation like levels of an independent variable. Rather, they must be inferred from the data from orderly patterns of covariation among sets of dependent measures. Next, having identified the operation of alternative strategies we have sharpened our hypotheses concerning the nature of these strategies, and we have sought converging evidence for their operation by deriving testable consequences of alternative strategy use. Third, we have attempted to assess the flexibility of strategy adoption by seeing whether isolated cases of strategy use could be changed by introducing manipulations of task demands or structural problem characteristics designed to favor the use of one strategy or another. Finally, an ongoing objective has been to explore the interactions between strategies revealed in this fashion and other indices of spatial skill.

The overall plan of our studies of complex spatial problem solving is as follows. We began with a large sample of engineering students and classified them with respect to level of aptitude using a combined measure from three spatial aptitude tests. A subset of these students (those scoring at the upper and the lower ends of the combined measure) returned to participate in laboratory tasks which can be viewed as discrete-trial versions of items on aptitude batteries. The idea behind this phase of the experimental design was to determine whether values of information processing parameters estimated from the laboratory tasks were related to problem solving skill, to conventional aptitude measures, or to both, as might be expected under a traditional information processing account of sources of individual differences in spatial skill.

These subjects then engaged in solving orthographic compatibility problems, and we attempted to classify their solution strategies in ways that will be described below. We then designed new sets of problems that were intended to incorporate certain features of the alternative strategies, and subjects whose strategies and aptitude levels had been analyzed in initial experiments participated in a modified problem solving situation. Strategy use was assessed again with these new problems, and the entire experimental sequence was repeated with additional students and other selected groups of subjects.

There are a number of salient features of the initial problem solving experiment to be presented here. Although a variety of problem-solving tasks had been included in pilot experiments, only data from the orthographic compatibility problems will be considered here, primarily for comparability with subsequent experiments. The sequence of events on a typical trial in our initial experiment was as follows: First, a slide containing two orthographic views and an empty placeholder was presented, and the subject could initiate when so desired a second slide containing the potential completion in the form of a third orthographic view. The subject was allowed to alternate between the two slides as many times as he or she felt necessary, up to a maximum allowable solution time of 70 seconds.

The dependent measures of interest included the accuracy of the "compatible/incompatible" choice response, the number of alternations between the first and second slides, and various measures of the distribution of solution time over the first and subsequent presentation of each of the two problem slides. Of particular interest was the proportion of total solution time spent in the initial viewing of the first slide, containing two "given" orthographics and a placeholder indicating the location of the upcoming completion view. In addition, subjects were interrogated at the end of the entire problem solving session as to the methods they used in solving the spatial problems. That is, in this experiment a single retrospective verbal protocol was elicited.

In an initial analysis, we examined correlations obtained between accuracy on the orthographic compatibility task and a variety of other measures of spatial skill. No compelling patterns emerged from these simple correlations, except for modest relationships between problem solving accuracy and two of the spatial aptitude measures, as well as correlations with experience on problems similar to those in our task and correlations with intercept parameters in the timed laboratory tasks. These last correlations may well reflect the operation of general speed factors revealed by lower intercepts in the laboratory tasks and the tendency to solve more problems correctly within the alloted time in the problem solving situation.

Of considerably more interest are the results of our efforts to relate alternative solution strategies to measures of spatial skill. From a joint consideration of the content of the verbal protocols and two of the dependent measures, we were able to indentify two global strategies that capture the performance of most of the individual subjects. These strategies differ in both the nature of the mental representations and the operations on these representations used to solve the spatial problems. The first strategy, termed the constructive approach, seems to involve the generation of an internal representation of a three-dimensional model of the object that is consistent with the initial two orthographic views -- during the time in which those views are displayed -- followed by a quick check of the third view to determine whether or not it "fits onto" the constructed internal representation. The dependent measures diagnostic of use of this strategy are a large proportion of total solution time spent examining the first presentation of the initial orthographic projections (during which, by hypothesis, the mental construction is occurring) and relatively few alternations between the first and second parts of each problem. Protocols of subjects using this strategy are consistent with the patterns of dependent measures, and some example verbal protocols are provided in Figure 4-IV.

Engineering Studies -- Sample Protocols

I. Constructive Strategy

> "Looked at first two views and got an isometric picture and tried to decide what third view would look like without looking at it." (Student)

> "Looked at the two views and tried to visualize something that might look like something with these two views. Then switched to second slide and tried to fit it with what I was thinking." (Student)

> "I would try to take the first two views and see how they relate to each other, then try to visualize the missing view while looking at the first two views. Tried to form a three-dimensional picture of the object." (Draftsman)

FIGURE 4-IV

Sample verbal protocols from subject inferred to solve spatial problems using a constructive strategy.

A second strategy, termed the analytic approach, is revealed in the dependent measures by many alternations between problem parts and relatively small proportions of total solution time spent on any given part. This strategy appears to involve individual, local comparisons of portions of the initial two orthographic views with corresponding sections of the third flat projection, a number of times if necessary to obtain an answer. Verbal protocols of some subjects who reported using this strategy, at least part of the time, are provided in Figure 4-V.

Engineering Studies -- Sample Protocols

II. Analytic Strategy

> "Tried to see if it would fit in ... Just match of little parts of third view with the other two views that they gave you. Just used what was supplied. Isometric used on simple forms ... others just matched. Began to picture object in easy forms, but the others -- forget it!" (Student)
>
> "Looked to see if object was symmetrical on first slide. On second slide, looked for planes to see if surfaces shown on first slide were flat or slanted. If there were hidden lines, checked other views for them. Also anticipated kinds of lines on second slide. From looking at first slide, got an idea what to look for on second slide -- hidden lines, number of solid lines." (Draftsman)

FIGURE 4-V

Sample verbal protocols from subjects inferred to solve spatial problems using a constructive strategy.

Having identified the constructive and analytic strategies from covariation in the content of verbal protocols, frequency of alternations, and distribution of viewing times, we examined data addressing the consequences of alternative strategy adoption and how alternative strategy use might be related to other indicators of level of spatial skills. Before examining these data, it is useful to consider -- in terms of the analysis of skill offered earlier-- just what some possible relationships between skill and strategy use might be.

The first possibility is that low skill individuals might not have access to the seemingly "spatial" constructive strategy and thus would tend not to use it. A second related possibility is that aptitude levels might drive strategy selection such that high aptitude people would tend to use the constructive strategy and low aptitude people would select the analytic procedure. If we add the possibility that the constructive strategy might produce better performance than the analytic strategy on this face valid spatial task, then the constructive users should perform better than the analytic users. The third possibility relates the ability to switch strategies to level of skill. This experiment was not designed to assess switching, so the issue will be discussed in the context of a subsequent study. The fourth possibility is that aptitude essentially reduces to efficiency, so high skill people should simply perform better (in terms of speed and/or accuracy) than low skill people, regardless of which strategy is selected. Finally, strategic factors could interact in various ways with level of skill or aptitude, resulting in any of a number of performance patterns.

Figure 4-VI shows data relevant to those possible relationships between skill or aptitude and type of strategy employed. Specifically, performance on the orthographic compatibility task, in terms of solution time and overall accuracy, is displayed as a function of both aptitude level and type of strategy selected. The cells are further subdivided into relatively slow and fast solution times. Examination of these data leads to several clear conclusions. First, any simple version of the first two possibilities for relations between strategies and skill offered above -- based on strategy repertoire and strategy selection considerations -- is incorrect. That is, if aptitude level controlled either the content of a strategy repertoire or the type of strategy selected, then most of the high aptitude subjects should select the constructive strategy, and their low aptitude counterparts should select the analytic strategy. From Figure 4-VI, the distribution of selected strategies over aptitude levels is certainly more uniform than either of these accounts would predict. Second, note that in terms of overall accuracy in problem solving, neither the constructive nor the analytic strategy leads to consistently superior performance. There is, however, an effect of aptitude on performance apparent in Figure 4-VI, showing higher aptitude individuals solving problems more efficiently overall than low aptitude persons.

Figure 4-VI also reveals clear joint effects of both aptitude level and strategy choice on performance in solving orthographic compatibility problems. In order to understand these joint effects, note, first, that the best problem solving performance -- in terms speed, accuracy, and their tradeoff -- results when high aptitude individuals use the constructive strategy (upper lefthand cells in Figure 4-VI). And, the lower lefthand cells in Figure 4-VI, corresponding to low aptitude individuals using the constructive strategy, reveal the poorest performance, which is basically at chance. Is this poor performance of low aptitude individuals using the constructive strategy to be attributed to general efficiency factors (i.e., that low aptitude individuals are generally poorer solvers of problems than are high aptitude individuals) or to the selection of a maladaptive strategy by students with this aptitude configuration?

Figure 4-VI shows that both efficiency and strategy-related factors operate to some extent in producing the poor performance of the low aptitude individuals using the constructive strategy. To appreciate this interaction, note that low aptitude individuals do indeed perform less efficiently overall than do high aptitude individuals; however, this general aptitude difference in efficiency is attenuated to some extent when performance resulting from use of the analytic strategy is considered. A comparison of the lower lefthand and lower righthand cells in Figure 4-VI (corresponding to low aptitude constructive and analytic strategy users, respectively) demonstrates that low skill students perform somewhat better on orthographic compatibility problem solving when they adopt the analytic strategy instead of the constructive approach. Moreover, not only do low aptitude individuals perform better with the analytic than with the constructive strategy, but also their performance using the analytic strategy is roughly comparable to performance of the high aptitude group of subjects that opted for the analytic approach (i.e., compare the lower and the upper righthand cells in Figure 4-VI, corresponding to low and to high aptitude subjects both adopting the analytic strategy). So, while the interpretation of these data is a bit complicated, it seems reasonable to conclude that general efficiency factors related to aptitude level do operate in determining problem solving performance, but this general effect is observed primarily when the constructive strategy is adopted for solving the orthographic compatibility problems.

ORTHOGRAPHIC COMPATIBILITY PROBLEMS

APTITUDE		STRATEGY: CONSTRUCTIVE	STRATEGY: ANALYTIC
HIGH	SLOW	N = 9 average solution time = 52.91 secs. accuracy = 72%	N = 6 average solution time = 55.62 secs. accuracy = 63%
HIGH	FAST	N = 9 average solution time = 38.52 secs. accuracy = 62%	N = 7 average solution time = 43.72 secs. accuracy = 59%
LOW	SLOW	N = 7 average solution time = 61.55 secs. accuracy = 60%	N = 6 average solution time = 57.55 secs. accuracy = 56%
LOW	FAST	N = 6 average solution time = 38.97 secs. accuracy = 46%	N = 2 average solution time = 46.45 secs. accuracy = 58%

FIGURE 4-VI

Summary of results from initial orthographic compatibility problem solving experiment.

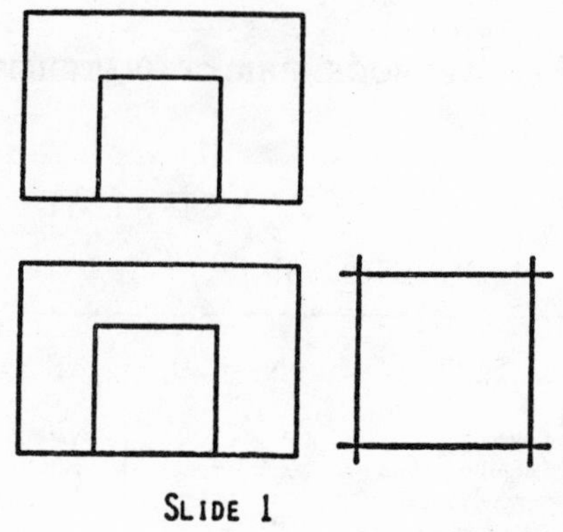

SLIDE 1

SLIDE 2 CORRESPONDING ISOMETRIC VIEW

FIGURE 4-VII

An example of a problem of the emergent feature variety

An additional source of converging evidence for the distinction between constructive and analytic strategy use emerged from a consideration of performance -- broken down by strategy type -- on individual problems in this experiment. (Recall, from Figure 4-VI, that neither strategy led to consistently superior performance over all problem types.) Figure 4-VII gives an example of a problem on which constructive strategy users did consistently better than analytic users. Note that a salient characteristic of this problem is that the wedge in the structure (shown in the isometric) emerges as a property of constructing the corresponding three-dimensional object and is not discernable from any features of the flat orthographic views in their given form. Contrast the cognitive requirements of that problem with those of the problem shown in Figure 4-VIII, on which analytic strategy users performed better than constructive strategy users. In this problem, all of the crucial details concerning left-right and top-bottom relations, which are sufficient to solve the problem, are available from local comparisons of the directions shown in the flat orthographic views themselves. And, this is just the nature of the mental operations presumed to be central to the use of the analytic strategy. Thus, an internal analysis of the individual problems provides both converging experimental evidence for the reality of the proposed strategy distinction and also the beginnings of an account of the problems as cognitive tasks.

We consider, next, a second problem-solving experiment designed to generate data more directly relevant to certain issues raised by the first experiment -- in particular, the question of possible relationships between skill and strategy flexibility. There are four salient differences between the present experiment and the earlier study. First, the subjects in the present experiment had participated in the earlier experiment and thus they were already tentatively classified, on the basis of their performance in that previous study, as to whether they would tend to use the constructive or the analytic strategy as a general solution mode for orthographic compatibility problems. Second, the problem composition was changed to include 10 problems of the "emergent property" variety (in an effort to elicit constructive strategy use), 10 problems of the "feature matching" sort (to elicit the analytic strategy), and 10 "miscellaneous" problems. We included this manipulation of the structure of the problem ensemble specifically to assess the extent of strategy switching -- in particular, to evaluate the hypothesis that high skill individuals are characterized by strategy flexibility and thus can adapt their strategy selection to the processing demands of a particular problem. Third, verbal protocols were requested from each subject after each problem was solved (as oppossed to a single retrospective protocol) in order to determine more accurately which strategy each subject used on each problem.

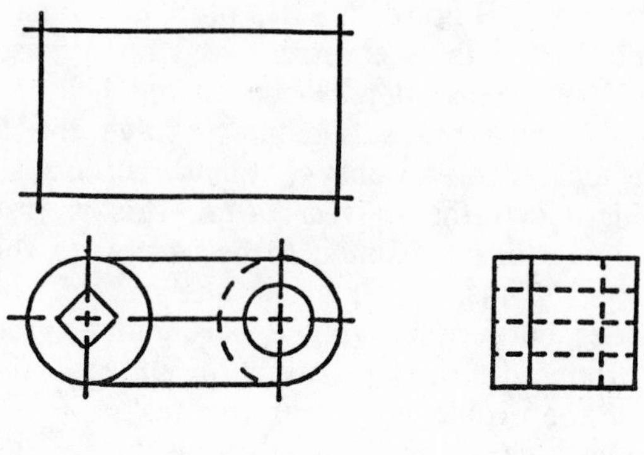

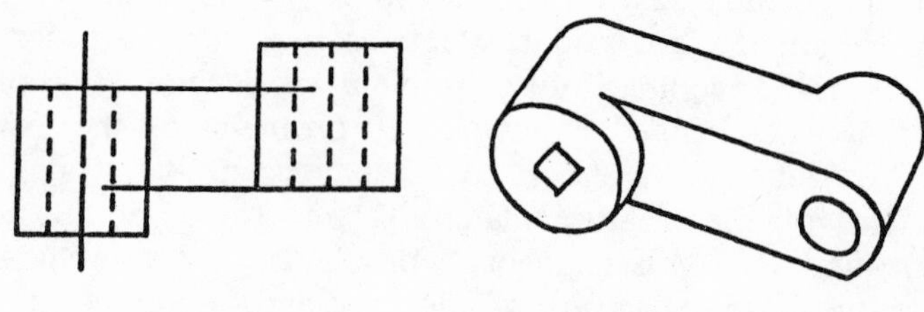

FIGURE 4-VIII

An example of a problem of the feature matching variety

Finally, the entire experimental session was concluded with a surprise recognition memory test for <u>isometric views</u> of objects that did or did not correspond to the same three-dimensional objects as had sets of orthographic projections displayed during the problem solving phase of the experiment. Figure 4-IX provides a schematic diagram of the isometric recognition task. This new experimental task is important, because with it we hoped to determine more directly than in the earlier experiment the nature of the mental representations that subjects had used while solving the problems. Our initial idea was that the constructive strategy users would be more likely to recognize the appropriate isometric views than would analytic strategy users because, by hypothesis, these isometrics were structurally similar to the mental representations that constructive strategy users had generated as problem solving tools.

THE ISOMETRIC RECOGNITION TASK

Provided during problem solving:

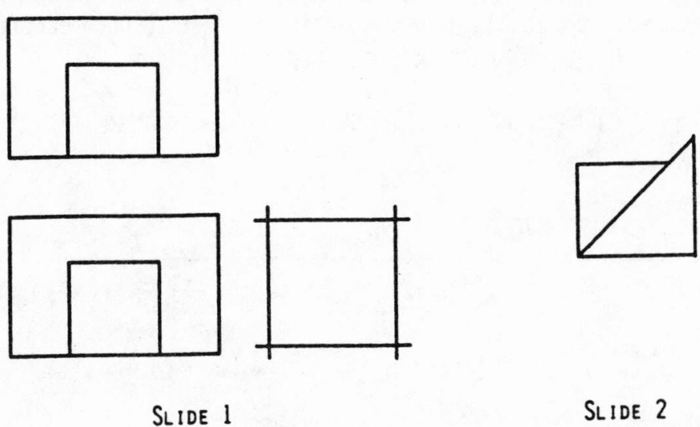

Shown for "yes-no" recognition:

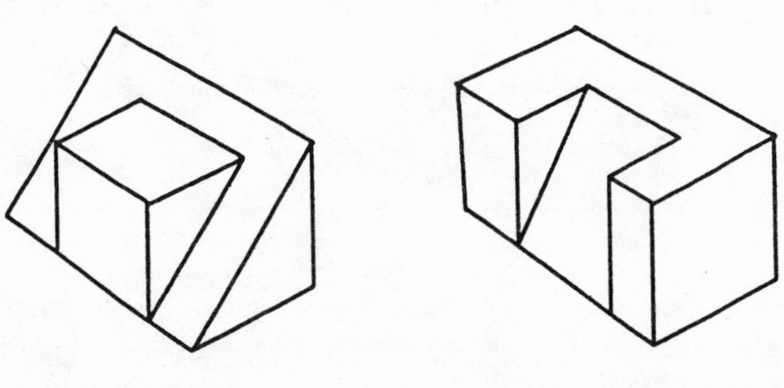

FIGURE 4-IX

A schematic illustration of the isometric recognition task.

The overall results in terms of speed and accuracy of orthographic problem solving are displayed as a function of aptitude level and strategy use in Figure 4-X. For purposes of this figure, strategy classification was determined by each individual subject's performance in the earlier experiments. Figure 4-X shows a replication of the essential results obtained in that earlier experiment. Note that again the high aptitude individuals using the constructive strategy give the best overall performance, and the worst performance is obtained when the low aptitude individuals use the constructive strategy. As in the earlier experiment, problem solving success is at least partially dependent upon strategy selection, in that analytic strategy users of both aptitude levels fall between the extremes found with the constructive strategy, and the high and low aptitude subjects perform in a roughly equal fashion when using the analytic approach.

ORTHOGRAPHIC COMPATIBILITY PROBLEMS

APTITUDE	STRATEGY: CONSTRUCTIVE	STRATEGY: ANALYTIC
HIGH	N = 10 average solution time = 57.31 secs. accuracy = 65%	N = 13 average solution time = 64.13 secs. accuracy = 64%
LOW	N = 6 average solution time = 67.95 secs. accuracy = 53%	N = 6 average solution time = 63.15 secs. accuracy = 58%

FIGURE 4-X

Summary of results from the second orthographic compatibility problem solving experiment.

A central question addressed in the present experiment concerns the possibility that high levels of aptitude or skill are associated with a greater tendency to switch strategies flexibly in accordance with structural properties of particular sorts of problems. Two kinds of analyses failed to find any striking evidence for this type of relationship between strategy flexibility and spatial skill. The first analysis compared the performance of high and low aptitude individuals, as well as their strategy selections, on problems of the "features matching" and the "emergent property" types. We were unable to obtain evidence that high aptitude individuals switched strategies more often in response to changes in problem types than did low aptitude subjects, nor were we able to find evidence that high aptitude individuals were generally more successful on one problem type or the other.

A second analysis of strategy flexibility required a determination -- from the verbal protocols and the time distributions of each individual subject on each individual problem -- of the extent of strategy switching of high and of low aptitude individuals during the course of the entire experimental session. For purposes of an overall analysis, we defined a marked tendency to switch strategies as a rate of switching that exceeded 40% over the series of 30 problems. Using this measure, high aptitude individuals as a group were only slightly less consistent in their use of strategy than were low aptitude individuals as a group, with 58% of the high skill students consistently (i.e., on 60% of the problems) using the same strategy and 69% of the low skill students showing consistent strategy use.

However, a third sort of analysis revealed that high aptitude individuals do demonstrate more strategy flexibility than low aptitude individuals, if strategy flexibility is considered **within** the solution of any given problem rather than **across** an entire problem solving session. To reveal this form of strategy flexibility, we considered in detail the verbal protocols that each subject produced after solving each in the series of 30 orthographic compatibility problems. From these verbal protocols, we generated a "strategy tree" that characterized the sequence of alternative strategies adopted in the solution of individual problems by individual subjects. Figure 4-XI illustrates four such strategy trees -- two for a high aptitude subject solving a constructive (emergent property) problem and an analytic (feature matching) problem -- and two for a low aptitude subject solving the same two problems.

Several features of these diagrams in Figure 4-XI are important. First, while both subjects began using a constructive approach to both problems (involving the generation of an isometric model of a three-dimensional object), the high aptitude individual in the case of both problems turned to an alternative strategy when the initial one failed. The low aptitude individual persisted with the use of the initially-selected strategy, and in the case of both problems this subject ended up guessing (correctly on one problem and incorrectly on the other). Second, note that the high aptitude individual seems to have had a finer-grained differentiation among strategies than did the low aptitude individual, using different versions of an analytic approach (line extension and line comparison) when the constructive approach failed. Third, in terms of the tendency to switch flexibly from one strategy to another, the solution trees of the high aptitude individual in Figure 4-XI are considerably richer than are the trees of the low aptitude individual. This characteristic of the strategy paths for individual subjects shown in Figure 4-XI is quite representative of the trees generated for all subjects on each of the problem. So, while high aptitude individuals do not tend to switch strategies substantially more than low aptitude individuals across the series of problems in the experimental session, the high skill people do show more strategy flexibility than the low skill people at the level of richness of their strategy solution trees for individual problems.

We consider, next, the results of the surprise isometric recognition test conducted at the end of the orthographic compatibility problem solving session. Recall that the purpose of this test was to probe more directly the nature of the mental representations that subjects had used during problem solving. Our initial hypothesis was that subjects who used the constructive strategy during problem solving would show recognition performance superior to that of subjects using the analytic strategy. This prediction derived from the idea that use of the constructive strategy involves, in part, the generation of an internal model corresponding to an "objectlike" or "isometriclike" view from the flat views given in the orthographic projections provided for problem solving. Use of the analytic strategy does not require the generation of such an "objectlike" mental model. Thus, constructive strategy users should be more likely than analytic strategy users to have information concerning the three-dimensional structure of objects corresponding to the orthographic views available at the time of the recognition test, and hence they should show better recognition performance than the analytic strategy users.

"STRATEGY TREES" FOR APTITUDE AND PROBLEM TYPES

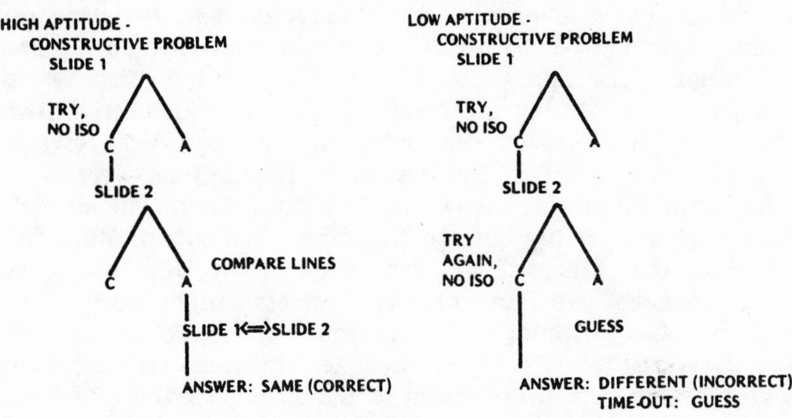

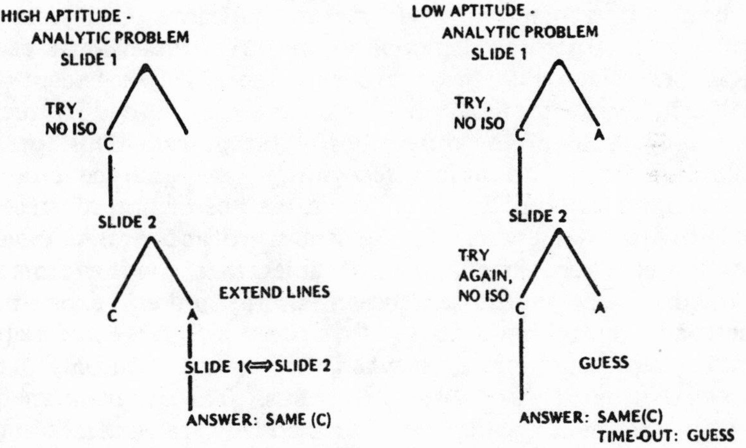

FIGURE 4-XI

Trees as representations of the sequence of strategies used by a high-aptitude and a low-aptitude subject on two orthographic compatibility problems.

Figure 4-XII shows hit rates and false alarm rates for isometric recognition for both high and low aptitude groups and for constructive and analytic strategy users. Note that at the level of overall accuracy our prediction concerning the relative recognition performances of the constructive and analytic strategy groups was not confirmed. However, latency for isometric recognition does appear to be sensitive to the differences in strategies used during problem solving. Constructive strategy users recognized isometrics with an average latency of 3.5 seconds, while analytic strategy users required an average of 8 seconds for correct isometric recognition. These latency differences suggest that the constructive strategy might produce "direct access" to the results of the generation of an "objectlike" mental model, whereas analytic problem solvers might recognize the isometrics by "stripping off" individual orthographic views from the displayed isometric and then testing these flat projections against a memory representation of the original problem slides.

Although the overall levels of recognition performance were not sensitive to the use of different strategies during problem solving, an unexpected and potentially important outcome is that for all strategy and aptitude classifications, recognition of isometrics was well above chance. Consider just what this relatively high level of recognition performance indicates: Subjects are recognizing a structural depiction of a three-dimensional object (an isometric view) that they have never seen before except in a radically different surface form, namely, the individual orthographic projections of the three sides of the object. This finding, here in the context of object recognition, is reminiscent of the work of Bransford and Franks 1971 on the abstraction of meaning from individual sentences. In the Bransford and Franks experiments, subjects recognized the gist rather than the surface form of individually presented sentences. In the present experiment, subjects apparently have access to a deep "objectlike" level of perceptual representation, even when they are exposed only to flat projections of surfaces of visual structures. The experiments presented in the next section are directed toward extending and exploring further this unexpected finding of high levels of isometric recognition accuracy given only previous exposure to flat, disconnected orthographic views of the corresponding objects.

ISOMETRIC RECOGNITION RESULTS

APTITUDE	STRATEGY: CONSTRUCTIVE	STRATEGY: ANALYTIC
HIGH	HR = .78 FAR = .28	HR = .76 FAR = .27
LOW	HR = .72 FAR = .33	HR = .82 FAR = .27

FIGURE 4-XII

Hit rates (HR) and false alarm rates (FAR) for isometric recognition following orthographic problem solving.

EXPERIMENTS ON MENTAL REPRESENTATIONS IN OBJECT RECOGNITION

The series of experiments described briefly below was designed to replicate and to begin exploring the "isometric recognition effect" that emerged unexpectedly from the experiments on complex problem solving. We undertook these experiments because we viewed the recognition finding as potentially significant for a number of reasons. First, the generally high level of recognition accuracy indicated that subjects had access to a constructed mental representation of a very different form from the representations of objects provided during problem solving. This suggests that the process of problem solution involves the obligatory construction of a mental model corresponding to the structure of a three-dimensional object, even though such a construction is not required by the problem solving task. Second, high levels of recognition accuracy characterized the performance of both analytic and constructive strategy users, even though their latencies for recognition were markedly different. This suggests that subjects using the analytic strategy (as well as subjects using the constructive strategy) have access to information about three-dimensional structure even though they do not verbally report generating such representations during problem solving. Third, our initial recognition findings make contact with results from other perceputal and cognitive domains and hence may have some degree of generality. In particular, these findings can be viewed as extensions to the domain of object recognition of the earlier findings of Posner and Keele 1968 -- showing that prototypes of visual categories are abstracted and remembered even when only non-prototypical exemplars are displayed for initial category learning -- and of Bransford and Franks 1971 concerning the abstraction of core meaning from individually presented sentences.

The first experiment in this series was a replication of the earlier recognition findings with a more sensitive experimental procedure. As in the earlier experiments, subjects solved a series of orthographic compatibility problems designed specifically for use in the present experiment. At no time during the problem solving phase of the experiment were subjects either shown isometric views of the objects displayed in the problems as sets of orthographic views or told that isometric views were relevant to the experimental task.

After solving the orthographic compatibility problems, the subjects were informed that there was a second phase of the experiment in which they would be asked to recognize isometric views of objects that had been shown previously in orthographic projection. On each recognition trial, a display containing two isometrics views was presented, and subjects were required to determine which of the two isometric corresponded to any of the same objects that had earlier been displayed as sets of orthographic projections. Figure 4-XIII illustrates two of the orthographic compatibility problems from a series of 20 such problems, and Figure 4-XIV shows the corresponding target/distractor recognition stimuli.

The central results from the problem solving task, the recognition task, and the relationship between performance on both of the tasks can be summarized as follows: Overall accuracy on solving the orthographic compatibility problems was 76.5%, and average solution time was 45.6 seconds. Average accuracy in discriminating target isometric views from distractors was 85.5%. Furthermore, accuracy on the problem solving and the recognition tasks were not independent ($X^2_1 = 8.85$; $p < .01$). The probability of correctly recognizing an isometric view of an object, given that the corresponding orthographic compatibility problem had been solved correctly, was .90. The probability of correct recognition, given an incorrect problem solution, was .72; and, these two recognition probabilities are significantly different ($t_9 = 2.29$; $p < .05$).

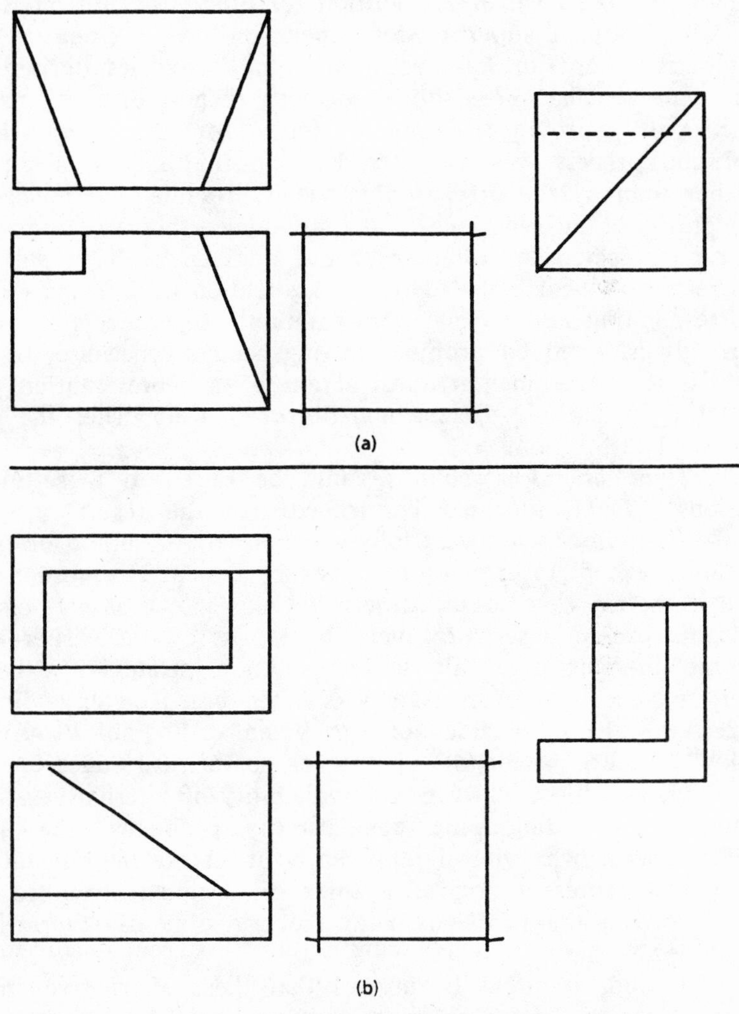

FIGURE 4-XIII

Two examples of orthographic compatibility problems used in the series of recognition experiments described in the text.

These results are consistent with the idea that solving orthographic compatibility problems is accomplished by construction of an internal representation of a three-dimensional structure--permitting later recognition of isometric views -- **even though the form in which the problem was presented contained only separated,** flat views of individual sides of a visual structure. The generally high level of recognition for previously unseen isometric views of objects supports this conclusion. More importantly, the significant superior later recognition of isometrics deriving from problems that had been solved correctly than from problems solved incorrectly, provides strong evidence for the claim that the solution process was mediated by a mental model of an object rather than by the orthographic views presented in the problems. Retention of information about individual orthographic views need not be affected by whether or not a given problem was solved correctly or incorrectly. However, retention of information about corresponding isometric representations of objects should be strongly affected by problem solving accuracy because, by hypothesis, it is the mental construction of a representation corresponding to a three-dimensional object that underlies the process of problem solution.

Two general objections could be raised to these interpretations. First, it could be argued that the results are hardly surprising, in that viewers have no alternative method of problem solution except to attempt to construct a mental representation of the isometric view of the object initially shown as sets of orthographic projections. However, the results of our earlier experiments indicate that alternative solution strategies exist. In particular, the analytic strategy is often based on extending lines from the different sides of the given orthographic views that allow a determination of whether or not critical edges could join to form an object. Given the availability of alternative strategies for solving orthographic compatibility problems, the question remains as to why viewers apparently undertake the constuction of a mental representation of a three-dimensional structure, rather than solving the problems with the two-dimensional projections provided.

Second, it could be argued that these alternative strategies may indeed mediate problem solution and that the present recognition results derive from the possibility that subjects have more information available about problems successfully solved than about the structures depicted in problems that were solved incorrectly. That is, in the case of problems solved correctly, more information relevant to the later recognition test is encoded than in the case of problems solved incorrectly. This additional encoded information might take any of several forms, including information about the flat orthographic views that could be used to advantage at the time of recognition.

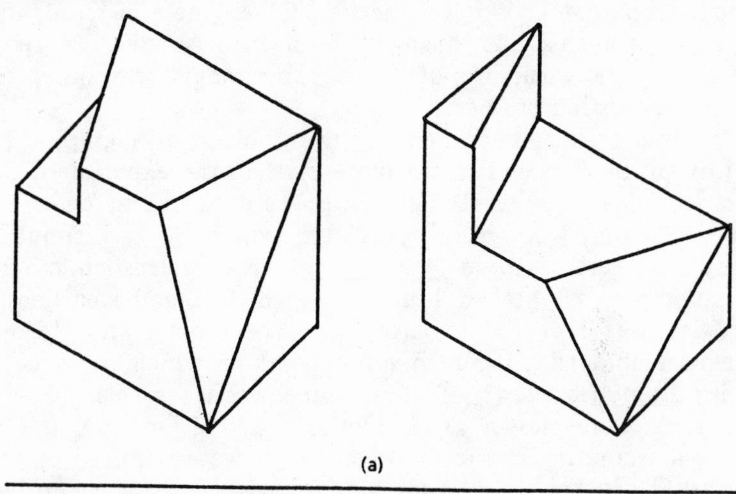

(a)

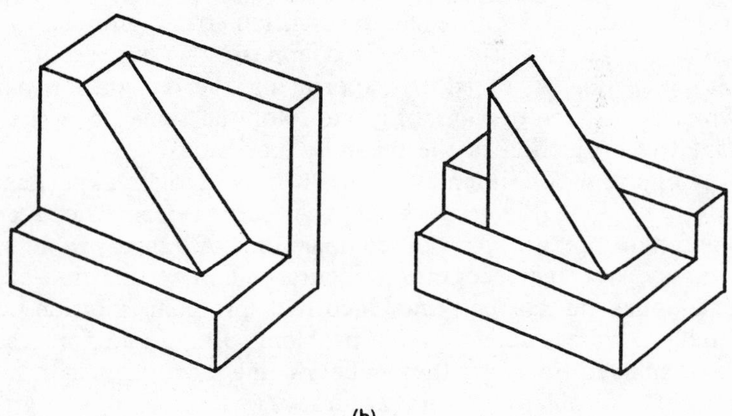

(b)

FIGURE 4-XIV

"Target/distractor" recognition pairs of isometrics corresponding to the orthographic compatibility problems shown in Figure 4-XIII

In order to evaluate this and related objections to our interpretation of the isometric recognition results, we performed additional experiments that might be viewed as controls for sources of information other than three-dimensional structure mediating later recognition of isometric views. In each experiment, separate groups of mechanical engineering students solved spatial problems and engaged in a surprise delayed recognition test, but the structure of these experiments was quite different from our earlier studies.

In the first experiment, subjects solved orthographic compatibility problems identical to those used in the experiment described above. The surprise recognition phase consisted of trials on which subjects were required to indicate which of two simultaneously displayed sets of three orthographic views corresponded to orthographic views that had been displayed during the earlier problem solving phase of the experiment. The second and third experiments employed a problem solving task in which subjects reasoned with isometric views of three-dimensional objects. Specifically, subjects were shown an isometric view of an object, alternated with a second isometric view, and they were required to determine whether the two isometrics were views of the same object (i.e., rotational variants) or views of different objects. The second experiment had a recognition test in which the recognition pairs were the same isometrics used in the initial experiment reported in this section. On each recognition trial, subjects indicated which of the two isometrics had appeared in the earlier problem solving series. In the third experiment, the recognition pairs were two sets of three orthographic views of the same objects shown in isometric projection in the second experiment.

Figure 4-XV summarizes the results of these experiments, and shows as well the results of the earlier isometric recognition experiment for purposes of comparison. Average problem solving accuracy, average recognition accuracy, and recognition accuracies conditional on correct and incorrect problem solution are presented. Average latencies for problem solving and for recognition are displayed in parentheses below the accuracy scores. Note, first, that problem solving accuracy was reasonably high for all experiments and that considerably more time was required to solve the orthographic compatibility problems than to perform the isometric comparisons. Overall recognition performance was reasonably good in all conditions. Not surprisingly, the lowest recognition scores and the longest recognition latencies were obtained when subjects were asked to discriminate target from distractor orthographic views after solving problems based solely on exposure to isometric projections. Note, also, that the best performance was obtained when isometric problem solving was followed by isometric recognition.

SUMMARY OF INCIDENTAL RECOGNITION RESULTS

PROBLEM SOLVING TASK	ACCURACY, PROBLEM SOLVING	RECOGNITION TASK	ACCURACY, RECOGNITION	ACC|PR$_C$ / ACC|PR$_I$
ORTHOGRAPHIC COMPATIBILITY (N=10)	76.5% (45.00)	ISOMETRIC VIEWS	85.5% (9.32)	90% (t_9=2.29; $p<.05$) 72%
ORTHOGRAPHIC COMPATIBILITY (N=10)	86% (48.87)	ORTHOGRAPHIC VIEWS	89.5% (13.65)	90% NS 85%
ISOMETRIC COMPARISON (N=10)	72.5% (21.82)	ISOMETRIC VIEWS	96% (3.75)	96% NS 97%
ISOMETRIC COMPARISON (N=10)	73.5% (21.55)	ORTHOGRAPHIC VIEWS	75.5% (26.08)	75% NS 79%

FIGURE 4-XV

Problem solving and recognition accuracies and latencies for the series of surprise recognition experiments described in the text. Recognition accuracy conditional on correct and incorrect problem solution is displayed in the rightmost column.

The conditional recognition scores displayed in the rightmost column of Figure 4-XV are of considerable importance to an interpretation of the nature of isometric recognition following orthographic compatibility problem solving. Only in the case of isometric recognition following reasoning with orthographic views are the recognition probabilities obtained for problems correctly solved significantly different from the recognition probabilities obtained for problems incorrectly solved. Consider, in particular, the difference between isometric recognition following orthographic compatibility problem solving and orthographic recognition following the same type of problem solving. The data in Figure 4-XV clearly show that subjects are capable of recognizing sets of orthographic projections following orthographic compatibility problem solving, but this recognition performance is not differentially affected by the accuracy of initial problem solution. This suggests that the amount of information encoded in a problem (assessed by the accuracy of solution) is not always a potent determinant of subsequent recognition performance. The clear implication is that recognition -- in the case of isometric views following problem solving with orthographic projections -- **depends on whether or not the encoded information enables the constuction of a representation incorporating aspects of three-dimensional structure.**

Many questions remain concerning (a) the nature of the mental model of a three-dimensional object that is apparently constructed during problem solving, and (b) precisely why the construction of such a representation should occur, given that it is not required by the problem solving task itself. With respect to the first of these questions, a central thrust of our ongoing program of research has been to use the isometric recognition technique to ask whether constructed mental representations of objects contain view-independent information about three-dimensional structure or whether such representations specify object structure only from a particular point of view. In addition to articulating further the nature of the mental models used in spatial problem solving, research like this is relevant to questions concerning the accessibility of different levels of perceptual representation postulated by Marr 1982.

CONCLUDING REMARKS

One central aim of the experimental work described here has been to elucidate the nature of the mental representations and processing operations that contribute to skill in solving complex spatial problems. The results of our studies of problem solving indicate that two distinguishable global strategies, with corresponding differences in internal representations and operations, are used when people are asked to reason about whether disconnected sets of flat, two-dimensional projections correctly depict possible three-dimensional structures.

Our results suggest, further, several ways in which these strategies might be related to spatial skill. First, high levels of aptitude result in greater processing and problem solving efficiency, regardless of which global strategy is selected. Nonetheless, one strategy (the constructive strategy) seems particularly ill-suited to subjects of low aptitude and particularly well-suited to subjects high in spatial ability. Differences between the two levels of aptitude in complex problem solving is notably attenuated by use of the second, analytic strategy. Finally, examination of protocols of subjects solving individual problems suggests that high levels of skill are characterized by the flexible use of multiple strategies within the confines of single problems.

Our view of the relationship between alternative strategies and spatial skill is reinforced by findings from other laboratories using quite different experimental tasks and dependent measures (see, for example, Just and Carpenter's 1985, elegant analysis of strategies in relation to aptitude for a mental rotation task, using evidence from eye fixation data, as well as Sternberg and Weil's 1980 explanation of individual differences in syllogistic reasoning by differences among subjects in overall aptitude profiles). Furthermore, this emphasis on the contribution of alternative strategies to differences in patterns of performance is consistent with conclusions from earlier work in this laboratory on strategic factors in the execution of simple "same-different" visual comparisons (see, for example, Cooper 1976, 1980a, 1980b, 1982, Cooper and Podgorny 1976; and Cunningham, Cooper and Reaves 1982). Thus, the emerging view of spatial, as well as other forms of cognitive skill, must take account of differences in strategies in providing a comprehensive picture of sources of differences in performance (see, Cooper and Mumaw 1985 and Snow and Lohman 1984 for additional discussions).

In addition to our demonstration that the process of solving complex spatial problems is under strategic control, the research described here also has implications for how spatial information is **represented** internally for purposes of solving problems. The delayed recognition procedure used in our experiments provides a sensitive method for probing the nature of mental models used to solve spatial problems involving reasoning about two-dimensional projections of three-dimensional objects. Our results indicate that mental representations embodying information about three-dimensional structure are generated even when such a mental construction is not required by the problem solving situation.

Given that the construction of an internal model corresponding to a three-dimensional object must require time, effort, and processing resources, why should such a construction occur when the problem solving task does not require it? We suggest that representing information about visual surfaces in the form of a mental model corresponding to a three-dimensional object could be an efficient problem solving method for several reasons. Such a representation contains information about structure that makes relationships among surfaces of an object directly accessible and obviates the need for additional symbolic computations on separate pieces of stored information in memory. In addition, such mental models provide a reflection of the structure of the world in which we normally perceive and act (cf., Gibson 1979). Thus, mental representations that preserve three-dimensional structure may serve as modes of encoding information for many tasks requiring spatial reasoning. The range of reasoning situations that use such mental models and the nature of the information embodied in the models themselves are areas of current investigation in our laboratory.

NOTES

1. The research reported in this chapter was funded by contract N00014-81-C-0532 from the Office of Naval Research.

5

Perceptual Representations: Meaning and Truth Conditions

Donald D. Hoffman and Bruce M. Bennett

All acts of perception, regardless of modality, share a common formal structure. In this regard, the field of perception is like any other scientific field; behind the diversity of specific phenomena studied by each field there is, or at least one hopes there is, a fundamental unity that can be expressed precisely, perhaps in the language of mathematics.

In this paper we propose a formal, though admittedly partial, account of the structure common to all acts of perception. A central aspect of this structure, according to our account, are formal entities we call "observers". We propose a definition of an observer, a definition intended to be a formal counterpart to the informal claim that perception is a process of inference and that the inferences typical of perception are not deductively valid.

Before presenting the formal definition of an observer, we first consider two examples of visual observers. These examples are chosen to illustrate the principles that underlie our definition of an observer. They are chosen for their perspicuity and their mathematical simplicity, and are not intended to be a representative sampling of all the work done in perception. In fact, the first example is fabricated. Against the background of these examples, we present the definition of an observer and discuss its properties. As the definition uses some elementary concepts from measure theory, we include an appendix on these concepts for the convenience of the reader. Given the definition of an observer, we discuss, first, under what conditions an observer's performance is ideal; we discuss, second, the inferences of observers in the presence of noise; and we give, third, four examples of observers, all drawn from the field of computational vision.

A theory of perception cannot, of course, stop with a theory of observers. A complete theory must also discuss the objects of perception -- those entities with which an observer interacts in an act of perception -- and the relationship between observers and their objects of perception. On this issue we face a fundamental choice. We can propose that the objects of perception have the same formal structure as observers, or we can propose that they have a different formal structure.

Were we to propose that objects of perception have a formal structure different from that of observers we would have to explain why we adopted the ontologically less parsimonious course. We would also have to provide convincing arguments that the new formal structure was indeed appropriate for the objects of perception. And we would have to demonstrate that the two distinct formalisms, one for observers and one for objects of perception, could somehow be integrated so that observersand their objects of perception could interact.

We choose the ontologically parsimonious course. Specifically, we propose that the objects of perception are themselves observers (as formally defined in section four). In the concluding sections of this paper, we develop this idea a little. In Bennett et al. 1988 we develop it quite a bit further, introducing "reflexive observer frameworks" as a formal account of the interaction of observers with their objects of perception.

We turn first to some introductory examples.

BUG OBSERVER

Imagine a world in which there are bugs and one-eyed frogs that eat bugs. The bugs in this world come in two varieties -- poisonous and edible. Remarkably, the edible bugs are distinguished from the poisonous ones by the way they fly. Edible bugs fly in circles. The positions, radii, and orientations in three-dimensional space of these circles vary from one edible bug to another, but all edible bugs fly in circles. Moreover, no poisonous bugs fly in circles. Instead they fly on noncircular closed paths, paths that may be described, say, by polynomial equations.

The visual task of a frog in such a world is obvious. To survive it must visually identify and limit its diet to those bugs that fly in circles. How does the frog determine which bugs fly in circles? First, the frog's eye forms a two-dimensional image on its retina of the path of the bug. If the path is a circle, then its retinal image will be an ellipse.[2] The contrapositive is also true: If the retinal image is not an ellipse, then the path is not a circle. Therefore the frog may infer with confidence that if the retinal image of a path is not an ellipse then the bug is poisonous. In this case the frog does not eat the bug.

The frog needs to eat sometime. What can the frog infer if the retinal image is an ellipse? It is true, by assumption, that if the path is a circle then its retinal image will be an ellipse. But the converse, viz., if the image is an ellipse then the path is a circle, is in general not true. For example, elliptical paths also have elliptical images. With a little imagination one can see that many strangely curving polynomial paths have elliptical images. In fact, for any unbiased measure on the set of polynomial paths having elliptical images, the subset of circles has measure zero. So the converse inference, from elliptical images to circular paths, is almost surely false if one assumes an unbiased measure. Putting this in terms relevant to the frog, if the image is an ellipse then the bug is almost surely poisonous, assuming an unbiased measure. If the image is not an ellipse then the bug is certainly poisonous.

This situation presents the frog with a dilemma each time it observes an elliptical image. It can refuse to eat the bug for fear it is poisonous, in which case the frog starves. Or it can eat the bug and thereby risk its life. Regardless of its choice, the frog will almost surely perish.

This is a world harsh on frogs, but one which can be made kinder by a simple stipulation about the paths of poisonous bugs. Stipulate that poisonous bugs almost never trace out paths having elliptical images. So, for example, poisonous bugs almost never trace out elliptical paths. (This is not to say, necessarily, that poisonous bugs go out of their way to avoid these paths. One can get the desired effect by simply stipulating, say, that there are approximately equal numbers of edible and poisonous bugs and that all polynomial paths are equally likely paths for poisonous bugs. Then only with measure zero will a poisonous bug happen to traverse a path having an elliptical image.) This is equivalent to stipulating that the measure on the set of pathshaving elliptical images is not unbiased, contrary to what we assumed before. In fact it is to stipulate that this measure is biased toward the set of circles. With this adjustment to the world frogs have a better chance of surviving. Of course it is still the case that each time a frog eats a bug it risks its life. The frog stakes its life on the faith that the measure on bug paths is biased in its favor. But then the frog has little choice.

Presumably the frog makes visual inferences about things other than bugs, so we will call its capacity to make visual inferences about bugs its "bug observer". This bug observer is depicted in Figure 5-I. The cube labelled X is the space of all possible bug paths, whether poisonous or edible.[3] An unbiased measure on this space will be called μ_x. The wiggly line labelled E denotes the set of circular bug paths. E has measure zero in X under any unbiased measure μ_x. This is captured pictorially by representing E as a subset of X having lower dimension than X. A biased measure on X that is supported on E will be called ν. The square labelled Y is the space of all possible images of bug paths, whether poisonous or edible. The map π from X to Y represents orthographic (parallel) projection from bug paths to images of bug paths. An unbiased measure on the space Y will be called μ_y. Y is depicted as having dimension lower than X because the set of all paths in three dimensions which project onto a given path in the plane is infinite dimensional (by any reasonable measure of dimension on the set of all paths). The curve labelled S represents the set of ellipses in Y, i.e., $S = \pi(E)$. S has measure zero in Y under any unbiased measure μ_y. This is captured pictorially by representing S as a subset of Y having lower dimension than Y.

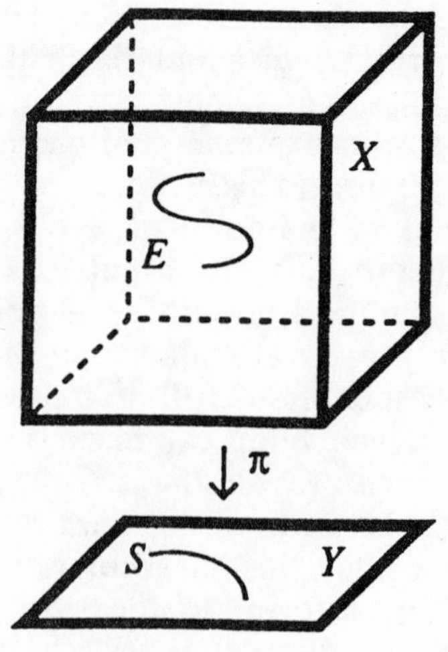

FIGURE 5-I

Bug observer

We now interpret Figure 5-I in terms of the inference being made by the bug observer. The space Y is the space of possible premises for inferences of the observer; the space X is the space of possible paths. Each point of Y not in S represents abstractly a set of premises whose associated conclusion is that the event E of the observer has not occurred. Each point of S represents abstractly a set of premises whose associated conclusion is a probability measure supported (having all its mass) on E. To each point of S is associated a different probability measure on E. This probability measure can be induced from the probability measure ν on E and the map π by means of a mathematical structure called a conditional probability distribution, discussed in the appendix. We call π the "perspective" of the bug observer.

In summary, a lesson of the bug observer is this: the act of observation unavoidably involves a tendentious assumption on the part of the observer. The observer assumes, roughly, that the states of affairs described by E occur with high probability, even though E often has small measure under any unbiased measure μ_X on X. (More precisely, the observer assumes that the conditional probability of E given S is much greater than one would expect under an unbiased measure.) This is to assume that the world effects a switch of event probabilities such that the observer's interpretations have a good chance of being correct. The kindest worlds switch the probabilities so that an observer's interpretation is almost surely correct. In this case the measure in the world is not unbiased; it is completely biased towards the interpretations of the observer.

One can put this another way. The utility of the bug observer depends on the world in which it is embedded. If it is embedded in a world where states of affairs represented by points in $\pi^{-1}(S)$ are all equally likely, then it will be useless. Put it in a world where states of affairs represented by points of E occur much more often than those represented by all other points of $\pi^{-1}(S)$, and it is quite valuable. An observer must be tuned to reality. And no finite set of observers can ever determine if the world in which they are embedded effects the necessary switch from the unbiased to the biased measure. They must simply operate on the assumption that it does; perception involves, in this sense, unadulterated faith.

BIOLOGICAL MOTION OBSERVER

The bug observer discussed in the previous section was chosen primarily for its simplicity; it permitted the examination of some basic ideas with minimal distraction by irrelevant details. In this section we construct an observer that solves a problem of interest to vision researchers.

The problem is the perception of "biological motion," particularly the locomotion of bipeds and quadripeds. Johansson 1973 highlighted the problem with an ingenious experiment. He taped a small light bulb to each major joint ona person (ankle, knee, hip, etc.), dimmed the room lights, turned on the small light bulbs, and videotaped the person walking about the room. Each frame of the videotape is dark except for a few dots that appear to be placed at random, as shown in Figure 5-II. When the videotape is played, the dots are perceived to move, but the perceived motion is often in three dimensions even though the dots in each frame, when viewed statically, appear coplanar. One often perceives that there is a person, and that the person is walking, running, or performing some other activity. One can sometimes recognize individuals or accurately guess gender.

To construct an observer, we must state precisely what inference the observer must perform: we must state the premises, the conclusions, and the biases of the inference. Now for the perception considered here, the relevant inference has, roughly, this structure: the premise is a set of positions in two dimensions, one position for each point in each frame of the videotape; the conclusion is a set of positions in three dimensions, again one position for each point in each frame of the videotape. Of course, this is not a complete description of the inference for we have not yet specified how many frames of how many points will be used for the premises and conclusions, nor have we specified a bias.

A bias is needed to overcome the obvious ambiguity inherent in the stated inference: if the premises are positions in two dimensions, and the conclusions are to be positions in three dimensions, then the rules of logic and the theorems of mathematics do not dictate how the conclusions must be associated with the premises; given a point having values for but two coordinates there are many ways to associate a value for a third coordinate. We are free to choose this association and, thereby, the bias.

Figure 5-II

One frame from a biological motion display

If we wish to design a psychologically plausible observer, we must guess what bias is used by the human visual system for the perception of these biological motion displays. To this end, let us consider if a bias toward rigid interpretations will allow us to construct our observer.

When we observe the displays, we find that indeed some of the points do appear to us to move rigidly: the ankle and knee points move together rigidly, as do the knee and hip points, the wrist and elbow, and the elbow and shoulder. Our perception does indicate a bias toward rigidity. We observe further, however, that not all points move rigidly: the ankle and hip do not, nor do the wrist and shoulder, the wrist and hip, and so on. It appears, in fact, that our bias here is only to see some **pairs** of points moving rigidly.

This suggests that we try to construct a simple observer, one that has as its premises the coordinates in two dimensions of just two points over several frames, and that associates the third coordinate in such a way that the two points move rigidly in three dimensions from frame to frame. We assume that each point can be tracked from frame to frame. (This tracking is called "correspondence" among students of visual motion and is itself an example of a perceptual bias, namely an assumption, unsupported by logic, that a point in a new position is the 'same' point that appeared nearby in the preceding frame.)

Now this inference must involve distinguishing those premises that are compatible with a rigid interpretation from those that are not, for as we noted above, we see some pairs of points as rigidly linked and others as not. This is to be expected: of what value is an observer for rigid structures if its premises are so impoverished that they cannot be used to distinguish between rigid and nonrigid structures? This suggests what is, in fact, an important general principle, the discrimination principle:

■ An observer should have premises sufficiently informative to distinguish those premises compatible with its bias from those that are not.

We shall now find that it is not possible to construct our proposed observer so that it satisfies this principle. To see this, we must first introduce notation. Denote the two points O and P. Without loss of generality, we always take O to be the origin of a cartesian coordinate system. The coordinates in three dimensions of P relative to O at time i of the videotape are $p_i = (x_i,y_i,z_i)$. We denote by $\hat{p}_i = (x_i,y_i)$ the coordinates of P relative to O in frame i that can be obtained directly from the videotape. This implies that $\hat{p}_i$ can be obtained from p_i by parallel projection along the z-axis. If the observer is given access to n frames of the videotape, then each one of its premises is a set $\{\hat{p}_i\}_{i=1,\ldots,n}$.

We will find that no matter how large n is, all premises $\{\hat{p}_i\}_{i=1,\ldots,n}$ are always compatible with a rigid interpretation of the motion of O and P in three dimensions over the n frames. That is, there is always a way to assign coordinates z_i to the pairs (x_i,y_i) so that the resulting vectors always have the same length in three dimensions. Therefore this observer violates the discrimination principle.

To see this, we write down a precise statement of the rigidity bias using our notation. This bias says that the square of the distance in three dimensions between O and P in frame 1 of the tape, namely the distance $x_1^2 + y_1^2 + z_1^2$, must be the same as the square of this distance in any other frame i, namely the distances $x_i^2 + y_i^2 + z_i^2, 1 < i \leq n$. We can therefore express the rigidity bias by the equations in (1).

1) $x_1^2 + y_1^2 + z_1^2 = x_i^2 + y_i^2 = z_i^2, \quad 1 < i \leq n$

This gives n-1 equations in the n unknowns $z_1,...,z_n$. Clearly this system can be solved to give a rigid interpretation for any premise $\{(x_i,y_i)\}_{i=1,...,n}$ $(=\{p_i\}_{i=1,...,n})$. Therefore the observer contemplated here violates the discrimination principle and is unsatisfactory.

Ullman 1979 has shown that one can construct an observer using a bias of rigidity if, instead of using two points as we have tried, one expands the premises to include four points. He found that three frames of four points allow one to construct an observer satisfying the discrimination principle. This valuable result can explain our perception of visual motion in many contexts. Unfortunately we cannot use Ullman's result here, for in the biological motion displays only pairs of points move rigidly, not sets of four.

Perhaps we could resolve the problem by selecting a more restrictive bias. Further inspection of the displays reveals the following: pairs of points that move together rigidly in these displays also appear, at least for short durations, to swing in a single plane.[4] The ankle and knee points, for instance, not only move rigidly but swing together in a planar motion during a normal step. Similarly for the knee and hip. The plane of motion is, in general, not parallel to the imaging plane of the videotape camera. All this suggests that we try to construct an observer with a bias toward rigid motions in a single plane. We will find that we can construct an observer with this bias, an observer that requires only two points per frame and that satisfies the discrimination principle.

Equations expressing this bias arise from the following intuitions. If two points are spinning rigidly in a single plane then the points trace out a circle in space, much like the second hand on a watch. (The circle may also be translating, but by foveating one point such translations are effectively eliminated.) The circle, when projected onto the xy-plane, appears as an ellipse. Therefore if two points in space undergo rigid motion in a plane their projected motion lies on an ellipse. If we compute the parameters of this ellipse we can recover the original circle and thereby the desired interpretation.

To compute the ellipse, we introduce new notation. Call the two points P_1 and P_2. Denote the coordinates in three dimensions of point P_i in frame j by $p_{ij} = (x_{ij},y_{ij},z_{ij})$. Denote the two-dimensional coordinates of P_i in frame j that can be obtained directly from the videotape by $\hat{p}_{ij} = (x_{ij}, y_{ij})$. If the observer is given access to n frames of the tape, then its premise is the set $\{\hat{p}_{ij}\}_{i=1,2;j=1,...,n}$.

The x_{ij} and y_{ij} coordinates of each point $\hat{p}_{ij}$ satisfy the following general equation for an ellipse:

2) $ax_{ij}^2 + bx_{ij}y_{ij} + cy_{ij}^2 + dx_{ij} + ey_{ij} + 1 = 0$

Each frame of each point gives us one constraint equation of this form, where the x_{ij} and y_{ij} are known and a, b, c, d, e are five unknowns. Note that (2) is linear in the unknowns. Two frames give four constraint equations (one equation for each point in each frame), but there are five unknowns. Therefore each premise is compatible with an interpretation of rigid motion in a plane.

Three frames give six constraint equations in the five unknowns. For generic choices of x_{ij} and y_{ij} these six equations have no solutions, real or complex, for the five unknowns.[5] This is exactly what we want. To say that for a generic choice of x_{ij} and y_{ij} our constraint equations have no solutions is to say that, except for a measure zero subset, all premises are incompatible with any (rigid and planar) interpretation. Furthermore, the constraint equations are all linear, so that if the equations do have solutions then generically they have precisely one solution for an ellipse. This ellipse, in turn, can be the projection of one of only two circles, circles that are reflections of each other about a plane parallel to the xy-plane. So if a premise is compatible with at least one interpretation then generically it is compatible with precisely two interpretations (the two circles). Thus to each premise in S is associated, generically, a conclusion measure supported on two points of E (where E is the set of rigid planar interpretations).

It is not true that if the premise is compatible with at least one interpretation then it always has precisely two interpretations. Within the set of premises that are compatible with at least one rigid-planar interpretation there is a subset of measure zero that is compatible with infinitely many such interpretations -- namely, those $\{\hat{p}_{ij}\}_{i=1,2;j=1,...,3}$ for which the Equations (*) give infinitely many solutions.

The abstract structure of the biological motion observer is the same as that of the bug observer shown in Figure 5-I; the meaning of the sets X, Y, E, S, and of the map π is different, but the abstract structure is the same. In fact, we propose that all observers have this same abstract structure, and capture this proposal formally in the next section where we define the term observer. For the biological motion observer the space X is the space of all triples of the three-dimensional coordinates of the second point relative to the first point, i.e., $X = \mathbf{R}^9$. This space represents the framework for expressing the possible conclusions of the biological motion observer. Each point in X represents some motion over three units of time of two points in three-dimensional space, where one of the two points is taken to be the origin at each instant of time. The space Y is the space of all triples of the two-dimensional coordinates of the second point relative to the first, i.e., $Y = \mathbf{R}^6$. This space represents the possible premises of the biological motion observer. Each point in Y represents three views of the two points. The map π is a projection from X to Y induced by orthographic projection from $\mathbf{R}^3$ to $\mathbf{R}^2$. E is a measure zero subset of X consisting of those triples of pairs of points in three-dimensional space whose motion is rigid and planar. S is the image of E under π, $S = \pi(E)$. Each premise in S consists of three views of two points such that the motion of the points is along an ellipse. To each premise in S is associated a conclusion, viz., a probability measure on E. This structure, represented abstractly in Figure 5-I, can also be represented as follows:

3)
$$\begin{array}{ccccccc} X & = & \mathbf{R}^9 & \supset & \mathrm{E} & = & \textit{rigid planar motions} \\ & & \downarrow{\scriptstyle \pi} & & \downarrow{\scriptstyle \pi} & & \\ Y & = & \mathbf{R}^6 & \supset & S & & \end{array}$$

DEFINITION OF OBSERVER

In this section we propose a formal definition of the concept "observer". We suggest that every act of perception, regardless of modality, is an instance of this formal structure.

The appendix to this paper reminds one of the definitions of the measure theoretic concepts used in the following definition of an observer.

4) **Definition:** An <u>observer</u> is a six-tuple, $((X,\mathcal{X}), (Y,\mathcal{Y}), E, S, \pi,\eta)$ satisfying the following conditions:

1. $(X,\mathcal{X})$ and $(Y,\mathcal{Y})$ are measurable spaces. $E \in \mathcal{X}$ and $S \in \mathcal{Y}$.
2. $\pi: X \longrightarrow Y$ is a measurable surjective function with $\pi(E) = S$
3. Let $(E,\mathcal{E})$ and $(S, \mathcal{S})$ denote the measurable spaces on E and S respectively induced from those of X and Y. Then η is a markovian kernel on $S \times \mathcal{E}$ such that, for each s, $\eta(s, .)$ is a probability measure supported in $\pi^{-1}\{s\} \cap E$.

The constituents of an observer have the following names:

5) X --- *configuration space*
Y --- *premise space*
E --- *distinguished configurations*
S --- *distinguished premises*
π --- *perspective*
η --- *conclusion kernel*, or *interpretation kernel*

We also say that, for $s \in S$, $(s, .)$ is a <u>conclusion measure</u>.

Discussion

In what follows, we sometimes write X for $(X,\mathcal{X})$ and Y for $(Y,\mathcal{Y})$ when the meaning is clear from the context.

Fundamentally, an observer makes inferences with one notable feature: the premises do not, in general, logically imply the conclusions. In the definition of observer, the possible premises are represented by Y and the possible conclusions by the measures $\eta(s, .)$.

An observer O works as follows. When O observes, it interacts with its object of perception. It does not perceive the object of perception, but rather a representation of some property of the interaction. X represents all properties of relevance to O. Suppose some point $x \in X$ represents the property that obtains in the present interaction. Then O, in consequence of the interaction, receives the representation $y = \pi(x)$, where $y \in Y$. Informally, we say that y "lights up" for O. If x is in E, then y is in S; if x is not in E and not in $\pi^{-1}(S) - E$, then y is in $Y - S$. All O receives is y, not x. O must guess x. If y is not in S, then O decides that x is not in E and does nothing. If y is in S, then O

decides that x is in E. But O does not, in general, know precisely which point of E. Instead, O arrives at a probability measure $\eta(s, .)$ supported on E. This measure represents O's guess as to which point of E is x. If there is no ambiguity, then O's measure is simply a Dirac measure supported on the appropriate point of E.

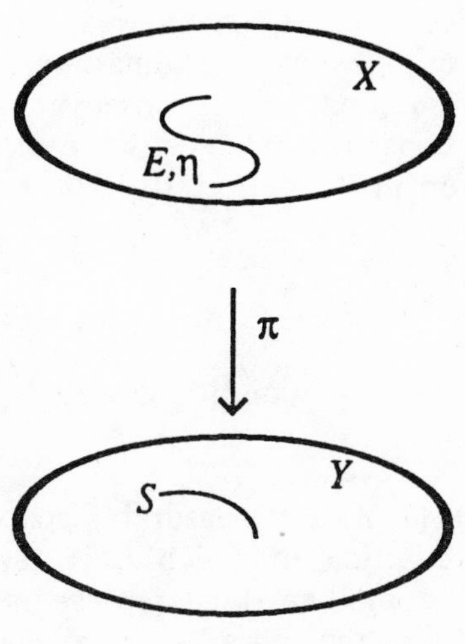

FIGURE 5-III

Illustration of an observer

From this description we see that an observer deals solely with representations: x and y are elements of the representations X and Y respectively, and $\eta(s, .)$ is a measure on X. What these representations signify we discuss in the last four sections of this paper.

One notes at once that the definition of observer is quite general. The class of observers is large, almost surely containing observers for which there is no human, even no biological, counterpart. Given this, of what use is observer theory to those interested in human perception? Roughly, it is of the same use as formal language theory is to those interested in human, or "natural", language. That is, formal language theory provides a framework within which one can formulate precisely the question, "What are the human languages?" Similarly, observer theory provides a framework within which one can formulate precisely the question, "What are the observers of relevance to human or, more generally, biological perception?" And just as the answer in the case of language has not come from formal language theory alone, so one would expect that the answer in the case of perception will not come from observer theory alone. In both cases the theory provides not an answer but a framework within which to seek an answer.

The framework should, of course, allow one to describe concrete instances of relevance to human perception. Therefore we present below four such examples. Moreover the framework should guide one in the construction of new results. Examples of such new results are given in Bennett et al. 1988.

The Conditions on Observers

We discuss the three conditions listed in the definition of observer.

Condition 1: (X,X), (Y,Y) are measurable spaces. $E \in \mathrm{X}$ and $S \in \mathrm{Y}$.

X is a representation in which E is defined. X itself is not the real world, but a mathematical representation. Y represents all premises from which the observer can make inferences. We stipulate that X and Y are measurable spaces because this is the least restrictive assumption that always allows us to discuss the measures of events in these spaces. It would be unnecessarily restrictive to specify that X must be, say, an Euclidean space or a manifold.

Condition 2: π: $X \longrightarrow Y$ is a measurable surjective function with $\pi(E) = S$

π must be surjective, for otherwise there would be premises in Y unrelated to the configurations in X: the observer would have premises that were gratuitous. π must be measurable for the premises Y must, at the very least, be syntactically compatible with the configurations X. $\pi(E) = S$ is a necessary condition for the distinguished premises to be good evidence for the conclusion measures.

Condition 3: η is a markovian kernel on S x **E** such that, for each s, $\eta(s, .)$ is a probability measure supported on $\pi^{-1}\{s\} \cap E$.

η represents the conclusions reached by an observer for premises represented by S. For each $s \in S$, η assigns a probability measure whose support is $\pi^{-1}\{s\} \cap E$; the measure has this support because, from the perspective π of the observer, only the distinguished configurations in $\pi^{-1}\{s\}$ are compatible with the premise represented by s.

IDEAL OBSERVERS

Let μ_X denote a measure class on (X,X) that is "unbiased": its definition makes no reference to properties of E or π. We think of μ_X as expressing an abstract uniformity of X which exists prior to the notion of the distinguished configurations E. For example, μ_X might be a measure class invariant for some group action on X. μ_X provides an unbiased background measure class by which one can determine if an observer is an "ideal decision maker" (discussed below), and to which one can compare the actual probabilities of obtaining configuration events in some concrete universe.

By an abuse of notation, we sometimes use the same symbol, μ_X, to denote both a measure class and a representative measure in the class.

6) **Definition:** An observer satisfying the condition

$$\mu_X(\pi^{-1}(S) - E) = 0$$

is called an <u>ideal observer</u>.

This condition states that the measure of "false target" is zero. A false target is an element of $F = \pi^{-1}(S)$ - E. False targets "fool" the observer; they lead the observer to perceptual illusions. Here is why. Note that since F is a subset of $\pi^{-1}(S)$, $\pi(F)$ is a subset of S. Now suppose that some point $x \in X$ represents the property of relevance to the observer that obtains in the interaction of the observer with the object of perception. Call such a point the <u>true configuration</u>. Assume that the true configuration is in F. Then the observer receives a premise $s = \pi(x) \in S$ and arrives at the conclusion measure $\eta(s, .)$. However, this measure is supported off F (and on E), and therefore gives no weight to the true configuration x in F. The conclusion measure represents, in this case, a misperception.

An ideal observer is an ideal decision maker in the following sense: **Given that the true configuration is not in E, an ideal observer almost surely recognizes this** . We emphasize the "almost surely". We claim not that observers, ideal or otherwise, are free of perceptual illusions; to the contrary, we claim that perceptual illusions, such as the cosine surface and 3-D movies, illustrate important properties of observers. But illusions are of two kinds: those that arise from a true configuration of relevance to the observer, i.e., from E itself, and those that do not. For an ideal observer the latter kind of illusion is rare, in a sense described formally by μ_x.

Also true is the following: **Given that the true configuration is in E, an observer, ideal or otherwise, always recognizes this.** True configurations in E always lead an observer to reach a conclusion measure (which measures are always supported on E), simply because $\pi(E) = S$ and η assigns a measure on E for every point in S.

True Configuration

Decision	E	-E
E	1 "Hit"	0 "False Alarm"
-E	0 "Miss"	1 "Correct Reject"

FIGURE 5-IV

Decision diagram for ideal observers.

Figure 5-IV summarizes these ideas in a decision diagram. The diagram displays two kinds of true configurations across the top: E, which indicates that the true configuration is in E, and -E, which indicates that the true configuration is in $X - E$. The diagram displays the two possible decisions of the observer along the left side. Inside each box in the right column is a number which is a conditional probability, namely the unbiased (μ_x) conditional probability that an ideal observer arrives at the decision indicated to the left side of the diagram given that the true configuration is in $X - E$. Inside each box in the left column is a number; in this left column the number 1 is a shorthand for "certainly" and 0 for "certainly not". The numbers in this left column hold simply by the definition of observer; if the true configuration is in E, then since $S = \pi(E)$ and the observer always decides that the true configuration is in E given a premise in S, the observer always decides correctly. Also inside each box is a label in quotes which describes the type of decision represented by that box.

As an example of how to read this diagram, consider the box labelled "false alarm". It contains a 0. This means that the conditional probability is zero that an ideal observer will decide that the true configuration is in E given that in fact it is not. (The one in the box labelled "correct reject" is the complementary conditional probability).

A sufficient condition for an observer to be ideal is the following:

7) $\pi_* \mu_x(S) = 0$

This condition states that $\mu_x(\pi^{-1}(S)) = 0$, which implies that $\mu_x(\pi^{-1}(S) - E) = 0$, and therefore that the observer is ideal. This condition often obtains in observers whose distinguished configurations are defined by algebraic equations.

The definition of an ideal observer makes essential use of the measure μ_x, a measure defined without regard to properties of any external world. Therefore an ideal observer is ideal regardless of the relationship between the ideal observer and any external world. However, μ_x may not accurately reflect the measures of events in the appropriate world external to the observer. We discuss this in later sections.

That aspect of the inference presented in Figure 5-IV is not the only one of interest. An observer decides not only if the true configuration is in E; it produces in addition a probability measure supported on E which is its best guess as to which events in E are likely to have occurred, together with their likelihoods. One can ask if this measure is accurate. The answer to this requires the establishment of a formal framework in which observer and observed can be discussed. This is the subject of the last four sections of this paper.

NOISE

Thus far we have considered only observer inferences whose premises are represented by single points $s \in S$. Such inferences are free of noise in the sense that the premise is known precisely. But if there is noise, if the premise is not known precisely but only probabilistically, what conclusions can an observer reach? A natural way to represent a noisy premise is as a probability measure λ on Y. A precise premise $s \in S$ is then the special case of a Dirac measure supported on s.   models noise or measurement error as follows: for $B \in \mathrm{Y}, \lambda(B)$ is the probability that the set of premises B contains the "true premise".

Given a probability measure λ on Y the natural conclusion for the observer to reach is the following:

8) with probability $\lambda(Y - S)$ there is no interpretation;
with probability $\lambda(S)$ the distribution of interpretations is ν,

where, for $\Delta \in \mathcal{E}$,

$$\nu(\Delta) = \lambda(S)^{-1} \int_S \eta(s, \Delta \cap \pi^{-1}(s)) \lambda(ds).$$

Intuitively, $\lambda(S)$ is the probability of having received a "signal", i.e., a distinguished premise, and $\lambda(Y - S)$ is the probability of not having received a signal.

Thus the definition of observer provides a formalism which, by means of the interpretation kernel η, unifies perceptual inferencing "policies" in the presence of noise. Moreover the effects of various kinds of noise can be analyzed within a given inferencing system. (For example, there may be regularities of the noise worth exploiting. A common approach to noise represents the set of noisy signals as a markovian kernel K on Y x Y, where $K(y,.)$ is computed by, say, convolving a fixed gaussian distribution with the Dirac measure $\epsilon_y(.)$ located at y.) These ideas need to be studied systematically and to be compared with the ideas of signal detection theory and various decision theories.

EXAMPLES OF OBSERVERS

In this section we consider several current explanations of specific perceptual capacities and exhibit these explanations as instances of the definition of observer.

Example: Structure from Motion (Ullman 1979)

One can devise dynamic visual displays for which subjects, even when viewing monocularly, report seeing motion and structure in three dimensions. This perceptual capacity to perceive three-dimensional structure from dynamic two-dimensional images is often called "structure from motion".[6] To explain this capacity, Ullman proposes what he calls the rigidity assumption: "Any set of elements undergoing a two-dimensional transformation which has a unique interpretation as a rigid body moving in space should be interpreted as such a body in motion." (1979:146) Moreover, he proves a theorem which allows one to determine whether a given collection of moving elements has a unique rigid interpretation. This structure from motion theorem states: "Given three distinct orthographic views of four noncoplanar points in a rigid configuration, the structure and motion compatible with the three views are uniquely determined [up to reflection]." (1979:148)[7]

Because of the rigor and clarity of Ullman's explanation it is possible to state precisely to which observer it corresponds. It is the observer whose configuration space consists of all three sets of four points, where each point lies in $\mathbf{R}^3$. Since Ullman takes one of the four points to be the origin, we find that the configuration space X is $\mathbf{R}^{27}$. The premise space is the space of all triples of four points, where each point lies in $\mathbf{R}^2$ (i.e., in the image plane). We find that the premise space Y is $\mathbf{R}^{18}$. Now denoting a point in $\mathbf{R}^3$ by (x,y,z) and recalling that the map p: $\mathbf{R}^3 \longrightarrow \mathbf{R}^2$ given by $(x,y,z) \longmapsto (x,y)$ is an orthographic projection, we find that the perspective π of Ullman's observer is the map π: $X \longrightarrow Y$ induced by p. E, the distinguished configurations, consists of those three sets of four points, each point in $\mathbf{R}^3$, such that the four points in each set are related to the four points in every other set of the triple by a rigid motion. One can write down a small set of simple algebraic equations to specify this (uncountable) subset of X, but this is unnecessary here. It happens that E has Lebesgue measure zero in X. S, the distinguished premises, consists simply in $\pi(E)$. Intuitively, S consists of all three views of four points that are compatible with a rigid interpretation. S happens to have Lebesgue measure zero in Y; therefore the Lebesgue measure of "false targets", i.e., elements of $\pi^{-1}(S) - E$, is also zero. Finally, for each $s \in S$, $\eta\ (s, .)$ can be taken to be the measure that assigns weight of 1/2 to each of the two points of E which, according to the structure from motion theorem, project via π to s. This would correspond to an observer that saw that saw each interpretation with equal frequency. If one interpretation was seen 90% of the time then the appropriate measure would assign weights of .9 and .1.

Example: Stereo (Longuet-Higgins 1982)

Because one's eyes occupy different positions in space, the images they receive differ subtly. Using these differences, one's visual system can recover the three-dimensional properties of the visual environment. This capacity to infer the third dimension from disparities in the retinal images is called stereoscopic vision.[8] To explain this capacity, Longuet-Higgins assumes that the planes of the horizontal meridians of the two eyes accurately coincide. He then proves several results, of which we consider the following: "If the scene contains three or more nonmeridional points, not all lying in a vertical plane, then their positions in space are fully determined by the horizontal and vertical coordinates of their images on the two retinas."

The observer corresponding to Longuet-Higgins' explanation has a configuration space consisting of all two sets of three points, where each point lies in $\mathbf{R}^3$. Longuet-Higgins does not take one of the three points to be the origin, so the configuration space X is $\mathbf{R}^{18}$. The premise space is the space of all two sets of three points, where each point lies in $\mathbf{R}^2$. Therefore the premise space Y is $\mathbf{R}^{12}$. The perspective of Longuet-Higgins' observer is the map $\pi : X \longrightarrow Y$ induced by the map p of example (6). E, the distinguished configurations, consists of all pairs of sets of three points, each point in $\mathbf{R}^3$, such that the three points in each set are related to the three points in the other set by a rigid motion whose rotation is about an axis parallel to the vertical axes of the two retinal coordinate systems. One can write down straightforward equations to specify this (uncountable) subset of X. S, the distinguished premises, is $\pi(E)$. And for each $s \in S, \eta(s, .)$ is Dirac measure on the unique (generically, according to Longuet- Higgins' result) point of E that projects via π to s.

Example: Velocity Fields along Contours in 2-D (Hildreth 1984)

Because of the ubiquity of relative motion between visual objects and the viewer's eye, retinal images of occluding contours (and other salient visual contours) almost perpetually translate and deform. For smooth portions of a contour, attempts to measure precisely the local velocity of the contour must face the so-called "aperture problem": if the velocity of the curve at a point s is $V(s)$, only the component of velocity orthogonal to the tangent at s, $v^{\perp}(s)$, can be obtained directly by local measurement. The visual system apparently overcomes the aperture problem and can recover a unique velocity field for a moving curve. This capacity to infer a complete velocity field along a two-dimensional curve given only its orthogonal component is called the measurement of contour velocity fields.[9] To explain this capacity, Hildreth proposes that the visual system chooses the "smoothest" velocity field (precisely, one minimizing $\int |\frac{\partial V}{\partial s}|^2 ds$) compatible with the given orthogonal component. She then proves the following result: "If $v^{\perp}(s)$ is known along a contour, and there exists at least two points at which the local orientation of the contour is different, then there exists a unique velocity field that satisfies the known velocity constraints and minimizes $\int |\frac{\partial V}{\partial s}|^2 ds$)."

The observer corresponding to Hildreth's explanation has a configuration space X consisting of all velocity fields along all smooth contours in $\mathbf{R}^2$. S, the distinguished premises, consists of all velocity fields along one-dimensional contours such that the velocity assigned to each point s of the curve is orthogonal to the tangent of the curve at s. The premise space Y is the same as S. (Because of the aperture problem the only premises are those in S.) The perspective of Hildreth's observer is the map $\pi : X \longrightarrow Y$ which takes each velocity field in X to its orthogonal component field in S. Thus π takes X onto S. For $s' \in S$, $\pi^{-1}(s')$ is all velocity fields which have s' as their orthogonal component. According to Hildreth's result, in each fibre $\pi^{-1}(s')$ there is a unique velocity field e which minimizes her measure of smoothness. E, the distinguished configurations, is the set of all these e'. For each $s' \in S, \eta(s',.)$ is Dirac measure on the corresponding e'.

Example: Visual Detection of Light Sources (Ullman 1976)

The visual system is adept at detecting surfaces which, rather than simply reflecting incident light, are themselves luminous. This perceptual capacity is called the visual detection of light sources. To explain this capacity, Ullman proposes that it is unnecessary to consider the spectral composition of the light and the dependence of surface reflectance on wavelength. He considers the case of two adjacent surfaces, A and B, with reflec-

siders the case of two adjacent surfaces, A and B, with reflectances r_A and r_B. (The reflectance of a surface, under Ullman's proposal, is a real number between 0 and 1 inclusive, which is the proportion of incident light reflected by the surface.)[10] He assumes that the light incident to surface A at some distinguished point 0 has intensity I_0 and that the intensity of the incident light varies linearly with gradient K. Thus a point 1 on surface B at distance d from 0 receives an intensity $I_1 = I_0 + Kd$. (Ullman restricts attention to a one-dimensional case and stipulates that d is positive if 1 is to the right of 0.) If A is also a light source with intensity L, then the retinal image of the point 0 receives, on Ullman's model (which ignores foreshortening), a quantity of light $e_0 = r_A I_0 + L$. On the assumption that the light source, if any, is at A (which can be accomplished by relabelling the surfaces if necessary) the retinal image of point 1 receives a quantity of light $e_1 = r_B I_1$. The gradient of light in the image of surface A is $S_A = r_A K$, whereas in the of surface B it is $S_B = r_B K$. Ullman then argues that the visual system detects a light source at A when the quantity $L = e_0 - e_1(S_A/S_B) + S_A d$ is greater than $e_1(S_A/S_B) - S_A d$; furthermore, L is the perceived intensity of the source.

The observer corresponding to Ullman's explanation has a configuration space consisting of all six-tuples:

9) (r_A, r_B, I_0, d, K, L),

where:

10) $r_A, r_B \in [0,1]$, $K, d \in \mathbf{R}$, $I_0, L \in [0, \infty)$,

and L is the light source intensity. Thus

11) $X = [0,1] \times [0,1] \times [0, \infty) \times \mathbf{R} \times \mathbf{R} \times [0, \infty)$.

The premise space consists of all five-tuples:

12) (e_0, e_1, S_A, S_B, d),

where:

13) $e_0, e_1 \in [0, \infty)$, $S_A, S_B, d \in \mathbf{R}$.

Thus

14) $Y = [0,\infty) \times [0,\infty) \times \mathbf{R} \times \mathbf{R} \times \mathbf{R}$

the perspective of Ullman's observer is the map $\pi: X \longrightarrow Y$ defined by:

15) $(r_A, r_B, I_0, d, K, L) \longmapsto (r_A I_0 + L, r_B(I_0 + Kd), r_A K, r_B K, d)$.

S, the distinguished premises, consists of that subset of Y satisfying:

16) $\hat{L} > e_1(S_A/S_B) - S_A d$

Similarly E, the distinguished configurations, consists of that subset of X satisfying:

17) $L > r_A(I_0 + Kd) - r_A Kd$

For each distinguished premise $s = (e_0, e_1, S_A, S_B, d) \in S$, $\eta(s,.)$ can be taken to be any probability measure supported on those distinguished configurations in $\pi^{-1}(s)$ satisfying $L = e_0 - e_1(S_A/S_B) + S_A d$ (since Ullman's explanation seeks to recover only the light source intensity, not the other aspects of the configuration).

OBSERVER/WORLD INTERFACE: INTRODUCTION

What are true perceptions? Without addressing this central question, no theory of perception can be complete. In observer theory the perceptions of an observer are represented by its conclusion measures so that, rephrasing, we may ask the question: What are true conclusion measures? Now clearly the truth of conclusion measures depends at least on two factors: (1) the meaning of the measures and (2) the states of affairs in an appropriate external environment. Recall, however, that the definition of observer in (4) nowhere refers to a real world or to an environment external to the observer. The spaces X and Y represent properties of the interaction between the observer and its environment but are not the environment itself. Therefore to study true perceptions we first propose a minimal structure for environments and for the relationship between observers and environments, thereby advancing a primitive theory of semantics for observers. We extend this theory in the penultimate section of this paper. In Bennett et al. 1988 we build a model for the theory by the introduction of "reflexive observer frameworks".

We described the observer-world relationship above as follows: When the observer (X, Y, E, S, π, η) is presented with a state of affairs in the world which corresponds to a point x of X, the point $\pi(x) \in Y$ "lights up". If $\pi(x) \notin S$ then the observer outputs no conclusion measure. If $\pi(x) = s$ is in S then the observer outputs the conclusion measure $\eta(s,.)$. Our task is to explain this statement.

We distinguish two levels of semantics: primitive semantics and extended semantics. In primitive semantics a "state of affairs" is an undefined primitive (much as, in geometry, a "point" is an undefined primitive); in extended semantics it is directly defined. Primitive semantics is the "local" semantics of a single observer, a minimal semantics which interprets the observer's conclusion measure η in terms of an external environment. Structure in addition to that of the observer is necessary for this purpose since conclusion measures are representations internal to the observer and have no a priori external interpretation. (In other words, the internal representation embodied in the conclusion measure is not itself a conclusion. For a conclusion is by definition a proposition: it is an assertion about states of affairs in some environment.) The necessary additional structure consists in a formal description of an environment; in terms of this description, meaning can be assigned to the representation η, and this meaning is the conclusion in the correct sense of the term.

In primitive semantics we assume that the "states of affairs" with which an observer is presented are undefined primitives, and that "presenting an observer with a state of affairs" is a primitive relation. States of affairs are not objects of perception. We reserve the term "object of perception" to refer to "that with which an observer interacts" in an act of perception. Rather, **states of affairs are relationships between the observer and its objects of perception**. For now these relationships are undefined primitives; the environment of states of affairs is, in the primitive semantics, an abstract formalism. The primitive semantics provides a dictionary between the internal representations of the observer and this abstract formalism.

By contrast, in extended semantics the states of affairs themselves -- not only the single observer -- are directly defined. At this level, the environment of the observer, as well as the states of affairs in it, have a priori meaning independent of the observer's conclusion measure.

This environment of states of affairs is not to be regarded as a theatre for all possible phenomena; it need only be rich enough in structure to provide a concrete model of the theoretical environment posited at the first-level. The environment is not accessible to the given observer; its perceptual conclusions are the most it can know in any instant. The environment may, however, be accessible to other "higher-level" observers under various conditions; this leads to the notion of "specialization" which we discuss in Bennett et al. 1988.

SCENARIOS

We begin with a fixed observer $O = (X,Y,E,S,\pi,\eta)$. As an abstract observer, O consists only of its mathematical components X,Y,E,S,π,η as set forth in the definition in (4). We want to view O as embedded in some environment as a perceiver. Therefore we must provide additional structure to represent such an embedding. We call this structure a scenario for O. Given a definition of scenario we can then discuss the semantics of O's conclusions.

The definition of scenario involves an unusual notion of time. Just as we assume no absolute environment, so also we assume no absolute time. We assume only that there is given, as part of each scenario, an "active time"; the instants of this active time are the instants in which O receives a premise. This active time is discrete. Perception itself is fundamentally discrete; any change of percept is fundamentally discontinuous. To put it briefly: we model perception as an "atomic" act. An atomic perceptual actis one whose perceptual significance is lost in any further temporal subdivision. This view is developed in Bennett et al. 1988 but a few remarks are in order here.

As we have indicated, observer theory is not a fixed-frame theory in which all phenomena are objectively grounded in a single connected ambient space -- an analytical framework which plays the role of an absolute "spacetime". Absolute spacetime is surely of interest both psychologically and physically, but in neither case is this due to a principled requirement that every scientific model must begin with it. In particular, this is true of absolute time. In building a theory which is centered on acts of perception there is no reason to assume, in general, that the active times of (the scenarios of) different observers bear any describable relationship to each other. Thus there maybe no natural way to embed the active times of two different observers into a third time-system (in some order-preserving manner). In special cases, however, it is natural to assume that the active times may be so embedded; this occurs, for example, when the observers occupy the same "reflexive framework" (Bennett et al. 1988). In other cases the active times of different observers admit comparisons of various kinds. For example, one instant of the active time of a "higher level" observer may correspond to an entire (random) subsequence of instants of the active time of a "lower level" observer.

18) **Definition:** A scenario for the observer $O = (X,Y,E,S,\pi,\eta)$ is a triple $(C, R, \{Z_t\}_{t \in R})$, where:

(i) C is a measurable space whose elements are called states of affairs;

(ii) R is a countable totally ordered set called the active time;

(iii) $\{Z_t\}_{t \in R}$ is a sequence of measurable functions, all defined on some fixed probability space Ω and taking values in $C \times Y$.

In other words, a scenario is a stochastic process with state space $C \times Y$ and indexed by R.

Z_t is called the observation at time t or the presentation of the observer with a state of affairs at time t or the channeling at time t. If Z_t takes the value (c_t, y_t) with $c_t \in C$ and $y_t \in Y$, we say that c_t is the state of affairs at time t and y_t is the premise (or sensation or sensory input at time t. For any sample point $w \in \Omega$, the sequence $Z_t(w)_{t \in R}$ corresponds to a sequence of points $\{(c_t, y_t)\}_{t \in R}$ in $C \times Y$. We call this an observation trajectory.

The "states of affairs" in the definition are external to the observer in the sense that they are not part of its structure. This does not imply that these states of affairs are states (or parts) of a physical world.[11] In fact, physical properties are an observer's symbols for these states of affairs, or for stable distributions of these states of affairs. Any attempt to ground a theory of the observer in an a priori fixed physical world encounters great difficulties from the outset. Contemporary physics, for instance, holds that physical theory itself must include the observer. This is evident at the quantum level, where it seems impossible to escape the conclusion that acts of observation influence the evolution of

the conclusion that acts of observation influence the evolution of physical systems. It is also seen in relativistic formulations, where the theory, by its very definition, consists in the study of statements which are invariant under certain specified changes in the perspective, or frame of reference, of observers. For such reasons it is scientifically regressive to cling to a fixed "physical world" as the ultimate repository for states of affairs. We do not deny the existence of physical worlds but suggest that, habit aside, it is more natural to ground physical theory in perceptual theory than vice versa.

To summarize: we distinguish between perceptual conclusions, states of affairs,and objects of perception. In primitive semantics the states of affairs are undefined primitives whose existence is assumed as part of a given scenario. These states of affairs are relationships between the observer and its objects of perception, which are not specified. The observer is presented randomly in discrete time with states of affairs. This presentation is a primitive, assumed as part of the scenario. The presentations consist in a stochastic sequence (in the given discrete time) of pairings of states of affairs with premises from the premise space Y of the observer. These elements of Y constitute the only information accessible to the observer about the scenario, i.e., about its "environment." The scenario provides the syntactical structure to which semantics can be attached.

However, in the scenario itself there is no semantics: there is no conclusion in the correct sense of theword. Namely, the data of the scenario alone contain no direct relationship between the states of affairs in C and the conclusion measure η or, for that matter, the observer's configuration space X. (We regard the indirect relationship, at each instant t, which exists because the conclusion measure $\eta(s,.)$ is deterministically associated to s, as a purely syntactical relationship: the symbol $\eta(s,.)$ is formally attached to the symbol s, which in turn is formally attached to c_t via $Z_t = (c_t, s)$.) The scenario directly relates states of affairs with points of Y -- not with points of X.

The only information an observer directly receives is a premise, a sensory input, at each instant of active time. The scenario is a minimal formalism for an external world whose states of affairs are related in some unknown manner to the successive production of these premises. This world must be external to the observer, because the internal structure of the observer, by definition, consists only in X, Y, E, S, π, η; these alone say nothing about the production in a time sequence of elements of Y. To go further, to posit a relationship between the states of affairs and X that is compatible with the scenario data, brings us to the issue of meaning.

MEANING AND TRUTH CONDITIONS

Let be given an observer O and a scenario (C,R,Z_t) (Definition (18)). We have been referring to the "conclusion of the observer" as the meaning of its conclusion measure. This meaning is a proposition regarding a relationship between the conclusion measure and the scenario. Now the truth or falsity of this proposition can be decided only in the presence of a concrete model of the scenario, i.e., only in the presence of an extended semantics. Prior to such a model,i.e., within a primitive semantics, we are free to assign meaning to O's conclusion measure by postulating a relationship between it and the scenario. In the definition to follow we state this relationship.

19) **Definition:** Let $t \in R$. Let pr_1 and pr_2 be the projections of $C \times Y$ onto the first and second coordinates respectively. The meaning of the conclusion measure η at time t is the following pair of postulates:

Postulate 1. There exists a measurable injective function $\Xi: C \longrightarrow X$ such that, if $Z_t = (c_t, y_t)$ then $y_t = \pi \circ \Xi(c_t)$.

Postulate 2. ν_t^S is a nonzero measure and η is its rcpd with respect to π.

Let $X_t = \Xi \circ \mathrm{pr}_1 Z_t$. Then X_t is a measurable function with the same base space as Z_t and taking values in X. Letting ν_t be the distribution of X_t, denote its restriction to $\pi^{-1}(S)$ by ν_t^S. for A $\in$X , we have $\nu_t^S(A) = \nu_t(A \cap \pi^{-1}(S))$.

To specify a particular meaning for η in a given scenario, we need only specify a Ξ such that $\nu_t(\pi^{-1}(S)) > 0$; the interpretation of is then established by Postulate 2.

The measurable function Ξ is the configuration map; $\Xi(c)$ is the configuration of c. If the definition in (19) holds, $(R, C, \{Z_t\}, \Xi)$, is called a primitive semantics (for O). A state of affairs $c \in C$ is called a distinguished state of affairs if $\Xi(c) \in E$.

Discussion of Postulate 1

The existence of the configuration map Ξ, asserted in Postulate 1 of (19), means that there is a time-invariant relationship between the states of affairs in C and the configurations in X; we therefore can now say what X represents. Until now X was simply part of the internal formalism of the observer, an abstract representational system. It is only by virtue of Ξ that X represents the states of affairs; indeed Ξ defines that representation. The postulate states further that the pairing in the scenario between c_t and y_t (via the channeling Z_t) is imitated within the observer by the pairing between $\Xi(c_t) = x_t$ and $\pi(x_t) = y_t$. We may say that $(x_t, \pi(x_t))$ is a picture of (c_t, y_t).

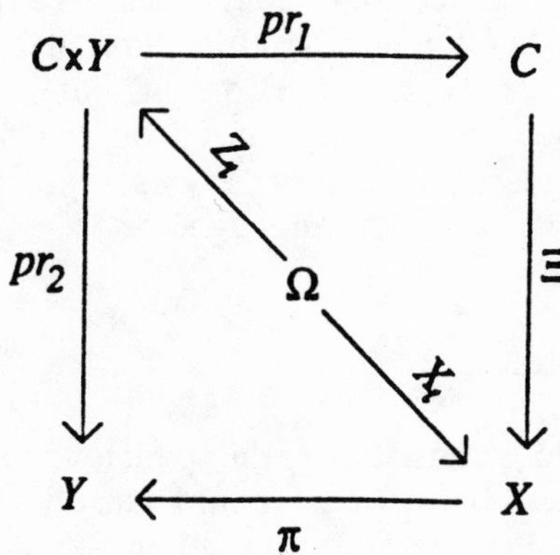

FIGURE 5-V

Postulate 1 says there exists a Ξ for which this diagram commutes.

Given the configuration map Ξ satisfying the properties of Postulate 1, we may effectively replace C with X, at least for the purposes of the primitive semantics. Because Ξ is one-to-one, the internal formalism of the observer, specifically X, Y and π, gives a good representation of the interaction of the observer with its environment (as provided in the scenario). Thus we can formally bypass C, and view the scenario as consisting, in essence, of a discrete-time probabilistic source of elements of X, i.e., as the sequence of measurable functions $\{X_t\}_{t \in R}$. These measurable functions take values now in X, and are related to the original measurable functions Z_t of the scenario by $X_t = \Xi \circ pr_1 Z_t$. To emphasize this simplification, we will sometimes use the word "configuration" in place of "state of affairs". Of course, this is an abuse of language; when we say, for example, "a configuration x channeled to the observer," we mean that a state of affairs c, for which $x = \Xi(c)$, channeled to the observer. Figure 5-V illustrates Postulate 1.

The condition that the X_t's have identical conditional distributions over points $s \in S$, namely the distributions $\eta(s,.)$, expresses an assumption built into the observer that its relevant environment is stationary: the distribution of states of affairs which channel to the observer, resulting in premises in S, does not vary with time. We mean neither that the observer has made a considered or learned inference to this effect, nor that it has made a scientific judgement about the stability of its environment. Rather, our viewpoint is that a de facto assumption of stationarity is fundamental to perceptual semantics; we are here modeling perception at the level where each instantaneous percept involves the output of a de facto assertion of some stationarity in the environment. The stationarity condition given above is the strongest such assertion that the observer can make without exceeding the capacity of its language.

Discussion of Postulate 2

The set $\pi^{-1}(S)$ consists of the configurations of those states of affairs whose channelings could result in a distinguished premise $s \in S$. Postulate 2 says, then, that there is a nonzero probability $\nu_t(\pi^{-1}(S))$ that such channelings occur. Moreover, it assigns meaning to the conclusion measures $\eta(s,.)$. Since $\eta(s,.)$ is deterministically associated to $s \in S$ it can be viewed as the "output" given s as "input"; in fact we have tacitly but consistently viewed it in this way up to now. Using this terminology, and given Postulate 1, the meaning assigned by Postulate 2 may be expressed as follows: If the premise at time t is $s \in S$, then the observer outputs the conditional distribution, given s, of the configurations of states of affairs whose channeling could result in s; this conditional distribution is $\eta(s,.)$. It is independent of the value of t. If the premise at time t is not in S, then the observer outputs no conclusion. This explains the description of the observer-world relationship.

For Postulate 2 to hold at all times t, it is necessary that the distributions of the X_t have identical rcpd's over S. Now the observer itself cannot verify such a stationarity in the distributions. For the observer has no language other than that provided by η, with which to represent information about the distributions of the X_t's. In fact, it can say nothing about what happens when $y_t \notin S$; the observer is necessarily inert at such instants t. Nevertheless this stationarity in the observer's environment is fundamental to our perceptual semantics; we as modelers can verify the existence of such a stationarity.

As noted in the section on Scenarios, truth conditions for the conclusions of an observer amount to giving additional conditions on the scenario under which these conclusions are true propositions. Thus the truth conditions will be satisfied in some models (of the abstract scenario formalism), and not in others. We reiterate that, for this reason, the truth conditions can only be verified in the extended semantics where a concrete model of the scenario is given.

Given an observer in a scenario and given a model of that scenario (i.e., an extended semantics for the observer) we say that <u>the observer's conclusion is true at time *t*</u> or that <u>the observer has true perception at time *t*</u> if the postulates of the definition in (19) are true in that extended semantics. If the observer has true perception at time *t* for all *t*, and if the map Ξ is the same for each *t*, then we simply say that <u>the observer has true perception</u>. This terminology allows truth an instantaneous character.

EXTENDED SEMANTICS

So far we have assigned meaning to the observer's conclusion measures, but not to the states of affairs. A "state of affairs" in *C* is a relationship between the observer and its objects of perception. The objects of perception do not appear explicitly in the definition of scenario, although each channeling arises from an interaction between the observer and these objects. In order to assign meaning to the states of affairs, i.e., in order to extend our semantics, we must construct models for the scenario in which the objects of perception are specified.

In the next section we propose one such specification of the objects of perception. Here we ask the following question: In order to be able to extend our primitive semantics, what relationship must obtain between the set of objects of perception and the primitive semantics? Let us denote the set of objects of perception by B. The primitive semantics, as above, is (R, C, Z_t, Ξ).In an extended semantics the set C of states of affairs plays a dual role, both as the set of referents for O's conclusions and as the set of relationships between O and B. The answer to our question must ensure a compatibility between these roles. The elements of B are the source of the channelings, they can in principle be individuated by O only to the extent that they are individuated by the relationships in C. We may now state our requirement of compatibility between B and (R,C,Z_t,Ξ).

Assumption

Suppose that we have a primitive semantics (R,C,Z_t,Ξ); in particular, suppose Ξ exists and has the property statedin Postulate 1. Suppose that we are given a set B such that at the instant t of O's active time there is at most one channeling to O, and that this channeling arises from the interaction of O with a single element of B. The class of such interactions is parametrized by C. Suppose further that the primitive semantics (R,C,Z_t,Ξ) induces an equivalence relation on B: two elements, say B_1 and B_2 of B, are equivalent if and only if any channeling at time t arising from the interaction of O with B_1 or B_2 results in the same value of the measurable function X_t, where X_t is defined as in the definition in (19). Since distinct elements of X_t correspond to distinct elements of C the equivalence classes are in one-to-one correspondence with elements of C. Let B_c denote the equivalence class in B which corresponds to the element $c \in C$ for the equivalence relation just defined.

We can now say precisely what is the meaning of the elements of C as relationships between O and B:

Condition

To say that an observer stands in the particular relationship c of C to B at time t means that the observer interacts with some element of the equivalence class B_c at time t, and that a channeling at time t arises from this interaction; the channeling results in the value $\Xi(c)$ for the measurable function X_t.

Since the state of affairs c is specified by the corresponding equivalence class B_c we can think informally of the relationship corresponding to c as the "activation" of the class B_c. As defined, the notion is instantaneous. The formal definition of extended semantics is then the following:

20) **Definition**: Given a primitive semantics (R,C,Z_t, Ξ) for the observer O, an extension of this semantics consists in a set B for which the hypotheses above hold (for some notion of "interaction"). B is then called the set of objects of perception. Such extensions of primitive semantics are called extended semantics. In an extended semantics, the meaning of the states of affairs as relationships between O and B is described immediately above.

Once we are in an extended semantics, it is usually convenient simply to bypass the states of affairs C and to speak only of the objects of perception B and the configuration space X of the observer. For the states of affairs map injectively to the configurations by Ξ, so no information is lost thereby. Moreover, by assumption, all channelings originate in interactions of O with elements of B. Thus the essential information in an extended semantics for O is R,B ,Φ, and X_t, where

21) Φ :B $\longrightarrow X$

is defined by $\Phi(B) = \Xi(c)$ for that c such that B_c is the equivalence class (described immediately above) which contains B. In this way, the equivalence classes now appear as the sets $\Phi^{-1}\{x\}$, for $x \in X$, so that the original information carried by the states of affairs is not lost.

Terminology

We refer to "the extended semantics defined by (R, B, Φ , X_t)." (B,Φ) is called the environment of the extended semantics. We retain the terminology "configuration map" for Φ ; now we can speak of the configuration $\Phi(B)$ of the object of perception B. We call B a distinguished object of perception if $\Phi(B)$ is in E. We say that B channels to O at time t if a channeling arises from the interaction of O with B at time t.

The postulates of the definition in (19) assume a new significance in the context of extended semantics. Postulate 1 is required to hold in order that the extended semantics exist.

Postulate 2 is now also a truth condition whose veracity can be tested in $(R, \mathrm{B}, \Phi, X_t)$.

HIERARCHICAL ANALYTIC STRATEGIES AND NONDUALISM

In an extended semantics for an observer O, the states of affairs C are relationships between O and a set B of objects of perception, as stipulated in the definition in (20). The objects of perception represent the minimal entities that can interact instantaneously with the observer: at each instant of the observer's active time a channeling occurs, and there is at most one channeling, corresponding to the interaction of the observer with exactly one element of B. Thus a channeling indicates an interaction of O with an object of perception. The conclusion of O -- expressed by the output of the conclusion measure $\eta(s,.)$ -- is an irreducible perceptual response of O to the channeling. The interaction is an irreducible perceptual stimulus for O. The word "irreducible" here refers not to an absolute indecomposability, but to an indecomposability relative to the observer's perceptual act: In some (hypothetical) decomposition of both the observer and its object of perception, a single channeling might involve many "microchannelings" between components of the observer and its object. But these microchannelings have no direct perceptual significance for the original observer -- neither a channeling nor a conclusion on the part of the original observer are associated to a single microchanneling.

Up to now we have been considering the interactions of systems without reference to their further decomposition -- what one might call direct interactions. In this section we direct attention, briefly and informally, to the problem of analyzing the interaction between "complex systems," i.e., systems each admitting more than one distinct level of structure. Assume for the moment that the levels have already been distinguished. We suggest that an appropriate analysis of such an interaction involves matching levels of the respective systems in such a way that the total interaction appears to consist of separate "direct interactions" between the constituents at each of these matched levels. The constituents of any given level, or stratum, are entities which are not decomposable in that stratum, although they may be decomposable in terms of entities at lower levels of the stratification. It may be that only one level of each system interacts directly with a corresponding level of the other system, or it may be that any pair of levels, one level from each system, interacts directly. We also assume that information flows between the various levels within each system separately, so that the effects of the direct interaction at any one level can propagate to other levels. Thus it is not restrictive to require that an interaction should admit a decomposition, for purposes of analysis, into separate direct interactions between entities at certain matched levels. Nor is such a requirement to be taken as a statement about the absolute character of reality.

It is rather a matter of choosing an analytical strategy. In practice we want the freedom to choose the stratifications so as to display effectively the total interaction in terms of direct interactions at appropriate levels. (We wish to understand the total interaction, not to embed some previously distinguished elementary levels in a larger context.) This kind of freedom requires that our concept of stratification has some flexibility, that its application is not rigidly determined in every case (although each application must produce strata whose mathematical relationship to one another is of some well-defined type). The question of what principles should govern the selection and "matching" of strata rests in turn on the question of what constitutes "direct interaction," because the purpose of the matching of strata is to display direct interaction. There need not be a unique answer to this question, even in a concrete situation. Indeed, because of the internal flow of information between the levels in each system, there may be many ways to select a certain set of levels as being the sites of direct interaction. But however the definitions of stratification and direct interaction are ultimately fixed in a particular case, we would adduce at least the following general requirements:

22a) **Irreducibility**. The notion of "level" is sufficiently robust so that irreducibility relative to a level makes sense: If P is an irreducible constituent of a level L in a system A (i.e., the constituent P of A is a site for direct interaction at level L), then although P may be decomposable in some way in the total system A, there is no such decomposition within L itself.

22b) **Matching**. To match levels L and L', in the respective systems A and A', means that every irreducible constituent of L can in principle interact directly with every irreducible constituent of L'.

22c) **Homogeneity.** There is homogeneity within any given level in the sense that the minimal syntax required to distinguish the level *L* from other levels is not sufficient to discriminate among the irreducible constituents of *L*.

22d) **Transitivity.** The notion of direct interaction is transitive: Given three entities P_1, P_2, P_3, if P_1 can interact directly with P_2, and P_2 can interact directly with P_3, then P_1 can interact directly with P_3.

Terminology

An approach to the analysis of any type ofinteraction of complex systems, which involves a notion of "direct interaction," and a corresponding notion of stratification of the respective interacting systems into levels at which direct interaction occurs, will be called a hierarchical analytical strategy if the requirements (22a) to (22d) above are fulfilled. This terminology is informal, since we have not rigorously grounded it. However it is useful as it stands for purposes of motivation and description. Here is how we apply the terminology in observer theory, in a particular perceptual context where a hierarchical analytic strategy has been adopted:

23) To specify the objects of perception for an observer is to specify what constitutes direct interaction for that observer.

This proposal is reasonable, for we have already characterized the objects of perception for *O* as "minimal entities with which *O* can interact instantaneously," or "irreducible perceptual stimuli of *O*" in a given extended semantics. If we imagine this semantics sitting at one level in a hierarchy, this characterization of *O*'s objects of perception models "direct interaction" at that level. Now suppose we are given a hierarchical system, say *A*, in which the observer *O* is an irreducible entity at some distinguished level *L*. If *B* is any other system, perceptual or otherwise, with which *A* can interact, then in virtue of (23) the level *L*' of *B* which is matched with *L* must consist of objects of perception for *O*. We claim that other entities, say *P*, in *A* at the same level *L* as *O* must also be be objects of perception for *O*. For by requirement (22b) above, the entities in *L*' can interact directly with these. And by (22d), *O* itself can in principle interact directly

these. And by (22d), *O* itself can in principle interact directly with such *P*. Thus, on the one hand the entities *P* at the same level *L* as *O* may be represented as objects of perception of *O*; they are structurally equivalent to objects of perception in the given analytical framework. On the other hand, by (22c), these *P* are structurally indistinguishable from *O*, at least in terms of the syntax associated to the level *L*. We finally conclude that the *P*'s also have some of the structure of observers.

Hypothesis

This suggests a hypothesis. The objects of perception for an observer *O* have the same structure as *O* in the following sense: the objects of perception share with *O* that part of *O*'s structure which defines it as an irreducible entity at the fixed level *L* of the given hierarchical analysis. Stated succinctly, the objects of perception of *O* may themselves be represented as observers.

This hypothesis makes sense only in the context of a hierarchical analytic strategy; since that notion is not rigorous, it is clear that the argument given above which leads to the hypotheis is not intended to be rigorous. However the hypothesis motivates the construction of rigorous models of extended semantics in Bennett et al. 1988, models which are designed to be incorporated in a particular, well-defined hierarchical analytic strategy. The hypothesis says that a fundamental nondualism is associated with the various levels of the hierarchy; more precisely the nondualism is a property of the syntax associated with each such level, which is the minimal syntax necessary to distinguish that level. Thus, in the presence of a hierarchical analytic strategy, the apparently "dualistic" interaction of two complex systems is decomposable into a set of "nondualistic" interactions between entities at matched levels, together with information propagation through the levels of each system. On the other hand, one could take an approach which simply begins with a suitable hypothesis of nondualism and observe that it suggests (though it certainly does not require) hierarchical strategies. For example we might begin with a metaproposition similar to the following.

Meta-Proposition

Insofar as any two entities interact they are congruent: the part of their respective structures which is congruent delineates the nature and extent of the primary aspect of their interaction. Any aspect of the interaction which cannot be described in terms of this congruence is secondary, and arises from the propagation of the effects of the primary interaction by the internal flow of information within the separate entities.

We can then take our notion of "direct interaction" to be the "primary interaction" of this meta-proposition, so that direct interaction is automatically nondualistic. Stratification of interacting systems can then be defined in terms of levels of structure at which congruence occurs.

Hierarchical analytic strategies differ significantly from "fixed frame" analytic strategies. In the latter, there is a single unchanging framework (such as spacetime) in which all phenomena of interest are embedded.

NOTES

1. We thank A. Bobick, M. Braunstein, T. Cornsweet, V. Brown, D.P. Hoffman, T. Indow, D. Laberge, E. Matthei, L. Narens, H. Resnikoff, W. Richards, J. Rubin, and J. Yellott for discussions. We expecially thank C. Prakash, who has collaborated with us during the two years since this manuscript was first submitted. This material is based on work supported by the National Science Foundations under grants IST-8413560 and IRI-8700924, and by Office of Naval Research contract N00014-85-K-0529.

2. For simplicity, we assume parallel projection from the world onto the retina.

3. This cubic representation implies no statement about the dimensionality of the space of all closed curves in ($\mathbf{R}^3$) represented by level sets of polynominals.

4. For some discussion on this, see Hoffman and Flinchbaugh 1982 and Hoffman 1983.

5. Remarkably, one can prove this by finding one concrete choice of the x_{ij} and y_{ij} for which the six equations have no (real or complex solutions. Proof by concrete example is possible in this case since, for systems of algebraic equations, the number of solutions is an upper semicontinuous function of the parameters. This fact often allows one to determine the number of interpre-

tations associated to each premise rather easily. For more on this, see Hoffman and Bennett 1986.

6. Among the formal studies of structure from motion are Ullman 1979, 1981, and 1984; Longuet-Higgins and Prazdny 1980; Webb and Aggarwal 1981; Hoffman and Flinchbaugh 1982; Hoffman and Bennett 1985 and 1986; and Koenderink and van Doorn 1986.

7. The comment in bracket is ours; there are actually two solutions which are mirror images of each other, as Ullman points out elsewhere.

8. Among the formal studies of stereoscopic vision are Koenderink and van Doorn 1976, Marr and Poggio 1979, Grimson 1980, Longuet-Higgins 1982, Mayhew 1982, and Richards 1983.

9. Among the formal studies of optical flow are Koenderink and van Doorn 1975, 1976, and 1981; Marr and Ullman 1981; Horn and Schunck 1981; and Waxman and Wohn 1987.

10. Among the formal theories of shading are Horn 1975, Koenderink and van Doorn 1980, Ikeuchi and Horn 1981, and Pentland 1984. Among the formal theories of reflectance are Land and McCann 1971, Horn 1974, Maloney 1985, and Rubin and Richards 1987. For reviews see Horn 1985 and Ballard and Brown 1982.

11. In particular, when we define the collection of states of affairs to be a measurable space C, we are not claiming that any part of a physical world is a set.

Appendix: Mathematical notation and terminology

The definition of observer given in this papermakes use of several mathematical concepts from probability and measure theory. In this appendix we collect basic terminology and notation from these fields for the convenience of the reader. (For more background, beginning readers might refer to Breiman 1969 or Billingsley 1979. For advanced readers we suggest Chung 1974 and Revuz 1984.)

Let X be an arbitrary abstract space, namely a nonempty set of elements called "points." Points are often denoted generically by x. A collection X of subsets of X is called a σ-algebra if it contains X itself and is closed under the set operations of complementation and countable union (and is therefore closed under countable intersection as well). The pair (X,X) is called a measurable space and any set A in X is called an event. If (X,X) is a measurable space and $Y \subset X$ is any subset, we define a σ -algebra Y on Y as Y = {A ∩ Y | A∈X}. This measurable structure on Y is called the induced measurable structure. A map π from a measurable space (X,X) to another measurable space (Y,Y), π: $X \longrightarrow Y$, is said to be measurable if $\pi^{-1}(A)$ is in X for each A in Y; this is indicated by writing $\pi \in$X/Y. In this case the set $\sigma(\pi)$ = { $\pi^{-1}(A)|A \in$ Y} is a sub -algebra of X, called the σ-algebra ofπ. It is also denoted π^*Y. A measurable function π is said to be bimeasurable if, moreover, $\pi(A)$ is in Y for all $A \in$ X. A measurable function whose range is **R** or $\overline{\mathbf{R}} = \mathbf{R} \cup \{-\infty, \infty\}$ is also called a random variable; the symbol X also denotes the random variables on X. (The σ-algebra on **R** or $\overline{\mathbf{R}}$ is described in the next paragraph.) A measure on the measurable space (X,X) is a map μ from X to R∪{∞}, such that the measure of a countable union of disjoint sets in X is the sum of their individual measures. A measure μ is positive if the range of μ lies in the closed interval [0,∞]. A measure μ is called σ -finite if the space X is a countable union of events in X, each having finite measure. A property is said to hold "μ almost surely" (abbreviated μ a.s.) or "μ almost everywhere" (μ a.e.) if it holds everywhere except at most on a set of μ-measure zero. A support of a measure is any measurable set with the property that its complement has measure zero. If X is a discrete set whose σ -algebra is the collection of all its subsets, then counting measure on X is the measure μ defined by $\mu(\{x\}) = 1$ for all $x \in X$. A probability measure is a measure μ whose range is the closed interval [0,1] and that satisfies $\mu(X) = 1$. A Dirac measure is a probability measure supported on a single point. If ν and μ are two measures defined on the same measurable space, we say that ν is absolutely continuous with respect to μ (written $\nu \ll \mu$) on a measurable set E if $\nu(A) = 0$ for every $A \subset E$ with $\mu(A) = 0$. A measure class on (X,X) is an equivalence class of positive measures on X under the equivalence relation of mutual absolute continuity. Given a measure space (X,X,μ) and a mapping p from $(X,\mathrm{X},)$ to a measurable space (Y,Y), one can induce a measure $p_*\mu$ on (Y,Y) by $(p_*\mu)(A) = \mu(p^{-1}(A))$. Then $p_*\mu$ is called the distribution of p with respect to μ, or the projection of μ by p or the pushdown of μ by p.

If X and Y are two topological spaces, a map $f\colon X \longrightarrow Y$ is continuous if $f^{-1}(U)$ is an open set of X whenever U is an open set of Y. A continuous f is a homomorphism if it has a continuous inverse. A basis for a topology is any collection of sets that are open and such that any open set is a union of sets in the basis. A topological space is called separable if it has a countable basis. The smallest σ-algebra algebra containing the open sets of a topology (and therefore also the closed sets) is called the σ-algebra generated by the topology or the associated measurable structure of the topology. A metric on a set X is a function $d\colon X \times X \longrightarrow \mathbf{R}_+ = [0,\infty)$ such that for all $x, y, z \in X$, $d(x,y) = 0$ iff $x = y$, $d(x,y) = d(y,x)$, and $d(x,y) + d(y,z) \geq d(x,z)$. Given $\epsilon > 0$, the set $B_d(x, \epsilon) = \{y \mid d(x, y) < \epsilon\}$ is called the ϵ-ball centered at x. A topological space is metrizable if there is a metric on the space such that the open balls in the metric are a basis for the topology. A standard Borel space is a separable metrizable topological space with a σ-algebra generated by the topology. The topology on R or $\overline{\mathrm{R}}$ is here taken to be that generated by the open intervals. The associated measurable structure constitutes the Borel sets. Lebesgue measure λ is the unique measure on the Borel structure such that $\lambda((a,b)) = b - a$ for $b \geq a$. The Lebesgue structure is the smallest σ-algebra containing all Borel sets and all subsets of measure zero Borel sets. Lebesgue measure λ then extends to a measure with the same name on the Lebesgue structure.

Let (X,X), (Y,Y) be measurable spaces. A kernel on X relative to Y or a kernel on X relative to Y is a mapping $N\colon Y \times \mathrm{X} \longrightarrow \mathbf{R} \cup \{\infty\}$, such that:

(i) for every y in Y, the mapping $A \longrightarrow N(y,A)$ is a measure on X, denoted by $N(y,.)$;

(ii) for every A in X, the mapping $y \longrightarrow N(y,A)$ is a measurable function on Y, denoted by $N(.,A)$.

N is called positive if its range is in $[0,\infty]$ and markovian if it is positive and, for all $y \in Y$, $N(y, X) = 1$. If $X = Y$ we simply say that N is a kernel on X In what follows, all kernels are positive unless otherwise stated. If N is a kernel on Y x X and M is a kernel on X x W, then the product $NM(y,A) = \int_x N(y,dx)M(x,A)$ is also a kernel.

Let (X,X) and (Y,Y) be measurable spaces. Let p: $X \longrightarrow Y$ be a measurable function and μ a positive measure on (X,X). A regular conditional probability distribution (abbreviated rcpd) of μ with respect to p is a kernel m_p^μ: Y x X $\longrightarrow [0,1]$ satisfying the following conditions:

(i) m_p^μ is markovian;

(ii) $m_p^\mu(y,.)$ is supported on $p^{-1}\{y\}$ for $p_*\mu$-almost all $y \in Y$;

(iii) If $g \in L^1(\mathrm{X})$, then $\int_X g d\mu = \int_Y (p_* \mu)(dy) \int_{p^{-1}\{y\}} m_p^\mu(y, dx)g(x)$.

It is a theorem that if (X,X) and (Y,Y) are standard Borel spaces then an rcpd m_p exists for any probability measure μ. In general there will be many choices for m_p^μ any two of which will agree a.e. $p_*\mu$ on Y (that is, for almost all values of the first argument). If p: $X' \longrightarrow Y$ is a continuous map of topological spaces which are also given their corresponding standard Borel structures one can show that there is a canonical choice of m_p^μ defined everywhere.

PART THREE

Cognitive Development

6

Cognitive Development in Childhood

Susan Carey

A pendulum swing in views of cognitive development has occurred over the past 20 years. The issue in this pendulum swing is the proper description of the child's cognitive capabilities -- the proper description of how the child's conceptual system differs from the adult's. Twenty years ago, we had all assimilated Piaget's description of the incompetent child. Today, we are coming to grips with the competent child -- SuperKid.

A sketch of this recent bit of intellectual history makes the point clearly. Piaget presented us with hundreds of phenomena that diagnosed (so the story went) the fundamental differences between the young child's thought processes and the adult's thought processes. Most of these phenomena have been replicated literally thousands of times. So, for example, hundreds of thousands of children have been submitted to conservation experiments -- asked to equate the size of two balls of playdough (Figure 6-I), asked to watch while one is flattened into a pancake, and then asked whether they both are still the same amount of playdough, whether they still weigh the same, whether they would still displace the same amount of water. One MIT professor's 5-year-old, upon being asked one of these questions, answered, "I don't know, ask my older brother, he's got conservation." What is universally found in all of these studies is that young children (say 4- to 7-year-olds) maintain that the quantity of substance, the weight, the volume, have changed, while older children look at you as if you are crazy to be asking such a silly question and tell you that quantity, weight, and volume are conserved, that the two blobs of playdough only look different, that they're really the same, and sure, this one's wider, but it's also thinner.

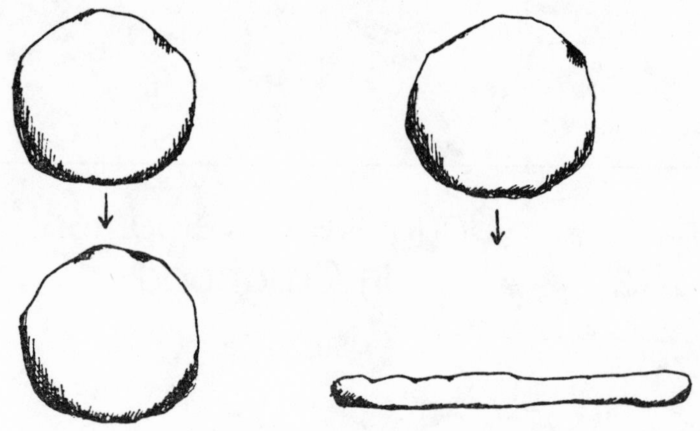

FIGURE 6-I

Example of Conservation

Conservation is only one in a range of phenomena, supposedly reflecting the preschool child's characteristic modes of thought, that Piaget, along with his coworkers and his followers, has given us. (In what follows, "young child" means 4-year-old; "old child" means 9 or 10-year-old.) Phenomenon 2: Seriation (Figure 6-II).

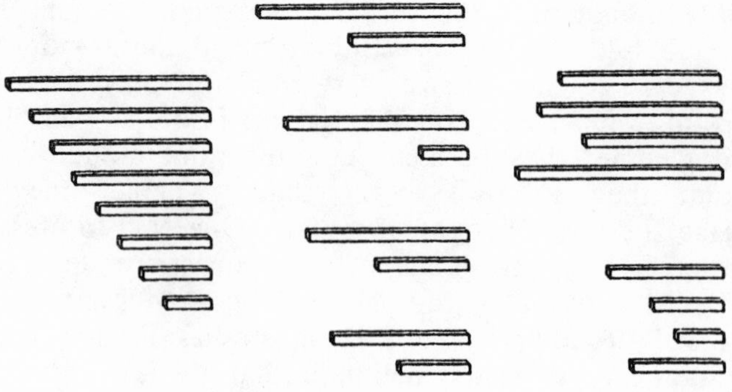

FIGURE 6-II

The Seriation Problem

Shown a series of sticks, arranged in order of length, and then asked to reproduce this series, young children cannot do so. They make two piles -- the short ones and the long ones, or else they alternate short-long, short-long, short-long. This problem is solved by age 8 or so. Phenomenon 3: Transitivity of shorter than, smaller than, heavier than, etc. If young children are taught that a particular red ball is heavier than an orange ball, and the orange ball is heavier than a yellow ball, they can draw no conclusion about the relative weights of the red and yellow balls. This problem is solved by age 8 or so. Phenomenon 4: Communications game. Children are seated on opposite sides of a barrier, so that they can see only the objects on their side. The experimenter indicates one of the objects of one of the children (e.g., the small, black, cube) and that child's task is to describe it so that the other child can pick the corresponding object from his or her side (Figure 6-III). A typical interchange between 5-year-olds is: Child 1, "It's this one." Child 2, (pointing at random, "This one?" Child 1, "Yes." This problem is solved by age 9 or 10.

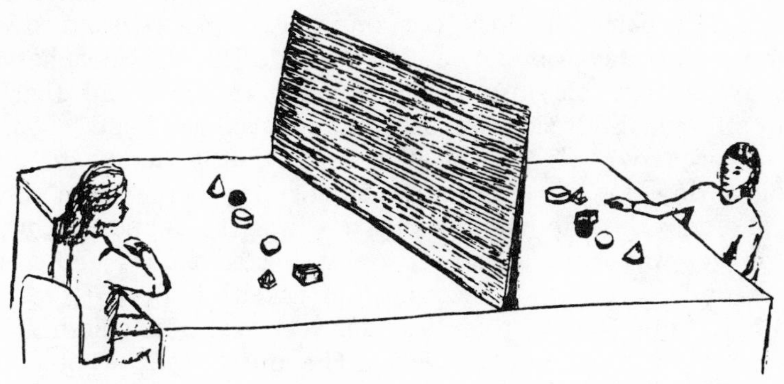

FIGURE 6-III

The Communications Game

Phenomenon 5: Mountains problem. The child is looking at a scale mountain with different objects on its sides (a ski-jump, a house, a road, etc., see (Figure 6-IV) He or she is asked to draw it as it appears to him or her, and also to draw it as it appears to the experimenter. At age 5 children draw the same picture under each instruction, namely, their own view.

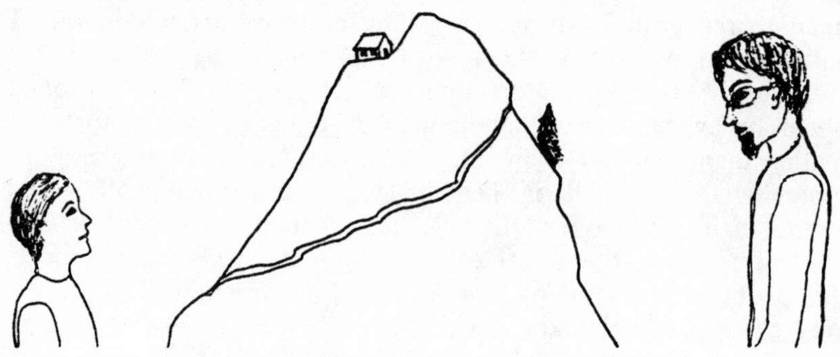

FIGURE 6-IV

The Mountains Problem

Phenomenon 6: How bad is the lie? Children are told two stories involving lies. In one, Bobby is very bad at school and his teacher warns him that she will soon have to take disciplinary action if his behavior does not improve. When asked by his mother how his day was, he replies, "Wonderful. The teacher told me today what a pleasure I am to have in class and that she wished all the children were as well-behaved as I am." In the other, George, who is afraid of dogs, makes a detour to avoid meeting a tiny dog on a sidewalk on his way home from school. When asked by his mother how his day was, he replies, "Wonderful. On my way home I saw a dog as big as a cow, and I went up to it and patted it." The question asked children is whether both Bobby and George told lies (answer, yes) and whether both were bad to do so (answer, yes). The question is whether one was a worse lie, whether one child was naughtier than the other in telling that lie. Young children say George's lie was worse and that George was naughtier, since it's not possible that a dog could be as big as a cow. Older children think that Bobby's lie was worse, for just the same reason -- because dogs are never as big as cows, there's no chance George's mother might believe him, but Bobby's might be actually deceived about an important matter. Phenomenon 7: Childhood animism. Young children maintain that the sun, the wind, clouds, cars, fires, and even rocks rolling down hills are alive. By age 10, life is attributed only to animals and plants. Phenomenon 8: Gender constancy. Young children maintain that one can change a girl into a boy by cutting her hair and inducing her to wear different clothes and play with different toys. Phenomenon 9: Class inclusion problem (Figure 6-V). Children are shown 8 flowers, 5 daisies and 3 roses. Asked to count the flowers, daisies, and roses, they do so correctly. Asked, which are there more of, more daisies or more flowers, young children answer, "more daisies."

The above is a very partial sampling of the questions to which 4-to 6-year-olds give sometimes surprisingly non-adult answers. Piaget's program was to bring order to this bewildering catalog of differences between preschool children, on the one hand, and 10-year-olds on the other. He sought an abstract, simplifying, characterization of how preschool children's thinking differed from that of late elementary school children's thinking. He tried many different formulations -- the 4-year-old child can focus on only one dimension of a task at once, the 10-year-old can coordinate two dimensions. The 4-year-old cannot represent linear orders, cannot form representations of classes nor of the inclusion relation among classes. The 4-year-old child cannot distinguish appearance from reality; the 4-year-old child has no notion of physical causality.

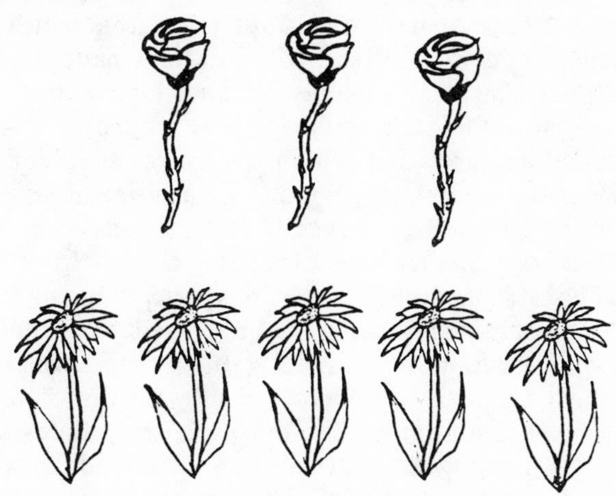

FIGURE 6-V

The Class Inclusion Problem

Let us return to conservation of amount. It does seem that the young child fails to distinguish appearance from reality where the older child succeeds; it does seem that the older child coordinates two dimensions where the young child focuses on just one. The difference seems to extend to all the other phenomena sketched above -- each putatively exemplifies one or more of the general shifts in thinking that occur in the first decade of life. Sometimes the phenomena Piaget described did not so transparently reflect the proposed underlying deficiency. Childhood animism, for example, was seen to be a reflection of the child's lack of a concept of physical causality. Here's how the story went -- the only causal schema the child has is intentional causation. But he sees the wind, clouds, the sun, moving cars, fires, rocks rolling down hills, as causal agents. They clearly affect other objects. Therefore, he attributes them beliefs, desires, and finally, life.

So how has the pendulum swung? First Piaget's descriptions of the developmental differences are vague and often obscure (I have given some of the clearer formulations of his claims.) Much effort has gone into making precise just what could be meant by the claim (for example) that young children cannot represent true concepts, nor the class inclusion relation, nor linear orderings. And for each reconstruction of what Piaget could have meant, the claim that young children are incompetent in that particular way has been denied. This denial has always taken the same form: a positive demonstration that preschool children have the representational or computational capacity in question. This is shown by their success at some task requiring that capacity. A second part of the denial is supplying an alternative explanation for the Piagetian phenomena that had previously been taken as evidence that the young child lacked the capacity in question.

I give an oversimplified example. The claims that the young child cannot construct linear orderings, nor make transitive inferences over linear orderings, were supported by phenomena 2 and 3 above (seriation and transitivity of length, weight, etc.). But consider the transitivity problem. It may be the case that the 4-year-old simply cannot remember the premises. Indeed, Bryant and Trabasso 1971 showed that given enough drill with the premises, children could construct 5 or 6 item series. They could impose a linear ordering on the following series: the yellow stick is longer than the orange stick; the orange stick is longer than the black stick, the black stick is longer than the red, the red is longer than the white, and the white is longer than the green. They could do this even though they never saw the lengths, and were presented the pairwise information in random orders. However, to do so, they needed to be drilled on the pairwise comparisons many hundreds of times. Further, they could easily make the relevant transitive inferences. In this example, this means being able to infer the relative lengths of the orange stick and the red stick. In sum, the Bryant and Trabasso work exemplifies both components of the denial of Piagetian claims -- a positive demonstration that the young child has the representational capacity in question and a diagnosis of the problem on the standard Piagetian task (memory limitations, in this case.)

The literature is now littered with demonstrations that the very young child has a notion of physical causality just like yours or mine, clearly distinguishes appearance from reality, can coordinate two dimensions, and so on. However, the stick example is misleading in one very important respect. In almost all cases, the source of difficulty for the preschool child is **not** some trivial artefact. We return to this point.

The upshot of the past two decades of research is the view that the young child does not have different computational and representational capacities than does the adult. However, many cognitive developmental psychologists have resisted this pendulum swing. It is perfectly obvious why -- if this view is correct, just what is there for the field to do? Nothing? Pack up and go home? Once one is seen the lessons of research like that sketched above, one doesn't want to make a lifetime career doing it -- discovering this artefact here, this artefact there, rediagnosing the real problem underlying the immature behavior in each of the thousands of Piaget's tasks. Why does this seem an uninteresting (an unimportant) enterprise? Because Piaget's theory characterized the <u>systematic</u> difference between the young child and the older child -- just a few systematic differences at that (e.g., appearance reality, coordinate 2 dimensions, linear ordering, classification, causality, egocentricity). This short list supposedly captures how 4-year-olds differ from 10-year-olds in a way that enabled us to understand the 4-year-olds limitations in reasoning about morality, spatial perspective, physical quantities, games of marbles, friendship, number, geometry, etc. By giving up this short list, we seem to be abandoning hope for a theory of cognitive development.

Let me put the dilemma in another way. There is no problem at all in finding differences between 4-year-olds and 10-year-olds. Indeed, it is news when children of such different ages perform the same on some task. But then 4-year-olds know less about just about anything you can mention, have less experience in almost every domain of endeavor of a child. A consequence of the pendulum swing has been (and should have been) to abandon the search for the essence of how 4-year-olds think differently from 10-year-olds or adults -- they don't. At issue, of course, is the existence of "stages of development," in the sense Piaget meant. The debate about stages concerns the correct level of abstractness to describe cognitive development. A commitment to stages is a commitment to there being a domain-general, i.e., conceptual content free, level of description of what changes in the course of cognitive development. The pendulum has swung away from a commitment to stages in the Piagetian sense. But does this mean that there is nothing unifying in the description of cognitive development?

A COUNTERPROPOSAL

I do not deny the competent child swing of the pendulum, but I also maintain that there are far reaching reorganizations of knowledge that unify the description of what might otherwise seem myriad piecemeal changes. These far reaching reorganizations can best be thought of as theory changes, or more precisely, as the emergence of new theories out of earlier ones. I have completed case studies of two such theory emergences. One charts the acquisition and reorganization of biological knowledge over the ages of 4 to 10 (Carey 1985b); the other charts the construction of a naive theory of matter over this same time period (Smith, Carey and Wiser 1985; see also Piaget and Inhelder 1941).

There are at least two broad types of theory changes in the history of science. In one, a well-developed domain of endeavor, say mechanics, undergoes revolution, as in the transition from the impetus theory to Newtonian mechanics, or from Newton's to Einstein's theory. In the other, a new theoretical domain emerges from a parent domain (or domains), as evolutionary biology, logic, psychology, and chemistry emerged as new domains of science in the 19th century. Even the latter are species of theory change, because they build on well-developed scientific traditions, and because some of the phenomena that motivate the new domain are studied earlier within a differnt scientific tradition. The developmental cases I have studied both fall into this latter type of theory change, those that witness the emergence of new theoretical domains. As in historical cases of the emergence of new theories, three developments are intertwined -- a new domain of phenomena is encountered, a new explanatory apparatus is developed, and new concepts come into being. Insofar as the new domain overlaps that of older theories, the changes in explanatory framework and concepts constitutes a theory change of the impetus theory/Newtonian theory variety. That is, these phenomena are reconceptualized, are articulated in terms of new concepts.

CASE STUDY

This will become clearer through a case study sketch -- the study of the emergence of the domain of biology from the domain of psychology. We examine all three kinds of change -- domain, explanatory framework, and core concepts.

Domain

There is no domain of phenomena that are strictly biological for the 4-year-old. Four-year-olds do not know the biological functions of eating, breathing, sleeping, having babies, having hearts, and so on. Activities such as eating, breathing and sleeping are part of the domain of human activities. They are phenomena of the same sort as playing and bathing. Important facts about eating include when one is allowed to eat candy, the difference between breakfast, lunch, and dinner, whether one is allowed to eat spaghetti with one's fingers, etc. The young child's knowledge about parts of the body is integrated into these same concerns -- the child knows one eats through one's mouth, that one's stomach gets full, even to the point sometimes of aching, etc. These activities and facts about people constitute a theoretical domain, because the child has an explanatory framework that accounts for them.

The Explanatory Framework

The explanatory structure in which these phenomena are embedded is social and psychological. The whys and wherefores of these matters, as the child understands them, include individual motivation (hunger, tiredness, avoiding pain, seeking pleasure and approval) and social conventions. Asked why people eat, 4-year-olds answer "because they are hungry," or "because it is dinner time." They might also say, "to grow," or "to be strong," but the ultimate explanation is still in terms of wants and beliefs--growing and being strong are desirable. The child knows no bodily mechanism whereby eating affects growth or strength.

Biological explanation, while also teleological, is not intentional. Supporting life is a bottomline goal; biological functions and bodily organs are explained in terms of their role in supporting life. The way eating, breathing, having babies, and so on, are understood in terms of biological explanation in the 10-year-old's conceptual system is different from the way these are understood in terms of intentional explanation in the 4-year-old's conceptual system. Thus, if my analysis is correct, the changes in both domain and explanatory structure characteristic of theory emergences are exemplified in this case study.

Changes in Individual Concepts

Sometimes theory changes involve changes in the core concepts that articulate the theories. The clearest cases are differentiations -- as Newton's distinction between mass and weight; Black's between heat and temperature. Coalescences also occur -- Galileo collapsed the Aristotelian distinction between natural and violent motion. Conceptual change entails cutting nature at different joints, and sometimes abandoning certain ontological commitments. For example, Aristotle was committed to "natural places" and "natural states" in his explanations of motion -- such notions played no role in Galilean or post-Galilean mechanics.

The emergence of an intuitive biology by age 10 involves conceptual change. The most radical is the coalescence of two distinct ontological types animal and plant into a single ontological type, living thing. For the 4-year-old, animals are fundamentally behaving natural kinds, like people; plants are fundamentally non-behaving natural kinds, like rocks. By age 10, both animals and plants are fundamentally the same kinds of things -- living things. Differentiations also occur -- the 4-year-old does not distinguish two different sense of "not alive" -- the sense of dead and the sense of inanimate. Indeed, every core concept in an intuitive biology, including animal, living thing, growth, death, baby, and the very notion of species, changes over this period. The status of people as animals also changes dramatically over these years.

Such are the simultaneous, mutually supportive, readjustments that constitute historical cases of conceptual changes as well.

Evidence

Several different methods yield a variety of phenomena that support the claim that an intuitive biology emerges during these childhood years. Six are briefly described below.

Inductive Projection. We constantly make inferences that are not deductively valid. Taught that people have membranes called omenta that hold our digestive organs in place, most adults infer that all mammals have omenta. Some infer all vertebrates do so, and some infer even more widely. Adults do not think that dolls have omenta, even though in many ways dolls appear more similar to people than are, say, dolphins. One role of our theories (naive or otherwise) is to constrain inductive projections of this sort. Our biological theory tells us that dolphins are similar to people in the relevant respects while dolls are not. Because this is so, patterns of inductive projection provide evidence about the thoeries held by the person making the inferences.

Four-year-olds, no less than adults, make sensible projections of newly taught biological properties. For example, when given some vague information about a new internal organ (such as that a spleen is a round, green thing found inside of people), subjects at all ages between 4 years and adulthood projected the new organ to other animals, with decreasing likelihood from mammals, through birds, through insects, through worms. At all ages there was significantly less attribution (usually none) to inanimate objects and plants (see Fig. 6-VI). Apparently, even for 4-year-olds enough information had been given for spleens to be interpreted as internal organs, and even 4-year-olds expect only other animals to share internal organs with people.

In spite of these constancies throughout development, patterns of inductive projection provided the best single piece of evidence that the 4-year-old's knowledge is organized differently from the adult's. The relevant data came in part from two other conditions in the same study. Other groups of subjects were shown a dog as the example of a spleen-haver (or omentum-haver, in the case of the older children and adults). Still others were shown a bee. As Figure 6-VII shows, in these cases, 4-year-olds did _not_ project spleens to other animals more than to inanimate objects, not even to other mammals (e.g., an aardvark) or insects

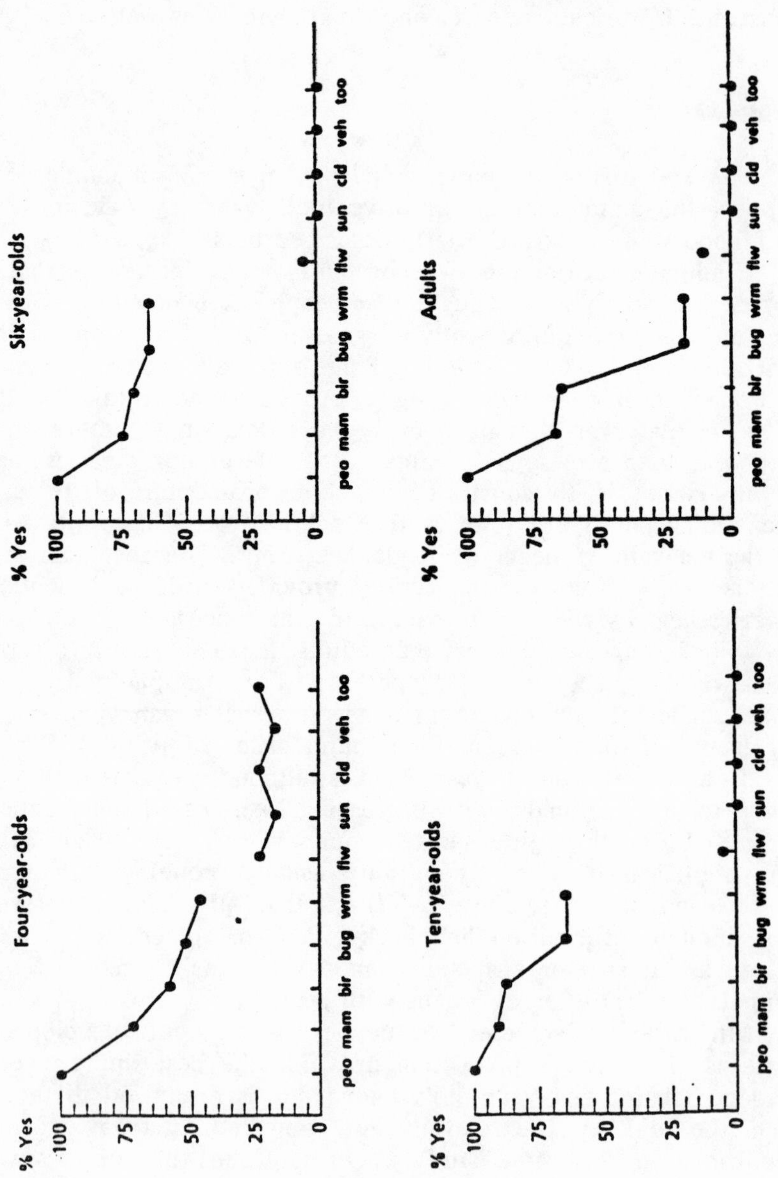

FIGURE 6-VI

Application of Biological Properties

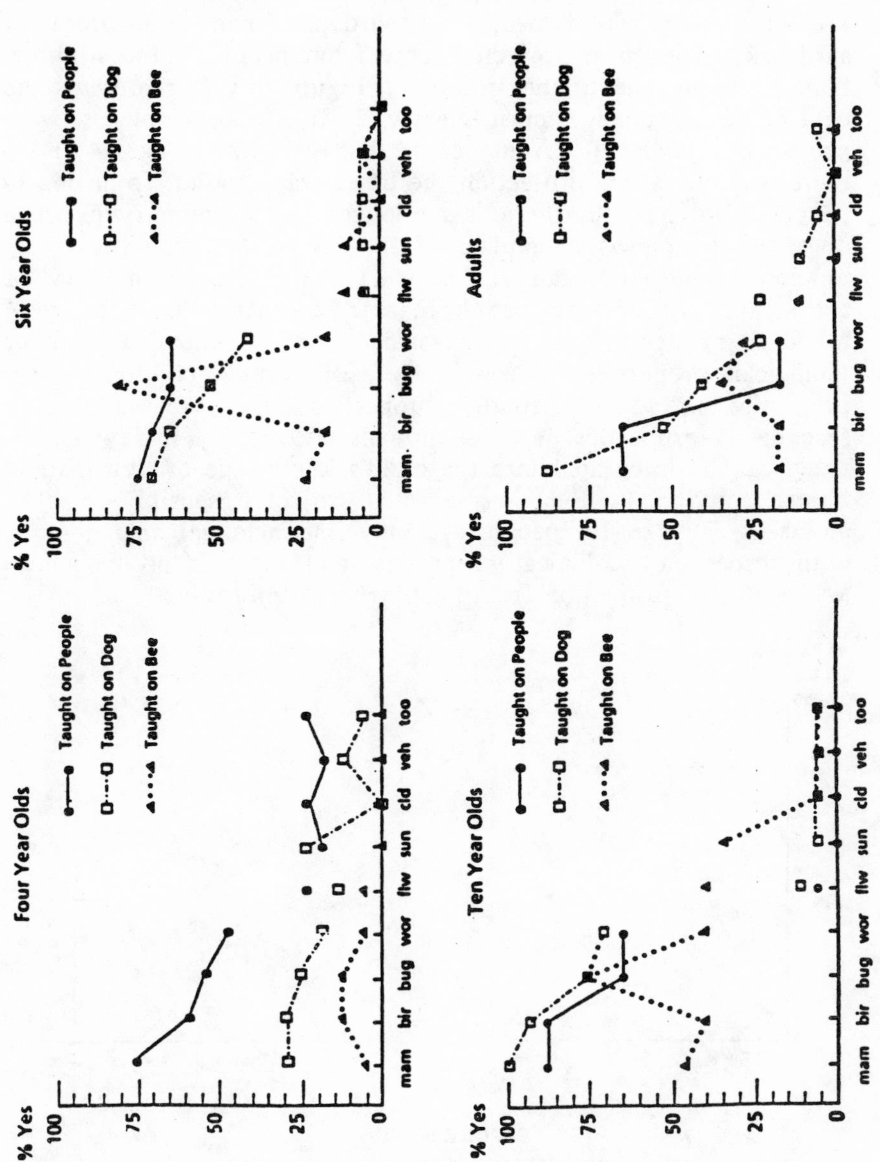

FIGURE 6-VII

Projection of Biological Properties

(e.g., a stinkbug). As the first graph in 6-VIII shows, 4-year-olds projected more from people to aardvark than from dogs to aardvark. They also projected more from people to the stinkbug than from the bee to the stinkbug. Figure 6-VIII represents the developmental change most clearly. At all ages spleens were projected significantly from people to dogs. But at ages 4 and 6 there was much less projection the other way around, from dog to people. But age 10, there is no longer any asymmetry between dogs and people as exemplars of the havers of some previously unknown internal organ. The shift from total asymmetry of projection (greater from people than from other animals) at age 4 to none at age 10 reflects restructuring of knowledge about biological properties. Apparently, for young children, these properties are fundamentally properties of people and only secondarily properties of other animals also. Only if new knowledge can be integrated into the child's knowledge of humans and human activities will the 4-year-olds project it sensibly to other animals. By age 10, people are only one mammal among many with respect to biological properties, and there is no longer an asymmetry of projection from people and from dog.

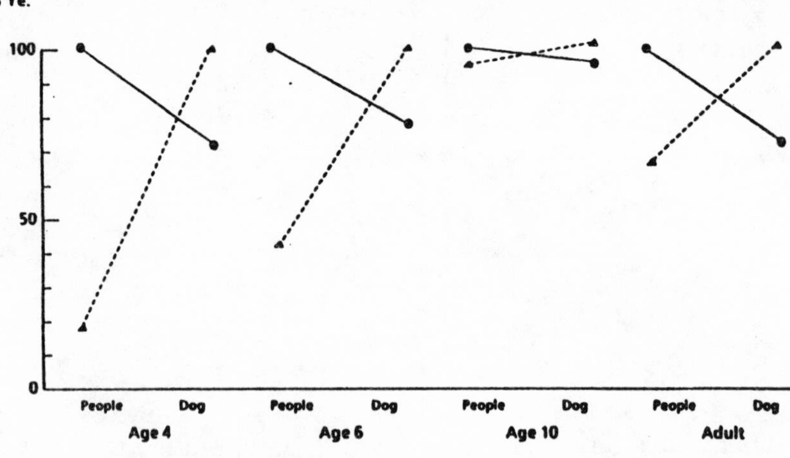

FIGURE 6-VIII

Projection from people to dogs compared to projection from dogs to people. —— taught on people --- taught on dogs

Patterns of Attribution of Biological Properties. If 4-year-olds' knowledge of biological properties such as eating, sleeping, breathing, having hearts, having bones, and having babies is structured in terms of the role of each in human intercourse, then they should not differentiate between those properties all animals must have from those that only some animals share with people. This prediction follows from the assumption that the child of this age does not know the biological functions of these properties.

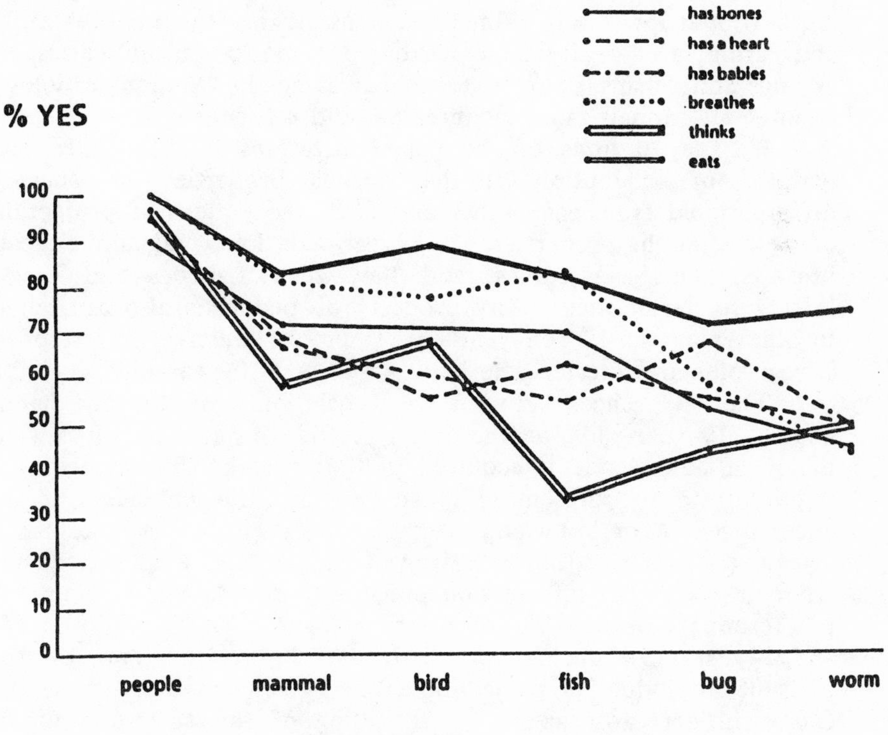

FIGURE 6-IX

Patterns of attribution for a 4-year-old

Children were probed as to what things in the world eat, breathe, sleep, think, have babies (always asked "Does x have baby x's?"), have hearts, have bones. To a first approximation, the 4-year-old's patterns of attribution of all these properties were identical to each other (Figure 6-IX). In each case, attribution was virtually 100% to people, and fell off thereafter according to similarity to people. Indeed, the patterns of attribution were the same as those for spleen. It seems that 4-year-olds answer the question, "Does an x breathe?" by recalling that people breathe and then projecting breathing to other objects according to similarity to people. These patterns of projection reflect paucity of biological knowledge in various ways. There is a drop in attribution of about 20% between people, on the one hand, and mammals such as dogs and aardvarks, on the other -- for having hearts, breathing, etc., as well as for having spleens. People are not just one mammal among many with respect to these properties. Also, properties of all animals such as having babies, breathing, and eating, are greatly underattributed to peripheral animals such as bugs and worms. The 4-year-old does not know enough biology to infer all animals must eat, breathe, and reproduce.

By age 10 none of these generalizations is still true. The patterns of attribution of the various properties are sharply differentiated from each other and from the pattern of projection of newly taught properties. Ten-year-olds know all animals eat, breathe, and have babies, and they restrict bones and hearts largely to vertebrates. Any property of people is also attributed to other mammals. Ten-year-olds resemble adults in this respect; 7-year-olds are intermediate between 4- and 10-year-olds.

The differences between the 4-year-olds, on the one hand, and the 10-year-olds, on the other, provide insights into just what biological knowledge is acquired in these years. But much more important to the present argument is the evidence these differences provide for knowledge restructuring. As in the case of the asymmetries of projection reviewed above, the evidence comes from the different information processing models that account for the responses of subjects of different ages. Young children (4- and 5-year-olds) decide what animals eat, breathe, etc., on the basis of an inductive projection from knowledge that people do. Older subjects are capable of reasoning of this sort, and use it when they have no other information to go on (as in the projection of omenta described above). However, 10-year-olds and adults use two quite different processes to generate their judgements about breathing, eating, having babies, having bones, etc. They base their judgements on deductive inferences from category membership (e.g., worms eat because worms are animals and all animals eat; worms do not have bones because they are not vertebrates, and only vertebrates have bones) or from reasoning about knowledge of biological function (e.g., worms must breathe because any living thing must burn oxygen for energy, and must therefore have a way of obtaining oxygen from the air). These information processing differences in turn reflect differences in the organization of knowledge. Four-year-olds' knowledge of what for us are biological properties is organized around their knowledge of people. Biological function does not affect the similarity metric underlying the projection of these properties to other things. By age 10 there is no evidence that knowledge that people have the properties in question is playing any role whatsoever in the child's attribution of these properties to other objects.

Projection From Two Animals. Suppose that instead of being informed that a dog is one of the things in the world that has a spleen, or a bee is one of the things in the world that has a spleen, the child is told "and here are pictures of two of the things in the world that have spleens," at which point pictures of both a dog and a bee are produced, and spleens drawn inside each. Adults might be expected to reason that if two such disparate animals share some unknown internal organ, then all animals of some minimal complexity must have that organ. Four- to 6-year-olds, in contrast, would not be expected to have this form of reasoning available to them, because they do not know the biological functions of internal organs, and do not understand that because some biological problems are universal, some aspects to the solution to them are also widely shared. How might young children decide whether some new object (say, a bird) has a spleen, given that they know that dogs have spleens and that bees have spleens? They might retrieve the known spleen-haver most similar to a bird, and then judge according to similarity to that spleen-haver. If this is how children do it, the pattern of projection from dogs and bees will be the intersection of the projection curve from dog alone and of the projection curve from bee alone.

The data from 17 6-year-olds are given in Figure 6-X. They almost perfectly fit the intersection pattern. Except in the case of projection to worm, projection to new animals is no greater from dog and bee than from dog alone (to people, another mammal, and a bird) or from bee alone (to another bug). Knowing that dogs **and** bees have spleens makes it no more likely to a 6-year-old that aardvarks do than knowing only that dogs have spleens. Analyses of individual patterns of projection showed that 6-year-olds were no more likely to judge that **all** animals have spleens, given that dogs and bees do, than they were to judge that all animals have spleens given that dogs alone do (or that bees alone do). In all three of these cases, about 5-10% of the subjects attributed spleens to all animals. Adults, in contrast, were significantly more likely to judge that all animals have omenta when taught that dogs and bees have omenta (about 50% of the time) than when taught that dogs alone, or bees alone, have omenta (5-10% of the time).

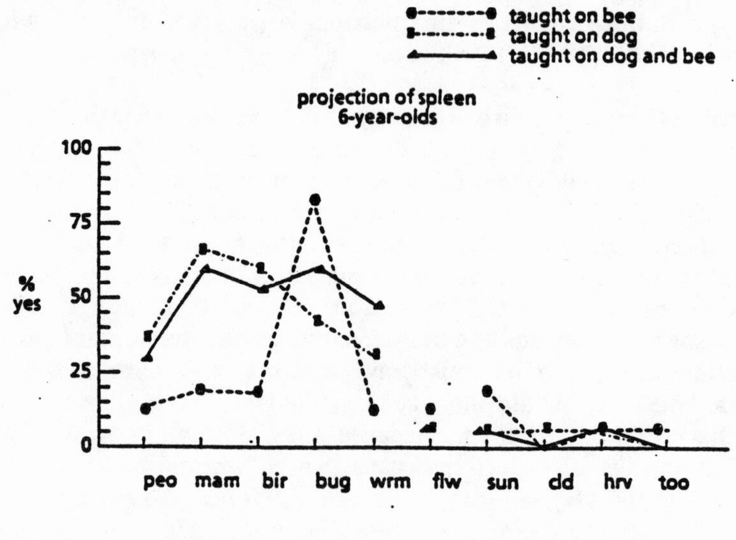

FIGURE 6-X

Projection of a spleen for 6-year-olds

One way to characterize this developmental difference is to say that the concept animal constrains inductive projection by 6-year-olds differently than it does for adults. That is, the concept animal constrains inductive projection in some sense even in the youngest children tested. As we saw above (Figure 6-VI), when taught that people have some internal organ, even the youngest children project it almost exclusively to new animals. However, the concept animal seems available as an inductive base in another sense by adulthood. Taught that dogs and bees have some animal property, the 6-year-old does not assume that all animals have that property, while adults do (at least sometimes). This is yet another difference between young children's inferential processes and adults. This third reflection of restructuring provided by differences in information processing models is interpretable as were the first two. Only when children understand some of the biological functions of activities like breathing and eating and of organs like stomachs and hearts can they begin to understand that there are some basic problems every living organism must have successfully solved in order to exist. Armed with this understanding the child can discover that some aspects of the solutions reappear throughout the biological kingdom. With such knowledge, the information that dogs and bees both share a biological property provides prima facie evidence that all complex animals do.

Clinical Interviews. The above discussion assumes that young children do not know the biological function of bodily processes and internal body parts. This assumption is supported by a vast literature on the young child's concepts of death, growth, gender, reproduction, illness, internal body parts, and bodily processes such as digestion. Almost without exception, the method used in this literature is the clinical interview. The child is asked a structured, semi-standardized, set of questions about his or her understanding of the issue under study. And without exception the young child (4-to 6-year-olds) conceives of these matters differently from the 10-year-old, who usually (but not in all cases) has achieved the naive adult conception.

This literature is much too vast to summarize here (see Carey 1985b for a review). It reveals the preschool child's ignorance of what's inside the body (4-year-olds commonly mention blood, food and bones). Insofar as internal organs are known, they are assigned functions on the principle: one organ -- one function. The stomach is for eating, the heart is for making blood, brain is for thinking, etc. Processes such as death, growth, reproduction, and ingestion are conceptualized in terms of the behavior of the whole person, and its consequences for the whole person. Thus, the 4-year-old might well know that if you eat too much dessert you will get fat, or that eating vegetables will keep you healthy. What the 4-year-old decidedly does not have is any knowledge of any mechanism by which the body mediates these input-output relations.

All this has changed by age 10. Ten-year-olds know of many internal body parts, and have constructed a model of how the integrated functioning of these internal organs supports life, growth, and reproduction (Crider 1981). The first model (achieved by age 9 or so) has substances being passed around -- air, food, blood -- and being used by the body. Different body parts are containers or conductors of these substances along the way. Only later does the child understand how the body breaks down and transforms substances. Even the first model, however, allows conceiving death as the cessation of internal bodily processes, and allows all animals to be seen as fundamentally alike in ways that do not involve being behaving beings. It also allows the conceptualization of plants as like animals. Finally, it allows the formulation of the general biological problems to which each animal is a solution, and therefore enables the child to see that the real nature of each animal is to be found in its unique solution to these problems.

Species as Natural Kinds. At least since John Locke, philosophers have distinguished between natural kind terms, such as *tiger*, *gold*, *water*, *proton*, *star*, *gene*, and so on, and non-natural kind terms, such as *box*, *thing*, *table*, and so on. While the distinction is easy to appreciate, it is not easy to state precisely, partly because many competing analyses have been offered in the philosophical literature. One thread running through the literature since Locke is that natural kind terms refer to kinds that have essences that are the proper business of science to discover. The essence of a natural kind is that property that kind must have in order to **be** that kind. The essence of water is being H_2O; the essence of gold is being the element with atomic number 69; the essence of tigers is presumably to be stated in terms of genetic structure. Note that we can believe that some kind is a natural kind, and therefore that its members have essences, without yet knowing the essence. Such is the case for tigers. We do know which science will discover the essence of tigers, namely biology, but we can only guess at the nature of the tiger's essence. We can see, then, that the specification of natural kinds is closely tied to our theories of the world. A rough and ready test for non-natural kinds is that they play no role in scientific theories. There is no essence of a box, a thing, or a table to be discovered; none of these is likely to play an important role in any present or future scientific theory.

When people treat a term as a natural kind term, they are willing to grant that those properties they know of things to which the term applies do not actually determine category membership. That is, they may have a prototype of members of the kind, but they are ready to defer to experts or to their own theory building to discover that their prototype is wrong. This is why if I show you a fruit with nubbly skin the size, shape and color of an orange, but **tell** you that it grew on a lemon tree, you are happy to conclude it is a funny looking lemon. Our current theories of the essences of biological kinds, being tied to genetics as they are, lead us to weight parentage very heavily. If something that looked exactly like a cactus had the genetic structure of a grapefruit, could cross with prototypical grapefruits, and so on, we would be surprised, but would accept that it is nonetheless a grapefruit.

Recently, Keil 1986 has asked at what age words for individual animals, such as "skunk" and "raccoon", fruits, such as "lemon" and "grapefruit," and plants, such as "cactus" and "palm," become natural kind terms in this sense. He used two converging paradigms. One pitted his best guess of the child's views of the nature of individual species' essences against his guess of what the child would consider merely characteristic features. The other left entirely open what the child might consider the essence. In the first experiment the child was shown a picture of an animal, say a skunk as in Figure 6-XI, and told various things about the behavior of that animal, such as that it was active at night, squirted smelly stuff when it was attacked or frightened, and so on. In other words, both its appearance and behavior fit the prototypical skunk. The child was asked what he thought it was a picture of, and of course, ventured it was a skunk. He was then told that scientists had studied this particular animal in great detail and had discovered that its parents had been raccoons, that its babies had been raccoons, and that its heart, brain, and blood were like the heart, brains, and blood of raccoons. He was then asked what the animal was -- a raccoon or a skunk. Subjects were 5-year-olds and 9-year-olds. The younger children insisted that the picture depicted a skunk; 9-year-olds said it was a raccoon that merely looked like a skunk.

As mentioned above, this study depended upon a guess as to what the child's views of the underlying essences of species would be like -- parentage and internal organs would loom large. The second study depended on no such guess. As before the child was shown a picture such as that in Figure 6-XI and asked what he thought it was -- skunk again being the answer. He was told that some veterinarians took that animal and shaved off all its fur, replaced it with black and brown fur, made it much fatter, removed its tail and replaced it with another, and so on, until the result looked as in Figure 6-XII. The question was what Figure 6-XI depicted. Five-year-olds were adamant that it was a raccoon, 9-year-olds equally sure that it was a skunk that merely looked exactly like a raccoon.

FIGURE 6-XI

Skunk

FIGURE 6-XII

Raccoon

FIGURE 6-XIII

Coffee Pot

FIGURE 6-XIV

Bird Feeder

An important control is to see that this shift does not occur for terms that do not refer to natural kinds. Parallel controls were carried out for the two studies; I describe those for the second study only. Subjects were shown a picture such as that in Figure 6-XIII, and all agreed it was a coffee pot. A transformation was described, where various parts were rearranged, excised, and added until the final result was as in Figure 6-XIV -- a bird feeder. The question is what the resulting object is -- a coffee-pot or a bird-feeder. Here children of both ages agreed that it is a bird feeder. There is no general tendency for 9-year-olds to conserve kind across transformations such as these.

Keil used many different examples, taken from the plant as well as the animal kingdom and from various types of non-natural kinds as well. He saw his data as reflecting a shift, between the ages of 5 and 9, in the nature of all the terms for biological species. For 5-year-olds these terms are non-natural kind terms, like coffee pot, while by age 9 they are natural kind terms. There is another way of describing the shift that is perhaps more familar to developmental psychologists: the 9-year-olds make a distinction between appearance and reality that the 5-year-olds do not. These two ways of describing the change are in fact closely related. Essences are the ultimate reality, the real nature of the things in nature, and are usually deeply hidden. It is the business of science both to discover essences and to discover deeper realities underlying surface appearances.

Keil does not argue for a general shift between these ages such that all terms that refer to natural kinds as far as adults are concerned begin to do so around age 9. Whether a term is a natural kind or not is a function of two factors: the world (is there a kind in nature picked out by the term?) and the user's knowledge (does he realize that the objects refered to have an underlying essence?). Thus, the words *atom* and *elm* may function as natural kind terms for me, but not for my 6-year-old daughter. Similarly, there is no general emergence of the appearance/reality distinction around age 9. Children as young as 3 command the distinction in some contexts (Flavell, Flavell, and Green 1982). After this age, grasp of the distinction develops in two respects: the child comes to appreciate it on a meta-conceptual level (Flavell et. al. 1982) and the child comes to know, through domain-specific conceptual change, more and more cases where surface appearances do not accord with deeper reality (Carey 1985a). Keil's phenomenon is an instance of the latter sort.

The discovery of the essences of the things in nature and the discovery of deeper realities underlying surface phenomena are two of the goals of theory development. Rudimentary biological knowledge is being acquired and restructured in the years 4 to 10. The reflections of this process described above provide some insight into Keil's phenomena. What for the adult are basic biological functions and crucial biological organs are seen by the 4-year-old in terms of their place in human activity. Other animals have these basically (for the child) human properties only insofar as they are similar to people. Suppose I am right that children do not understand these properties in terms of their biological functions until around age 10. Perhaps they cannot conceive of each animal or plant species as a unique solution to a basic set of common biological problems until then. In other words, if hearts, blood, stomachs are fundamentally properties of people, then the very notions of the heart of a skunk, the blood of a skunk, the brain of a skunk, and so on, are not meaningful to a 5-year-old.

Childhood Animism. The sixth phenomenon that reveals acquisition and reorganization of biological knowledge between ages 4 and 10 -- childhood animism -- is well known to developmental psychologists, although not usually interpreted in this light. Asked what things in the world are alive, young children include various inanimate objects -- the sun, the moon, cars, fires, stoves, clouds, rivers, the wind, televisions, rocks rolling down hills, and so on, have all been judged alive by many animistic young subjects (Piaget 1929; Laurendeau and Pinard 1962; Carey 1985b). Childhood animism disappears almost completely by age 10.

Piaget 1929 placed the phenomenon of childhood animism in the context of the child's notions of causality. He claimed that the preschool child had only one causal schema -- human intentional causation. Lacking any notions of physical causation, the child interprets cases of one inanimate object's affecting another in terms of the intentions and goals of the active object. The active object is seen as causal agent, as in the sun's warming a person, the fire's cooking food, the rolling rock's knocking loose another, and so on. Active agents, in turn, are endowed with life. Hence childhood animism. As Gelman and her collaborators have shown, the key presupposition of Piaget's account is false. The preschool child does **not** lack a notion of physical causality (e.g., Bullock, Gelman, and Baillergeon 1982; see also, Shultz 1982). Thus, although Piaget is right that young children do attribute intentional causal agency to inanimate objects, the reason for this cannot be that the child lacks any other causal schema. The root of childhood animism must be found elsewhere.

Object taught on	Percent inanimate objects attributed with golgi	Percent subjects making at least one attribution to inanimate object
dogs and flowers	38%	44%
flowers	11%	19%
dogs and bees	4%	15%

FIGURE 6-XV

Projection of golgi to inanimate objects

Here let us restrict our attention to developmental changes in the meaning of the word *alive*. In my monograph I argue that one major factor in the animistic attribution of life to inanimate objects is lack of biological knowledge. My argument is much too lengthy to go into here, but I can give the flavor of a part of it. Suppose that the child knows, because he has been told, that plants and animals are alive. Given that children under 7 do not yet know the biological functions of eating, breathing, growing, and so on, such that they do not even realize that all animals must share these functions, they could have no basis for rationalizing the inclusion of plants and animals in a single category. Having no basis for seeing why animals and plants are alike, other objects might be included among the living. Two results directly support this line of reasoning. First, a new property (having golgi) was taught as were spleen and omenta in the studies described above, only the child was told "and here are pictures of two of the things in the world that have golgi -- dogs and flowers." By hypothesis, the 6-year-old does not have the concept living thing available as an inductive base, and so should sometimes include inanimate objects among projected golgi havers. As

Figure 6-XV shows, this is what happened. Thus, it is possible to produce patterns of attribution like those for judgements of what is alive or not merely by telling the child that an animal and a plant share some property and asking him to judge what else might. Second, when tested in the standard Piagetian interview, 4- to 7-year olds gave animistic judgements only when they judged that plants were alive. If they judged animals to be alive, but not plants, they also did not include inanimate objects among the living (Carey 1985). In sum, one source of animistic attributions of life is not having the biological concept living thing available to rationalize the inclusion of animals and plants into a single category. The concept living thing becomes available as biological functions and properties become differentiated from general knowledge of people. As we saw above, this happens in the years between 4 and 10.

CONCLUSIONS

I have argued that these phenomena plausibly reflect the emergence of a new theoretical domain. I claim that such childhood cases of theory emergence involve restructuring of knowledge of just the same sort as occurs in the history of science. Insofar as there are only a very few intuitive theories represented by the child, and insofar as these intuitive theories encompass wide domains of phenomena, the study of theory changes in childhood will provide one source of unity in our description of development. Thus, if these two assumptions are correct, an undesirable consequence of abandoning the stage theory is avoided. We are not to be reduced to describing thousands of piecemeal developmental advances.

In Piaget's last work, he returned to questions that might be seen as the core of genetic epistemology -- the relations between the ontogenesis of scientific knowledge in childhood and in the history of science. In this context, the question of stages should be differentiated into two questions: (1) Are there developmental constraints on the types of theories children can construct? (2) Within any given theoretical domain, is ontogenesis characterized by large scale restructuring? If so, must we characterize the restructuring in cases of historical theory change in the same terms as we would characterize the restructuring in the case of individual development of scientific concepts? Some have taken large scale structural reorganizations as the hallmark of stages.

This is a merely semantic issue; any theorist is free to use the word "stage" however he or she pleases. But if "stage" is taken in the domain general sense adopted in this paper, a commitment to there being stages is a commitment to an affirmative answer to the first question. Here I would simply like to point out that the answer to each of these two questions constrains the other. Insofar as there are developmental constraints on the kinds of theories children can construct, the parallels between the characterization of conceptual change in childhood and in the history of science are limited. Insofar as the same representational and computational machinery is needed to characterize conceptual change in both cases, the role of domain general developmental change in childhood is limited. Thus, there is a certain tension between Piaget's work on the domain general characterization of changes in representational and inferential capacities and his work on the parallels between ontogenesis in the history of science and in childhood.

One example may make clear that these two questions are distinct. The difficulty in getting a child past a Piagetian hurdle is well known. Indeed, the hallmark of most of Piaget's phenomena is that it is nearly impossible to get the child to perform as would an adult. Upon seeing a non-conserving child for the first time, most people's initial response is that the child is failing to understand the question, for some trivial reason. The intuition is that given 20 minutes with the child, you could make clear what is wanted, and straighten the kid out. The literature is littered with failed attempts to do just that. So-called "training studies" just do not work -- unless the child is "ready" to be trained. This is to be understood on the assumption of domain general stages, since being "ready" meant having attained a new way of thinking or new information processing capacity -- only if you have passed into the new stage will you be able to benefit from training. But this is also to be understood on the theory change story.

Theories resist change. Discrepant phenomena are assimilated or ignored. Given the restructuring involved, it is no accident that the process is protracted -- over a 5 or 6 year period -- and it is not surprising that short training studies fail. Indeed, the science education literature now has myriad examples of failures of curricular materials to dislodge misconceptions, where the source of each misconception is alternative conceptual frameworks -- intuitive theories -- novices bring to science learning. A year of college level mechanics does not replace the pre-Newtonian ideas the college student brings to the physics class (see Chi, Glaser, and Rees 1982 for a review.)

I am arguing here that conceptual change in childhood must be analyzed in the context of theory changes in childhood. This commits me to the view that children, even babies, represent theory-like conceptual structures. Of course, I embrace this commitment; indeed, I believe that we will need to appeal to intuitive theories in any attempts to specify constraints on induction, ontological commitments, and causal notions. And, as I have tried to sketch here, appeals to theory change may provide some descriptive unity to diverse developmental changes, and may help us understand resistance to learning in at least some cases.

Just what is meant by "theory" and is it plausible to impute theories to young children? A theory is characterized by the phenomena in its domain, its law and other explanatory mechanisms, and the concepts that articulate the laws and the representations of the phenomena. Explanation is at the core of theories. It is explanatory mechanisms that distinguish theories from other types of conceptual structures, such as restaurant scripts. To see this, consider such questions as "Why do we pay for our food at a restaurant?" or "Why do we order before the food comes?" The answers to these questions are not to be found within the restaurant script itself; the answer to the first lies in the domain of economics, where questions of exchanges of goods and services sit, and that to the second in the domain of physics, where questions of the directionality of time sit.

The distinction between theory-like structures and other types of cognitive structures is one of degree. Probably all conceptual structures provide some fodder for explanation. My intuition, however, is that there are only a relatively few conceptual structures that embody deep explanatory notions -- on the order of a dozen or so in the case of educated non-scientists. These conceptual structures correspond to domains that might be the disciplines in a university -- psychology, mechanics, a theory of matter, economics, religion, government, biology, history, etc. On the view of development put forward in this paper, the child begins with many fewer such domains -- perhaps only a naive mechanics and a naive psychology. Conceptual developmental consists, in part, of the differentiation of new theoretical domains from these beginning ones, as in the differentiation of biology from psychology described in this talk.

I have not shown, of course, that theory-like structures are relatively few in number, and that such structures can be distinguished from other conceptual structures along the continuum of explanatory depth. Rather, I have attempted to make these claims at least plausible, so that they may be subjects to further scrutiny and test. I hereby confess that the ultimate interest of the arguments in this paper depend upon these claims being cashable.

One final caveat -- many will recognize that I have opened a can of worms. I have tried to show that developmental psychologists are up against the same set of problems that arise in the general problem of understanding theory change -- but what kind of step forward is this? All I can say is that I think it is important to know just what can of worms we are in.

7

Formal and Substantive Features of Language Acquisition: Reflections on the Subset Principle and Parametric Variation

Thomas Roeper

Robert Berwick 1985 has recently provided a beautifully articulated formal account of a principle that has been informally at work in much of the theoretical efforts in language acquisition: the subset principle.[1] The subset principle requires that set of sentences generated by earlier grammars must comprise a subset of sentences generated by later grammars. Less elegantly, languages grow from smaller to larger.

The scenario is this: Each step of a child's acquisition of grammar must involve movement from a smaller set to a larger set and cannot involve the reverse. The steps are motivated by pieces of input data (adult sentences) which fail to fit into the smaller set, thereby forcing an expansion of the set. In this sense, the formal, mathematical notion corresponds naturally to empirical reality. It is undoubtedly the case that children learn their native tongue by trying to incorporate new sentences they hear into existing grammar. The subset principle predicts thereby sequential growth, which again, corresponds to reality.

Berwick has not only formalized the idea within a computational model, but has provided numerous carefully reasoned examples of how a machine could follow such a principle. In short, he provides an argument about how linguistic computations can fit into a larger theory of mental computations.

In what follows we would like to place the subset principle in the context of substantive linguistic factors that interact with formal factors. We will not examine the subset principle in terms of its mathematical detail, but in terms of how it fits acquisition data. The principle has the virtue of simplicity, serving to clarify auxiliary or derivative principles which the acquisition mechanism must obey. We propose below that some principles of grammar can only be realized via an anti-subset constraint, which guarantees that a child's progressive grammars G_1 and G_2 are not in a subset relation.[2] We will concentrate on three examples, drawn from the domain of optional subjects, coreference, and optional inversions.

THE GENETIC PROGRAM

Chomsky 1965 originally distinguished between formal universals and substantive universals. The substantive universals involved notions like Noun, Verb, and Adjective, while formal universals involved principles which limited the possible form of transformations. There was an implicit interaction between a substantive linguistic component and general (but undescribed) "principles of mind." The crucial feature of the innateness hypothesis was not that every formal principle was uniquely linguistic, but rather, that the scope of interaction between substantive linguistic features and other aspects of mind was itself genetically controlled. A crude analogy might be helpful. We know that the mouth is used for both eating and speaking, but the way it is used for each of these activities is different and genetically controlled. We could say that language used "general mouth ability." While such a remark is mouthable, it tells us very little. What is of interest is the task specific organization of oral physiology.

Genetic Determination and Reductionism

The notion "genetic determination" does not mean that particular abilities are limited to a particular mental function, such as language.[3] The genetic component may simply determine which of a large set of general mental abilities are permitted to function in the language component, and in which fashion. Suppose we have a general concept of hierarchical (i.e. tree) structure, and a general capacity for recursion, or embedding, and a general notion of discrete category (like N, V, A). Each of these notions may have roots in broad mental capacities, or at least one can assert that similar formal features are found elsewhere in mental activity. In this sense every linguistic ability can be subject, in part, to reductionism. The domains where reductionism is possible, however, obscure the essence of language, namely, the genetically specific web of connections among various cognitive abilities. That is, the point where formal features combine in language is subject to exact restrictions. In the tree structure, it is the NP which dominates an adjective node ([$_{NP}$the[$_{A}$green]car$_{NP}$]), and not the reverse (*[$_{AP}$green[$_{NP}$the car]]). The NP and S, but not the VP or Art, or N, are available for recursion in the syntax, while N is available for recursion in the lexicon in the creation of compound nouns (e.g., *wallet hide distribution series*). While the general properties of language may be subject to reductionism, the connections between modules are genetically specified.

The reductionist program characterizes numerous anti-innateness arguments. They take the form of showing that a putative linguistically specific ability can be reduced to a more general cognitive ability. The argument misses the role of genetics in determining a limited set of abstract links between substantive features. The effect then of genetic determination is to stipulate that various cognitively possible generalizations never occur. For instance, *what* may be extracted from the object of a verb but not from a conjunction (**what did you see a house and*), although cognitively we can easily reconstruct what such a sentence should mean.

We can describe the cognitive/linguistic contrast in terms of restrictions on automatic or "on line" processes. Consider the different potentials of words and sentences. We can refer to any aspect of cognition by simply labelling it with a word, like trigonometry. Being the content of a word allows us to escape on-line trigonometic calculations. We do not have to run through a set of theorems before our minds allow us to utter the word "trigonometry"; the word by itself allows us to experience referentially (though not computationally) what we are talking about. A computational perspective is different. There are numerous operations and theorems in trigonometry which a human being cannot apply while in the course of processing a sentence (which usually happens within two seconds). This limitation is not necessarily a restriction on automatic processing. Complex tree structures might undergo trigonometic operations very rapidly (as our eyes do geometry rapidly). It is limitations on human on-line linguistic abilities which eliminate these options. They follow from no inevitable mathematical logic. It is precisely for this reason that it is a significant challenge to discover which parts of mathematics are appropriate for linguistic descriptions of on-line capacities. Vision calls for a different set of mathematical descriptions.

Once again, it is the genetic restrictions on the linguistic component which stipulates that the tree structure will be binary, or non-binary, that the discrete categories will correspond to Nouns and Verbs and not Wishes and Fears, that recursion will be possible for sentences and nounphrases and not articles (**the a house*). It is the genetic component that determines that for all human languages the top node in a tree will be the sentence node and that adjectives can be generated inside Noun Phrases. It is the genetic component that determines that grammar will have the potential of referring to objects and action for human beings. It can be argued that other species (e.g., Rhesus monkey) have a grammar of gestures for social relations which permits mating rituals. Their grammar communicates affection and dominace, but they are unable to unambiguously refer to a leg or a nose.

Language Acquisition and General Cognitive Ability

Chomsky has observed that in the history of science there have been numerous explanations where "general" properties of an organism are provided as an explanation. In each instance, the general explanation has eventually been replaced by a specific mechanism. In this respect we have been perhaps too generous to the cognitivists in the foregoing paragraphs. It is quite likely that properties of mind which appear to be general are separately represented in each relevant module. For instance, both seeing and hearing involve stereoscopic information-processing. But it is unlikely that there is a single stereoscopy center in the brain which divides its labors. The kinds of information computed in seeing and hearing are so dissimilar that the stereoscopic principle is undoubtedly built separately into the visual and auditory mechanisms.

An appeal to abstract "general" principles has been common in the field of language acquisition as well, both outside and within linguistic theory. Pragmatic approaches to language show that the whole realm of human cognition can be focused on the interpretation of brief utterances. If a parent says, "Lets go outside" and a one-year-old child says, "coat", then we are entitled to the extra-grammatical inference that the child thinks it is a good idea to wear a coat when you go outside so let's go and put our coats on. Likewise, an adult might walk into a party and say "beer"; we conclude that he is rather rude to complain about the absence of beer. Our interpretation of the communicative intent of both the child and the adult may use all of our cognitive abilities, but those abilities lie far beyond the content of the linguistic expressions. It is a mistake to think that we are talking about linguistic structure in these contexts. We are talking about the use of linguistic structure in life.

Chomsky's proposal that linguistic ability is innate challenged the view that learning language is like learning any other skill, like chess. The initial linguistic models as well appear to be too abstract in retrospect. In the earliest work on transformational grammar, the operative notion was the transformation itself. This concept was so abstract that one could not determine, from examination of two sentences, how they were related. In a word, did the sentence *John, Harry likes* come from *Harry likes John* or the reverse. In fact, one had to have a representative sample of all the sentences in a language in order to make a decision as to which deriviation was the most natural. Therefore no decisions could be made without making all decisions at the same time. In effect, the grammar had to be learned instantaneously. Another way to express that idea was simply to say that all earlier decisions could be re-analyzed in light of the last piece of data received. To do this one had to have, in effect, a sample of all previous sentences in one's head. One way, then, to look at early child grammars is as if they are data summaries which may not undergo incremental modification but rather total replacement with a new notation.

In addition, once all the data was present, it was possible that more than one grammar could fit the data. Then it was necessary to invoke an evaluation metric to decide which was the most natural. This evaluation itself could be carried out in either substantive or formal terms. The idealization to an instantaneous process was unavoidable under the transformational scheme. A system which avoids the idealization (or can decompose it in a natural way) will be an improvement by providing a closer fit to reality.

The Role of the Subset Principle

In the context of a learning device built to operate at a formal level, the subset principle is a very natural substitute for the evaluation metric. It stipulates a way in which a child can learn a formal system piecemeal, non-instantaneously, without the child being dependent upon the order in which sentences arrive. By hypothesis, the child orders the input such that grammars proceed from smaller to larger.[4] If the child chooses a set which is too large, there is no mode of "retreat."[5] Therefore it is categorically impossible for a child to move from a larger set to a smaller set.

THE SUBSET PRINCIPLE AND OPTIONALITY

Let us look more closely at how the subset principle works. It is usually illustrated with concentric circles which do not overlap, as in (1). Grammars in (2) are not in a subset relation but do have some sentences in common, while those in (3) have no sentences in common. In (1), a grammar which is smaller (A) is entirely within a larger grammar (B).

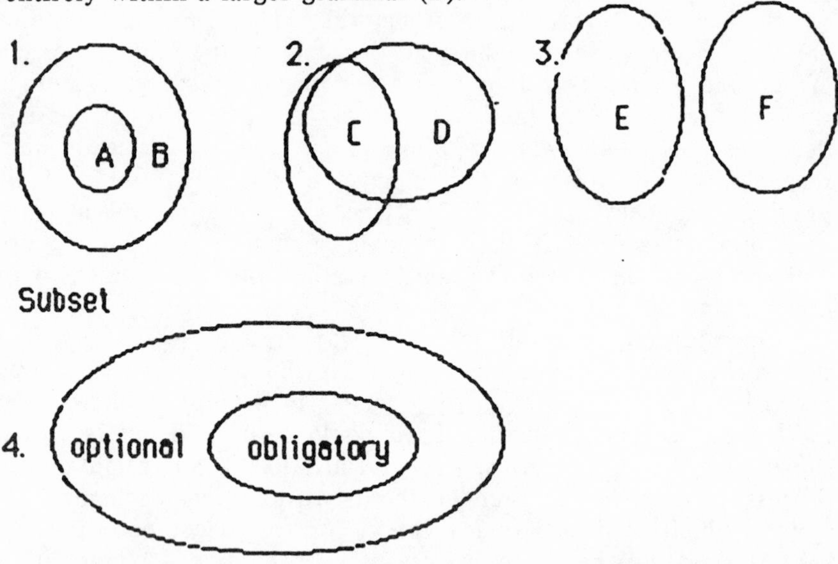

The classic case of a subset relation involves optional and obligatory rules (4). Suppose a child hears the sentence (a) *What can I do* and projects an optional inversion transformation. The grammar will allow both (a) *What can I do* and (b) *What I can do.* The inversion transformation in the adult language, however, could be (and, in fact, is) **obligatory** in that context. How can the child learn obligatoriness? How can the grammar be narrowed? Hearing (a), the child says "Fine," that's in my grammar. Then, however, the child happily produces either (a) or (b) since (b) is also in the grammar. What can show him that (b) is out? Nothing can directly lead to this conclusion. One can project complex frequency measures and argue that the child will drop the uninverted (optional) form after 100,000 inputs which have inversion, but none like (b). This makes the acquisition mechanism more complex.

Now suppose we follow the subset principle. The set of sentences with obligatory inversion is necessarily a subset of the set with optional inversion. With optional inversion, we have both (a) and (b) while with obligatory inversion we have only (a). If a child assumes Grammar_A with obligatory inversion, this will be right for English from the outset. If, however, the language allows both (A) and (B), then the child will rapidly encounter sentences which force a revision in Grammar_A, generating Grammar_B, with optional inversion. If the child's innate acquisition system organizes its hypotheses in this manner, then growth can occur efficiently. The principle is easy to apply: all rules are initially obligatory. This is the fundamental virtue of the subset principle. We will return to the question of what children actually do below.

For the sake of contrast, let us approach the issue from another perspective. What is the opposite hypothesis to the subset theory and why is it untenable? The opposite hypothesis is that a child begins with a broad definition of grammar which is large enough to accommodate any sentences in any language in the world. It has both **Subject-Verb-Object** (SVO) and **Subject-Object-Verb** (SOV) languages. It allows us to form questions in ten different ways. Then upon hearing real sentences from the environment, the child narrows the grammar to just the correct one. As I have described the phenomenon, it seems like common sense. However, when approached in detail, it fails to work. It fails because there can be more than one way to form questions in a single language. Therefore the existence of one form (say, wh-inversion) does not eliminate another form (yes/no questions). In a word, the approach fails because one must not only "include" one form, but "exclude" other forms since we assume that children begin with all possibilities in their incipient grammar. How and when do they decide that they have "not heard" something? The subset principle allows us to add new information rather than delete incorrect information.

Allied Assumptions

Now let us fill out the picture by stating some assumptions entailed in the subset approach. One assumption is that the child receives **no negative evidence**. That is, children are not sensitive to grammatical correction. This seems to be empirically correct for most cases. In the rare instances where parents do correct children, their advice is often ignored. In most instances, the grammatical deviation is so subtle that it is not detected and not easily corrected. For instance, when a child says, "I am strong to do that," an adult may know that it is not quite right, but not know how to correct it.

A second assumption is commonly known as the Continuity Hypothesis. This states that, all things being equal, children have all the adult principles of grammatical analysis at their command from the outset of acquisition. In other words, there is no significant maturation in the domain of grammar. There may, of course, be maturational pre-requisites for the full understanding of words which are themselves pre-requisite to the exercise of certain principles. For instance, a child may need some cognitive maturity to understand the word *puberty* or the word *seem*. Understanding *seem* may in turn be a pre-requisite to understanding Raising constructions like *John seems to be elected*. Thus **extraneous** forms of cognitive maturation can delay the realization of grammatical abilities which nonetheless may be latently present from the outset of acquisition.[6]

A third assumption is that the child organizes his hypotheses in a fashion that will maximize falsifiability (from Williams 1981, see also Williams to appear). The subset principle is an instantiation of this notion because it specifies how initial hypotheses can be falsified. If A is a subset of B, then A is falsified by a sentence that occurs in B. One might in fact think that the subset principle is the only possible instantiation of this idea. However, if there exist indirect means of "falsifiability," then they might conform to the principle but not create a subset relation. A fairly extreme case would be if there is relevant non-grammatical information. Suppose a neurological shift occurred which suddenly fixed as obligatory certain pathways that had been optional. Then a means would exist to "falsify" the earlier assumption. The concept of maximizing falsifiability is thus very general.

The concept of maximizing falsifiability is also a departure from earlier notions of what a child's first assumptions should be.

It was often assumed that a child's first assumptions are the "unmarked" set for human language. The "unmarked" set was determined by frequency in the world's languages. Because **SVO** is more frequent than **SOV**, then the former must be unmarked case. Under the falsifiability thesis, the child might have an initial hypothesis that was found in no language, as long as evidence existed which would lead him naturally to alter that hypothesis to fit his native language.

In conclusion, given these assumptions, the subset principle seems to be essential in describing the child's sequence of growth. In a word, if there is no negative evidence, it is impossible for a child to go from a larger to a smaller language. Therefore the subset principle must be correct. In what follows, we will not dispute this conclusion, but rather suggest that "parametric models" allow, in some domains of grammar, a substantively direct path for moving from G_1 to G_2 where G_1 and G_2 are not in a subset relation.

PARAMETRIC MODELS

In the late nineteen-seventies, it became apparent that the set of possible human grammars was much smaller than originally thought. If there is a finite number of grammars -- in fact a small number -- then the formal basis for grammar choice becomes theoretically unnecessary. That is, it is possible that there exists a substantive basis for grammar choice. The hypothesis that such substantive choices exist became known as the parameter-setting model. Several examples exist of how parameter-setting works, but how the model accounts for all parts of acquisition remains to be worked out in substantive detail. This project calls for close attention to both the logic of linguistic theory and the facts about how grammars emerge. One major virtue of the parameter-setting approach is that it inevitably makes specific predictions about the course of acquisition.

Parameters refer to substantive choices where the "complexity" of either choice is not an issue. It is the presence or absence of some datum which effects the choice. Either a language is an X language or a Y language. Either it has **SVO** or **SOV**. Either it allows clitics, or it does not; either it has an obligatory subject or an optional subject. These are substantive choices where no formal metric of complexity is involved. The result of these choices is automatically the creation of languages that are not in a subset relation. If a language chooses **SVO**, then it should have sentences which are **SOV** as a subset.[7]

The features which seemed to make transformations very complex, which in turn made a formal analysis necessary, have been relegated to other, equally substantive, subdomains of grammar. The subdomains are called modules. One module is the movement module, which has a very abstract definition because it is constrained by other modules. It says simply that constituents can move. Where they can move to is limited by other principles of grammar.[8] Instead of having landing sites built into the movement rule itself, the rule is free but it is externally constrained.

In the parametric model, language is composed of a set of independent modules, each with different primitives, which interact in specified ways. Thus a module of thematic roles (like AGENT, PATIENT, LOCATION) has a stipulated mapping onto a module of case relations (ACCUSATIVE, NOMINATIVE, POSSESSIVE). Nonetheless each module is satisfied by totally different kinds of expressions. The thematic module must coincide with an analysis of context (Is this Noun really an Agent), while the case module requires that a noun be present and that it have a particular phonetic realization (usually as an affix).

The existence of modules automatically simplifies the acquisition process because the modules are putatively independent. They may in fact be described in notations that are alien to one another. For instance, the structure of thematic roles has nothing to do with the definition of "move alpha". There is a point of connection -- like between a motor and wheels -- but the motion of wheels has no formal connection to combustion.

One caveat is necessary. We say the modules are "putatively" independent because they may interact if they project onto the same data in an ambiguous way. If we assume that the input data is not misanalyzed, then independence holds.

The subset principle contains an important truth, but it cannot be functional without the constraining effects of other features of grammar (as Berwick also argues). Therefore, if we ask how the subset principle is represented mentally, we must assert that it is written into the genetic specification for language as relevant at certain points. It cannot be an external mental ability which is accessed wherever possible. This should become clear when we consider applications of the subset principle in greater detail.

We turn now to empirical evidence and how it fits subset predictions.

OBLIGATORY VERSUS OPTIONAL SUBJECTS

The optional/obligatory story has several real applications. One arises in a well-known case of cross-linguistic variation. English contrasts with some Romance languages, like Italian, in the obligatoriness of subjects. In English we must say *he went*, while in Italian one can optionally say *went* with subject omitted (but with indications on the verb about the number and gender of the subject). Rizzi to appear has made the straightforward prediction that Italian and English children should both begin with the hypothesis that the subject is obligatory. When the Italian child hears a sentence with an absent subject, he will revise his grammar to make subjects optional. The English-speaking child never hears such a sentence and therefore his grammar remains the same.

Hyams to appear has explored the acquisition data and found quite a different state of affairs. Both English and Italian children begin with optional subjects; they both begin, as it were, speaking Italian. In English children utter sentences like, "Yes, is toys in the kitchen."

She provides a subtle explanation. A second difference between English and Italian exists: English has expletive subjects, while Italian does not. That is, we say *it appears to be rainy* where the *it* has no reference but fills the subject position, which is natural if the language has obligatory subjects.[9] In Italian, there are no expletives. One has, instead, an empty subject. Hyams argued that the expletive in English triggers a re-analysis under a substantive universal:

5) Subjects are obligatory if expletives are present.

In fact, she found that when expletive subjects appear in children's grammars, the subjectless sentences disappear. This is a good example of how a parametric theory makes subtle but exact predications.[10]

The general conclusion from this discussion is that English and Italian are not in a subset relation, as in (1), but rather overlapping as in (2), because the crucial sentences, which trigger obligatory subjects, lie outside the shared set.[11] It is important to note here that the axis of learning is substantive and not logical. There is no logical necessity that expletives are linked to obligatory subjects. One could have expletives for some verbs but allow empty subjects for others.[12]

The subset principle in this scenario is then irrelevant. One is then led to the following question: is it possible that the trigger for a grammatical decision is **always** linked to sentences which lie outside any subset relation. As we have seen, the crucial feature which decides whether the English obligatory Subject involves subsets has to do with the non-referential character of expletives. It is a decision about the semantic content of a frequent pronoun which is decisive. This might be called an anti-subset hypothesis. In the extreme case one might claim that (6) is true:

6) No two human languages are in a subset relation.

It should be clear from our discussion that such a proposal cannot be either confirmed or denied on abstract grounds. The hypothesis hinges on detailed analysis of every parametric variation available for scrutiny.

The hypothesis can undergo some analysis under an idealization, however.[13] It is in fact unlikely that two languages are in a subset relation with respect to all sentences. However, if one abstracts away from sentences that are irrelevant to a given parametric decision, then it is possible that two languages bear a subset relation to one another for a particular module. This idealization is a natural one if another theorem[14] is upheld:

7) Parametric decisions must be independent.

That is, if several parametric decisions hinge on each other, then the data required to set the system may be completely opaque or a misanalysis can result in an incorrect grammar. We can illustrate this state of affairs with a discussion of expletives and binding.

Binding

It has been argued that binding provides a classic instance where the subset principle can apply (Jacubowicz 1984), Wexler and Manzini to appear. The child begins with the assumption that anaphors apply only within a single clause: *John helps himself.* Ungrammaticality results when a clause boundary is crossed: *John thinks Mary likes himself.*

However, there are some languages where it is possible to have anaphors which refer outside their clauses. Under the subset system, the child assumes that they are impossible until such an example is encountered, whereupon the grammar is expanded to include the new sentence. Japanese, German, and Icelandic are a few of the languages which allow anaphors to refer outside of their respective clauses. The child must be programmed to examine the new sentences for grammatical criteria which allow violation of the clause-mate criterion. In German, for instance, the *sich* reflexive can refer beyond the clause only if it occurs in an infinitival clause, as the sentence:

8) Franz_1 bat Hans an [sich_1 zu kommen]
Frans asked Hans particle [reflexive to come]
'Franz_1 asked Hans to come to himself_i'

The child must therefore be on the lookout for sentences which warrant an expansion of the grammar and include a reference to infinitival contexts where appropriate.

The same situation arises in English in a fashion which allows the confounding of the optional subject parameter with the binding parameter. It turns out that the following sentence is acceptable in English:

9) They thought it was good for each other to win a game.

The *each other* refers outside of its clause to *they* and not to the *it* which is inside the clause. Now what is the criterial feature which allows this violation of the clause-mate restriction? The critical feature is the expletive. If an expletive subject is present, an anaphoric element can look up one sentence higher for a subject eligible for coreference. Without an expletive we have ungrammaticality:

10) *They thought the opportunity was good for each other to win a game.

We now see that the same expletive trigger affects two different parameters. This can be a good feature of grammars. We can in fact state a principle of efficiency in acquisition:

11) Maximize the consequences of individual triggers.

However, we also have a potential problem. What happens during the stage prior to the identification of expletive elements? When the child hears a sentence of the form of (9), but without knowledge that it is expletive, then the binding parameter could be set incorrectly, allowing coreference to occur over any NP if it is in an infinitive. In other words, if the expletive information is not present, the child could construe the evidence to mean that English is in fact German. When the expletive analysis arrived, the grammar would already have set the binding parameter in a fashion that allowed a superset larger than English.

In order to prevent this sequence of events we must order the acquisition of parameters. The indicated order is:

12) A. recognition of expletive
    B. fixation of obligatory subject
    C. fixation of binding domains

In other words, children must know not to establish binding domains until they have already determined whether or not expletives occur. We have now generated a theoretical sequence which makes empirical predictions.

What do the empirical results show? There has been no straightforward study of individual children and their acquisition of reflexives and expletives. From various experimental studies[15], one can make age-related judgements. Children before the age of 2 1/2 do not show clear control of reflexives and expletives. Somewhat after (perhaps 3 1/2 years) they acquire expletives and the obligatory subject, and they exhibit knowledge of domain restrictions on the interpretation of anaphora. Otsu 1981 has shown that some 3 year old children will reliably interpret *the hippos remembered that the monkeys hit each other* to allow coreference only with respect to the monkeys, that is, clause-internally. Other evidence suggests that children do not completely fix the domain restrictions on anaphora and pronominalization until between the ages of five to seven.[16] For instance, a number of the studies cited have shown that children do not know the clause-mate domain restriction on pronominalization: they allow coreference in a sentence like *John pointed at him.*[17] It is fair, at least, to conclude that domain restrictions are not fixed until after the expletive and obligatory subject parameters are set.

Therefore the evidence already exists to confirm the sequence of parameters which we have proposed.

We have argued the "independence" constraint cannot be upheld from a strictly instantaneous perspective, because the data relevant to different parameters may in fact be the same. Instead we have argued that we can achieve the effect of independence by a logical sequence in how parameters are set. The logical sequence is naturally reflected in a temporal sequence in acquisition, which we have projected in the foregoing paragraph. Thus we can see how substantive and formal factors interact. We have solved the logical "many parameters" problem, to use Matthews' terminology, by placing a constraint on how the acquisition device functions. The acquisition device must order the sequence of parametric decisions to guarantee that underanalyzed evidence (i.e. a failure to know that *it* can be an expletive) does not cause a domain-restriction parameter to be misset.

The Input Filter and Expletive

We have asserted that the child, if exposed to a sentence with an expletive and a reflexive, must not make the false judgement that it is a sentence with a referential subject. How can we place this injunction on the system? We can accomplish it via a natural limitation on the input filter discussed earlier. If the child lacks the cognitive maturity to comprehend an existential reference, then such sentences will be incomprehensible. The input filter automatically excludes incomprehensible sentences as input to the acquisition device, allowing grammar revision. That is, if we require semantic comprehensibility as a prerequisite for input into the acquisition device, then children will not allow expletive sentences to change the grammar until they understands expletives.

There remains one further possibility that is not excluded by our account. Suppose a child **incorrectly** thinks that she **does** understand a sentence which has both an expletive and a reflexive. Suppose the child is confronted with the sentence (11) where there is a big glass of chocolate in the context:

13) They think it is good for each other to drink.

An adult, following the grammar, will know that the *it* is an expletive. He is forced to this conclusion in order to allow the *each other* to be grammatical. The child, before she recognizes expletives, would be contextually led to think that the *it* refers to the glass of milk. She would then conclude that *each other* is not bound in its clause for all NP subjects and her grammar would be superset of English. She might then use such sentences.[18] The late fixation of the binding module could be a solution to this problem.

The Lexical Localization Constraint

There is another constraint which may serve to limit the degree to which parametric interaction can confound grammars. Nishigauchi and Roeper to appear[19] and Wexler and Manzini to appear argue for what we can call The Lexical Localization Constraint:

14) All parametric decisions are linked to the properties of individual lexical items.

We have found that the expletive plays a role in the optional-subject parameter and in fixing the environment of the binding parameter. Suppose, instead, that a complex set of if-then interactions were involved, rather than a single lexical item. Suppose that the expletive expands the binding domain only if the sentence is subjunctive unless the object is plural unless *each other* is involved. Each of these conditions has the effect of reversing the impact of the previous one. It is contingencies of this degree of complexity which the lexical localization hypothesis is intended to rule out.

This constraint follows the anti-subset principle. If languages always vary via the content of individual words, then one language will contain words that the other language does not contain. If so, then the sentence in which the special word occurs will be outside the set of sentences which had been the superset. Consequently the subset relation will not hold. Lexical localization may then guarantee learnability. Wherever non-subset relations hold, the information can be associated with lexical items.

It remains, however, an empirical hypothesis which must be tested in two ways. Can all of the parameters of grammar be formulated in a way which meets this constraint? Does acquisition follow the kinds of paths indicated? For instance, one can ask whether wh-movement can be associated with a unique lexical item. This becomes a particularly serious challenge when one considers two current claims: 1) some languages lack wh-movement, and 2) some languages exhibit wh-movement only at what is called the level of Logical Form. There is no phonetic element associated with such operations. In the next section we turn to a problem of inversion and wh-movement that does arise in the acquisition data available.

The lexical localization proposal remains to be worked out in detail. If correct, it is really a variant on the insight provided by the subset principle. In other words, the subset principle has articulated the logic of argumentation both for cases where it is obeyed and for those where it is overruled. We turn now to wh-movement, a domain where no obviously special lexical items are involved. It could provide evidence against the lexical localization hypothesis. As we shall see it may also challenge the subset principle. It is by the generation of empirical hypotheses that mathematically oriented analyses provide insights into biological processes.

Option Wh-Inversion

There is strong evidence from numerous sources that children fail to realize the obligatory nature of subject-verb inversion in wh-contexts. The children pass through a stage in which there is no inversion, to a stage where it is optional, and finally to a stage where it is obligatory. The problem for the subset principle is this: the rule appears to be optional **before** it is obligatory. We find that children will say both (a) and (b).[20]

15a)

"Where I going to sit"
"Where this one go"
"Where we are going"
"What you're doing to the TV"
"What he are"
"What it is it"
"What you've got Daddy"
"Where you're fixing"

15b)

"What's this"
"What can a dog jump with a leg"
"Where are Ria's sandals"

This directly contradicts the subset principles. One might therefore regard the subset principle as straightforwardly disproven. However there is a notable lack of an alternative explanation. What could cause a child to shift from an optional rule to an obligatory rule for questions? It is completely unclear especially since it is possible, in exclamations, for children to hear non-inverted forms. For instance, we can say (16) without inversion:

16) What a beautiful baby you are!

In the absence of an alternative explanation, it is worth exploring the possibility that additional assumptions should be made which continue to make the subset principle viable.

Let us articulate the question in greater detail. The primary fact is that children pass from a period where no inversion occurs in wh-contexts to a period in which it is optional. Some children allow the optionality to occur only with regular nouns and not pronouns. They will not allow inversion with pronouns. This has occurred in immediate proximity: "When is Tom coming?...When you are coming?" The pronoun/regular noun distinction can be found in the adult grammar of inversion as well. We can say:

17a) There the man goes
17b) There goes the man
17c) There she goes
17d) There goes she[21]

The absence of (17d) means that inversion is limited to full regular nouns in *there*-insertion contexts. The child apparently overgeneralizes there-insertion to include wh-contexts and must then make a restriction.

In addition, Pinker 1984 reports cases where the opposite occurs: overgeneralization of inversion to contexts where inversion is, exceptionally, disallowed: "how come is she here" instead of "how come she is here".[22] This kind of behavior runs against the subset principle rather directly. We have overgeneralizations of both the inversion and non-inversion cases. What tells the child that inversion is unacceptable in "how come" sentences but necessary in wh-sentences? A much more acceptable generalization would seem to be the one in (18), but for which we can see no escape route:

18) inversion is optional in both *wh-* and *how come* contexts.

We have a clear challenge to the subset principle, but no alternative in sight.

What is the conceivable range of possible solutions? Here are some:

I) Semantic: Suppose inversion carries the semantic notion of "question". The wh-word by itself, in contrast, may be linked to relative clauses. Therefore in order to signal "question", the child must use both a wh-word and inversion. This explanation has several weaknesses. First it is possible to ask questions without inversion as the *how come* cases illustrate. Second it is possible to use inversion in emphatic environments where no question exists: *are you ever beautiful!*

II) Dialects: It is possible that the child controls two dialects and that non-inversion belongs to one dialect. This is a fairly tenable option. It could be that children retain earlier grammars as dialects for a period which they use to communicate to younger siblings. If so, then the child would have two obligatory rules: obligatory inversion in one dialect and obligatory non-inversion in the other. This would allow successful acquisition when the earlier dialect was dropped.

III) Performance: Is it possible that inversion is dropped as a response to performance demands? This is a classic explanation. It has very low plausibility. Children who fail to perform inversion in four word sentences can utter extremely complex sentences involving several relative clauses. It is hard to imagine that any four word sentence involves significant performance demands.

IV) Parametric option: Is there a sophisticated aspect of acquisition which plays a crucial role here? Klein 1982 suggests that children who do not do inversion fail to have an articulated COMP node.[23] This could explain the stage before inversion was optional. As soon as it is possible to have inversion, then we must explain why non-inverted forms are not completely eliminated.

All of these proposed explanations, in effect, assume that the subset principle is true with respect to optional and obligatory inversions. They then attempt to find ways around the counter-evidence. Thus far, our empirical evidence against the subset principle merely forces us to recognize its necessity.

CONCLUSION

We have tried to illustrate how a formal principle can bring many questions into focus. At one extreme, the subset principle appears to be close to a truism: make a minimal assumption until you have evidence for more than a minimal assumption. At the other extreme, it makes predictions which appear to be contrary to fact: a child can only proceed from obligatory to optional rules. The principle, where it fails, nonetheless forces us to ask how an alternative explanation would work.

We have illustrated three problems for the subset principle: 1) a problem in learning where subjects are obligatory, 2) a problem with context and the learning of binding, and 3) a problem with the acquisition of obligatory inversions. Each problem forces us to make deviations from the subset principle precise. We have suggested that a substantive parametric violation can operate outside the subset principle, that the lexicon localizes hypotheses that are parametric, and that other problems remain, perhaps calling for "performance" explanations which in effect preserve the subset principle.

The value of formal principles as both explanatory devices and heuristic tools should be evident. The problem of "delearn-ability" or "retreat" remains a significant challenge to all accounts of acquisition.

NOTES

1. The earliest formulation may be as the principle of "maximization of falsifiability" by Williams 1981.

2. This constraint is not formulated as such by Berwick, but it is implicit in his use of the "uniqueness principle". The "uniqueness principle" was first formulated by Chomsky and Lasnick 1977, applied to acquisition by Wexler 1979, extended by Roeper 1981, and used in a variety of other contexts by Pinker 1984.

3. See Lightfoot 1982 for extensive discussion of these issues.

4. See Roeper 1978 for an argument that a child imposes an "input filter" on adult input data.

5. This is Randall's 1985 term.

6. Alternatively one can appeal to a notion of linguistic maturation. Borer and Wexler to appear have suggested that a movement transformation, NP-movement, is maturationally unavailable. Unfortunately it is difficult to disentangle linguistic and cognitive maturation, as the example above illustrates. Roeper et al 1985 argue that linguistic binding may be unavailable at young ages. Since one can argue that pragmatic binding is present at a young age, one can then argue that it is only linguistic binding which failed to mature. Using pragmatic binding, therefore, children allow a bound variable interpretation of sentences like *who does he think has a hat*. At a later age, bound variables emerge, ruling out the bound interpretation for that sentence, but allowing it for *who thinks he has a hat*.

7. This is of course crucial simplification. The result of transformations could be that there exist sentences that exhibit SOV order. For instance: *John is lumber hauling* has this structure. An acquisition theory must explain how a child avoids having such sentences misset his parameter. In principle, however, parameters generally create disjoint sets.

8. And they are limited by the constraint that transformational rules must be local.

9. Hyams provides two other possible triggers as well. The auxiliary system in English differs from Italian and differs in its relation to the subject position. In addition, there are unstressed pronouns in subject position in English, a situation which does not occur in Italian.

10. The issue is once again more complex with further interesting subtleties. It can be argued that Italian does have an expletive. However, in Hyams account other potential triggers exist. The existence of unstressed pronouns in English, such as *he RAN*, does not occur in optional subject languages. Moreover she proposes a third trigger that depends on the analysis of the auxiliary in English. Any one or all of these factors could serve as a trigger. By hypothesis, though, it is not the combination of them that is the trigger.

11. A fact noted by Hyams to appear, discussed by Lasnik 1985, Roeper 1985, and Williams to appear.

12. In fact, there are claims that some subjectless languages do have expletives, but the argumentation involved is not entirely clear.

13. Thanks to Edwin Williams for this suggestion.

14. Proposed by Matthews to appear, see also Wexler and Manzini to appear.

15. See Matthei 1981, Otsu 1981, Jacubowicz 1984, Wexler and Manzini to appear and references therein.

16. Solan 1983 shows sensitivity to the distinction between Sentence and Noun phrase in the interpretation of pronouns. See also papers in Lust to appear. Wexler (personal communication) has assembled extensive evidence that children do not control the domain restrictions on pronominalization until they are six.

17. Wexler and Manzini 1985 has assembled extensive evidence that children do not control the domain restrictions on pronominalization until they are six.

18. In fact, I have collected some examples of children misusing *each other* sentences. For instance, "I don't want each other to lean on each other", where the reference for *each other* is clearly contextual.

19. The lexical localization argument appears originally in Roeper 1981.

20. This data is drawn from my own corpus. The phenomenon is widely reported however. See Pinker 1984 for extensive references.

21. Semantic effects of presentational "there", versus locative "there" may be involved here. It is not clear when or how a child would make this differentiation. (See Gueron 1978.)

22. What is needed here is a fine-grained analysis of individuals acquiring wh-words. What is required is an attentive parent, since "how come" sentences might be fairly rare.

Pinker proposes that there are specific lexical limitations on each wh-word which a child must learn. This level of hypothesis must certainly be available to a child in order to capture exceptions. In addition a broader level, wh-category, seems necessary to capture overgeneralizations. The problem of what evidence the child uses to restrict generalizations is not addressed by the lexical approach.

23. See Nishigauchi and Roeper to appear for discussion of the growth of a COMP node. See Chomsky to appear for discussion of elaborated movement landing sites.

PART FOUR

Semantic Theory

8

Semantics and Semantic Competence

Scott Soames

The central **semantic** fact about language is that it carries information about the world. The central **psycho-semantic** fact about speakers is that they understand the claims about the world made by sentences of their language. This parallel suggests an intimate connection between semantic theories and theories of semantic competence. A semantic theory should tell us what information is encoded by sentences relative to contexts. Since competent speakers seem to grasp this information, and since the ability to correctly pair sentences with their contents seems to be the essence of semantic competence, it might appear that a semantic theory is itself a theory of competence.

Such a view has, I think, been quite common. We are all familiar with syntacticians who tell us that their grammars are attempts to specify the grammatical knowledge in virtue of which speakers are syntactically competent. This knowledge is generally thought to include, though perhaps not be limited to, knowledge of which strings of words are genuine (or grammatical) sentences of the language. By extension, it would seem that a semantic theory ought to specify the semantic knowledge in virtue of which speakers are semantically competent. Presumably, this knowledge will include, though perhaps not be limited to, knowledge of the truth conditions of sentences.

The reason for focusing on truth conditions arises from the representational character of semantic information. A sentence that represents the world as being a certain way implicitly imposes conditions that must be satisfied if the world is to conform to the way it is represented to be. Thus, the semantic information encoded by a sentence determines the conditions under which it is true. There may be more to semantic information than truth conditions, but there is no information without them. Thus, if semantic competence consists in grasping the information semantically encoded by sentences, then it would seem that it must involve knowledge of truth conditions.

The view that linguistic theories of syntax and semantics may double as psychological theories of competence comes in two main forms. The more modest form requires theories of syntax and semantics to provide theorems knowledge of which explains competence; however, it does not require these theories to specify the cognitive states and processes causally responsible for this knowledge. In particular, it does not require the theoretical machinery used in linguistic theories to derive theorems about grammaticality or truth conditions to be internally represented components of any psychologically real system. It simply leaves open the question of how the knowledge characterized by correct linguistic theories is psychologically realized.

The more robust form of the view that linguistic theories may double as psychological theories of linguistic competence tries to answer this question. According to this view, syntactic and semantic theories are required not only to characterize the linguistically significant properties of sentences, but also to do so on the basis of whatever internally represented cognitive apparatus is responsible for speakers' recognition of these properties. In short, linguistic theories are required to specify both the knowledge needed for linguistic competence, and the mechanisms from which that knowledge arises.

Although the robust approach has been accepted by many syntacticians, it has also been highly controversial. I believe it should be rejected for syntax as well as semantics (Soames 1984 and 1985b). However, it is not my present target. What I would like to argue is that, at least in the case of semantics, the modest approach is also incorrect. Semantic theories do not state that which a speaker knows in virtue of which he or she is semantically competent. Semantic competence does not arise from knowledge of the semantic properties of expressions characterized by a correct semantic theory.

KNOWLEDGE OF TRUTH CONDITIONS

Let us begin with the basics. The job of semantics is to specify the principles by which sentences represent the world. It is impossible to represent the world as being a certain way without implicitly imposing conditions that must be satisfied if the world is to conform to the representation. Thus, whatever else a semantic theory must do, it must at least characterize truth conditions. For certain languages, there are two standard ways of doing this. One involves the construction of a Davidson-style theory of truth for the language. The other involves the construction of a theory, or definition, of a relativized notion of truth for the language, truth-with-respect-to a world w. Both theories can be thought of as entailing statements that give the truth conditions of sentences. In one case, these statements are instances of schema T; in the other way they are instances of schema T*w*. (Instances are formed by replacing 'P' with a paraphrase of the sentence replacing 'S'.)

Schema T: 'S' is true (in L) iff P

Schema T*w*: 'S' is true (in L) w.r.t. w iff in w, P

Now it might be thought that knowledge of truth conditions is the key to semantic competence, and hence that competence is the result of knowing that which is stated by each instance of one or the other of these schemas. But this is false. Knowledge of truth conditions (in this sense) is neither necessary nor sufficient for understanding a language.

It is not sufficient since it is possible for even the logically omniscient to know that:

1) 'Firenze é una bella città' is true in Italian (w.r.t. w) iff (in w) Florence is a beautiful city

while failing to believe that:

2) 'Firenze é una bella città' means in Italian that Florence is a beautiful city

and believing instead that:

3) 'Firenze é una bella città' means in Italian that Florence is a beautiful city and arithmetic is incomplete.

All that is necessary for this is for the agent to believe that (for any w) Florence is a beautiful city (in w) iff (in w) Florence is a beautiful city and arithmetic is incomplete. In short, true beliefs about truth conditions are compatible with false beliefs about meaning.

One sometimes sees it suggested that this problem can be avoided by requiring the agent's knowledge of truth conditions to encompass everything forthcoming from a finitely axiomatized theory of truth for the entire language. But this is not so. Given a first order language, one can always construct extensionally correct, finitely axiomatizable truth theories **each of whose theorems** resembles (4) in correctly giving the truth conditions of an object language sentence, while failing to provide a basis for paraphrase or interpretation.

4) 'Firenze é una bella città' is true in Italian (w.r.t. w) iff (in w) Florence is a beautiful city and arithmetic is incomplete.

Now imagine a person ignorant of the object language being given a finitely axiomatized theory of truth. Unless he is also given information about meaning, he will have no way of knowing whether it can be used to paraphrase and interpret object language sentences. In particular, he will have no way of knowing whether the result of substituting 'means that' for 'is true iff' in its theorems will produce truths, as in (2), or falsehoods, as in (3). Knowledge of truth conditions, even of this **systematic** sort, is simply not sufficient for knowledge of meaning, or semantic competence.[1]

It is also not necessary. Knowledge of truth conditions, as I have described it, presupposes possession of a metalinguistic concept of truth. Thus, the claim that such knowledge is necessary for understanding meaning entails that no one can learn or understand a language without first having such a concept. But this consequence seems false. Certainly, young children and unsophisticated adults can understand lots of sentences without understanding 'true', or any corresponding predicate.

Must they, nevertheless, possess a metalinguistic concept of truth, even though they have no word for it? I don't see why. Perhaps it will be suggested that a person who lacked such a concept couldn't be a language user, since to use language one must realize that assertive utterances aim at truth and seek to avoid falsity. But this suggestion is confused. The child will get along fine so long as he knows that 'Momma is working' is to be assertively uttered only if Momma is working; 'Daddy is asleep' is to be assertively uttered only if Daddy is asleep; and so on. The child doesn't have to say or think to himself, "There is a general (but defeasible) expectation that for all x, if x is a sentence, then one is to assertively utter x only if x is true." It is enough if he says or thinks to himself, "There is a general (but defeasible) expectation that one should assertively utter 'Mommy is working' only if Mommy is working; assertively utter 'Daddy is asleep' only if Daddy is asleep; and so on for every sentence." For this, no notion of truth is needed.[2]

The point here is not that this truthless substitute says exactly the same thing as its truth-containing counterpart. In general, metalinguistic truth is not eliminable without loss of expressive power, and practical utility. The point is that it is not **necessary** to have such a concept in order to learn and understand a language. Thus, knowledge of that which is expressed by instances of schemas T and T*w* is neither necessary nor sufficient for semantic competence.

BEYOND TRUTH CONDITIONS

The problem with such accounts of semantic competence can be expressed as follows: Even if the sentence replacing 'P' is a strict paraphrase of the sentence replacing 'S', the "connective":

5) '...' is true (in w) iff (in w) ...

used to relate them is too loose to provide the information needed for understanding, or knowing the meaning of, a sentence. Thus, knowledge of truth conditions (in this sense) cannot explain semantic competence.

How might knowledge of meaning be expressed? A natural suggestion is that what one knows when one knows the meaning of a sentence is something of the form:

6) 'S' means that P

or:

7) 'S' says that P.

However, two qualifications must be noted.

First, in general if x means or says that P&Q, then x means or says that P and x means or says that Q. For example, if Reagan meant or said that defense spending would increase and taxes would be cut, then he meant or said that defense spending would increase, and he meant or said that taxes would be cut. However, the sentence 'Defense spending will increase and taxes will be cut' does not mean in English that defense spending will increase; nor does it mean in English that taxes will be cut. When we say that a sentence means in English that so-and-so, we are, I think, saying that it expresses the proposition that so-and-so. An unambiguous conjunction expresses a single, conjunctive, proposition; it does not also express the propositions that its conjuncts do.

Second, when an object language sentence contains an indexical element, we don't want to identify its meaning with any of the different propositions it may be used to express. For example, I don't want to say that 'I live in New Jersey' means (says) that I (S.S.) live in New Jersey. The sentence doesn't mean something specifically about me, any more than it means something about anyone else. Rather, its meaning is what allows it to be used in different contexts to express different (but systematically related) propositions.

These qualifications can be accommodated by suggestion (8).

8a) The meaning of a sentence is a function from contexts of utterance to propositions expressed by the sentence in those contexts.

8b) Knowledge of meaning is knowledge of that which is expressed by instances of schema K. (Instances are obtained by replacing 'C' with a description of a context of utterance, and 'P' with a sentence that expresses the proposition that the sentence replacing 'S' expresses in the context described.)

Schema K

'S' expresses the proposition that P relative to the context C.

In formulating this schema, we take 'express' to be a three-place predicate relating sentences, contexts, and propositions. A semantic theory utilizing this predicate will assign propositions to sentences, relative to contexts, while deriving the truth conditions of a sentence from the proposition it expresses. The suggestion for relating semantics to semantic competence, then, is that **a correct semantic theory will entail instances of schema K, knowledge of which explains semantic competence.**

But what are propositions, and how are they assigned to sentences? One familiar suggestion is that propositions are sets of metaphysically possible worlds assigned to sentences by recursive characterizations of truth with respect to a world. Given such a truth characterization, one can define the proposition expressed by a sentence S to be the set of worlds w such that S is true in w.

However, this won't do. On this approach, necessarily equivalent propositions are identified -- e.g., the proposition that Florence is a beautiful city is identified with the proposition that Florence is a beautiful city and arithmetic is incomplete. Thus, the approach predicts that anyone who believes the one believes the other, that any sentence which expresses the one expresses the other, and that anyone who knows that a sentence expresses the one knows that it expresses the other. These results are unacceptable.

It is important to note that the problem does not arise from the selection of metaphysically possible worlds as the truth-supporting circumstances in terms of which truth conditions are explicated, and propositions constructed. Given a background of relatively modest and plausible assumptions, one can reconstruct essentially the same problem for any fine-grained conception of truth-supporting circumstances that allows one to maintain the standard recursive clauses in a truth characterization for constructions like conjunction, quantification, and descriptions (Soames 1985a, 1987, and 1988). This means that **no matter what one takes truth-supporting circumstances to be, one cannot identify the proposition expressed by a sentence with the set of circumstances in which it is true; nor can one identify a semantic theory with a characterization of truth with respect to a circumstance.** What is needed is a reversal of familiar semantic priorities. Instead of viewing propositions as artifacts of conceptually prior truth characterizations, we should construct semantic theories that directly assign propositions to sentences, and derive truth conditions of **sentences** from theories of truth for the **propositions** they express. In order for these propositions to serve as fine-grained objects of the attitudes they should encode both the structure of the sentences that express them and the **semantic contents** of subsentential constituents. In this way, sentences with significantly different structures may express different propositions even though they are true in the same truth-supporting circumstances.

I believe that these ideas can best be implemented by an essentially Russellian conception of semantics and semantic content (See Soames 1985a, 1987, and 1988). This approach can be illustrated by considering an elementary first order language with lambda abstraction, a belief operator, and a stock of semantically simple singular terms, all of which are directly referential.[3] On the Russellian account, the semantic content of a variable relative to an assignment is just the object assigned as value of the variable; the semantic content of a closed (directly referential) term, relative to a context, is its referent relative to the context. The contents of n-place predicates are n-place properties and relations. The contents of '&' and '-' are functions, CONJ and NEG, from truth values to truth values.

Variable-binding operations, like lambda abstraction and existential quantification, can be handled by using propositional functions to play the role of complex properties corresponding to certain compound expressions.[4] On this approach, the semantic content of $\ulcorner[\lambda x\ Rx,x]\urcorner$ is the function g from individuals o to propositions that attribute the relation expressed by R to the pair $\langle o,o\rangle$. $\ulcorner[\lambda x\ Rx,x]t\urcorner$ can then be thought of as attributing the property of bearing R to oneself to the referent of t; and $\ulcorner\exists x\ Rx,x\urcorner$ can be thought of as "saying" that g assigns a true proposition to at least one object.

The recursive assignment of propositions to sentences is given in (9).

9a) The proposition expressed by an atomic formula $\ulcorner Pt_1,\ldots,t_n\urcorner$ relative to a context C and assignment f is $\langle\langle o_i,\ldots,o_n\rangle, P^*\rangle$, where P^* is the property expressed by P, and o_i is the content of t_i relative to C and f.

9b) The proposition expressed by a formula ⌜[λvS] t⌝ relative to C and f is <<o>,g>, where o is the content of t relative to C and f, and g is the function from individuals o' to propositions expressed by S relative to C and an assignment f' that differs from f at most in assigning o' as the value of v.[5]

9c) The propositions expressed by ⌜-S⌝ and ⌜S&R⌝ relative to C and f are <NEG, Prop S> and <CONJ, <Prop S, Prop R>> respectively, where Prop S and Prop R are the propositions expressed by S and R relative to C and f, and NEG and CONJ are the truth function for negation and conjunction.

9d) The proposition expressed by ⌜∃v S⌝ relative to C and f is <SOME, g>, where SOME is the property of being a non-empty set, and g is as in (b).

9e) The proposition expressed by ⌜t believes that S⌝ relative to C and f is <<o, Prop S>, B>, where B is the belief relation, o is the content of t relative to C and f, and Prop S is the proposition expressed by S relative to C and f.

9f) The proposition expressed by a sentence (with no free variables) relative to a context C is the proposition it expresses relative to C and every assignment f.

On this approach, the meaning of an expression is a function from contexts to propositional constituents. The meaning of a sentence is a compositional function from contexts to structured propositions. Intensions (and extensions) of sentences and expressions relative to contexts (and circumstances) derive from intensions (and extensions) of propositions and propositional constituents. These, in turn, can be gotten from a recursive characterization of truth with respect to a circumstance, for propositions.

For this purpose, we let the intension of an n-place property be a function from circumstances to sets of n-tuples of individuals that instantiate the property in the circumstances; we let the intension of an individual be a constant function from circumstances to that individual; and we let the intension of a one-place propositional function g be a function from circumstances E to sets of individuals in E that g assigns propositions true in E. Extension is related to intension in the normal way, with the extension of a proposition relative to a circumstance being its truth value in the circumstance, and its intension being the set of circumstances in which it is true (or, equivalently, the characteristic function of that set). Truth relative to a circumstance is defined in (10).

10a) A proposition <<$o_1,...,o_n$>, P*> is true relative to a circumstance E iff the extension of P* in E contains <$o_1,...,o_n$>.

10b) A proposition <<o>,g> is true relative to E (where g is a one-place propositional function) iff o is a member of the extension of g in E (i.e. iff g(o) is true relative to E).

10c) A proposition <NEG, Prop S> is true relative to E iff the value of NEG at the extension of Prop S in E is truth (i.e., iff Prop S is not true relative to E).

A proposition <CONJ, <Prop S, Prop R>> is true relative to E iff the value of CONJ at the pair consisting of the extension of Prop S in E and the extension of Prop R in E is truth (i.e., iff Prop S and Prop R are true relative to E).

10d) A proposition <SOME, g> is true relative to E (where g is as in (b)) iff the extension of g in E is non-empty (i.e., iff g(o) is true relative to E for some o in E).

10e) A proposition <<o, Prop S>, B> is true relative to E iff <o, Prop S> is a member of the extension of B in E (i.e., iff o believes Prop S in E).

Earlier we considered the suggestion that a semantic theory issues in instances of schema K, and that knowledge of that which is expressed by these instances explains semantic competence. The key idea behind this suggestion is that it is knowledge of the propositions expressed by sentences, rather than knowledge of truth conditions, that is fundamental to understanding a language. We now have a conception of semantics that pairs object language sentences with propositions of the right sort. Does this mean that we have a semantic theory that entails instances of schema K?

No, it does not. Instead, the above theory, when supplemented with a theory of object language syntax and an interpretation of its vocabulary, will issue in theorems of the kind shown in (11).

11) '∃x Lx,n' expresses (with respect to every context) the proposition which is the ordered pair whose first coordinate is the property SOME, of being a non-empty set, and whose second coordinate is the function g which assigns to any object o the proposition which is the ordered pair whose second coordinate is the relation of loving and whose first coordinate is the ordered pair the first coordinate of which is o and the second coordinate of which is Nixon.

Let us suppose, for the sake of argument, that (11) is true, and hence that the description it gives of the proposition expressed by '∃x Lx,n' is accurate. Still, the theorem is not an instance of schema K. Moreover, knowledge of that which it expresses is neither necessary nor sufficient for knowing the meaning of the sentence, let alone for explaining speakers' understanding of it.

In essence, the situation is this: We think of the instance (12) of schema K as containing a singular term t which denotes the proposition expressed by '∃x Lx,n'.

12) '∃ x Lx,n' expresses the proposition that something loves Nixon (with respect to every context C).

Corresponding to this, the semantic theory issues theorem (11), which contains a singular term t' that refers to the same proposition as t. However, t and t' are distinct, non-synonymous expressions; t is 'the proposition that something loves Nixon', whereas t' is the complicated definite description given in (11). As a result, (11) and (12) "say" different things. Thus, even if knowledge of meaning amounted to knowledge of that which is expressed by the latter, it would not amount to knowledge of that which is expressed by the former. Semantic competence is not the result of knowing **these** semantic theorems.

Suppose, however, that one were to make the assumptions in (13).

13a) The expression ⌜the proposition that P⌝ is a directly referential singular term that refers to the proposition expressed by P.

13b) 'Dthat' is an operator which can be prefixed to any definite description D to form a directly referential singular term dthat D whose semantic content is the referent of D. (See Kaplan 1979.)

13c) A proper semantic theory can be formulated so as to entail theorems analogous to (11) in which 'dthat' is prefixed to the description of the proposition expressed.

13d) If t and t' are directly referential singular terms that refer to the same thing, then substitution of one for the other in a sentence (outside of quotes) does not effect what proposition is expressed. Moreover, substitution of one for the other in propositional attitude constructions preserves truth value; if ⌜x knows (believes) that ...t...⌝ is true, then so is ⌜x knows (believes) that ...t...⌝.

From these assumptions it follows that knowledge of that which is expressed by (the newly formulated) semantic theorems just is knowledge of that which is expressed by instances of schema K.

In my opinion, these assumptions are more reasonable than commonly thought. Indeed, I am willing to accept them. However, even if they are accepted, they cannot be used to connect semantics with semantic competence. The reason they can't is that although they allow semantic theorems to be assimilated to instances of schema K, they make it possible to know that which is expressed by these instances without understanding object language sentences.

I take it that if propositions can be referents of directly referential singular terms, then they can be labeled using directly referential proper names. Suppose, then, that the proposition that mathematics is reducible to logic is labeled 'logicism'. Using the assumptions in (13), we can then conclude that (14) and (15) "say" the same thing, and that (16) and (17) have the same truth value.

14) Logicism is expressed by s.

15) The proposition that mathematics is reducible to logic is expressed by s.

16) x believes (knows) that logicism is expressed by s.

17) x believes (knows) that the proposition that mathematics is reducible to logic is expressed by s.

Thus, if it is possible to believe or know that logicism is expressed by a certain sentence without understanding that sentence, then it will be possible to believe or know the corresponding instance of schema K --namely (15) -- without being semantically competent.

But this is possible. The case is analogous to one in which someone believes that a particular person authored certain axioms without knowing very much about the person. For example, someone being introduced to elementary number theory might be told that certain axioms were first formulated by Peano. On the basis of this, he may come to believe that Peano first formulated those axioms, even though he is not able to identify Peano, distinguish him from other mathematicians, or to accurately characterize him using any uniquely identifying description.

Now consider a student attending his first lecture in the philosophy of mathematics. He may be told that logicism is a proposition about the relationship between logic and mathematics, that formalism is a doctrine about the interpretation of mathematics, and so on. At this stage, the student may not be able to distinguish logicism from other propositions about the relationship between logic and mathematics; or to describe it in any informative way. Nevertheless, he may acquire beliefs about logicism. For example, he may be told, "Russell was a defender of logicism", and thereby come to believe that Russell defended logicism. He might even be told, "Logicism is expressed by sentence s", and thereby come to believe that logicism is expressed by sentence s. In order to acquire this belief, it is not necessary that he understand s. It might, for example, be written on the board and labeled 's', but contain unfamiliar terminology. In such a case, the student's knowledge that s expresses logicism does not make him a linguistically competent user of s.

When combined with the assumptions noted above, this observation leads to the conclusion that one can know that which is expressed by an instance:

18) 'S' expresses the proposition that P (relative to C) of schema K without understanding the object language sentence that replaces 'S'. It would seem, therefore, that knowledge of semantic theorems is not necessary and sufficient for semantic competence, even under the most favorable assumptions.

To recapitulate: If one doesn't adopt the assumptions in (13), then one's semantic theory will not provide instances of schema K; if one does adopt the assumptions in (13), then one can construct a semantic theory whose theorems express the propositions expressed by instances of schema K -- however, under these assumptions knowledge of those propositions does not ensure understanding the object language. Either way, knowledge of semantic theorems is not necessary and sufficient for semantic competence.

SEMANTIC COMPETENCE AND "THE AUGUSTINIAN PICTURE" [6]

If this is right, then a familiar strategy for explaining semantic competence won't work. The strategy is based on the idea that competent speakers understand sentences in virtue of knowing precisely the information that a semantic theory provides -- namely, the truth conditions of, and propositions expressed by, object language sentences. In attacking this idea I have argued that semantic knowledge and linguistic competence do not always coincide; the presence of one does not guarantee the presence of the other. Thus, semantic knowledge cannot, in general, explain linguistic competence.

There is, however, a more fundamental point to be made. Even in cases in which a linguistically competent speaker is semantically knowledgable, his competence may not derive from his knowledge; rather, his knowledge may derive from his competence.

The examples in (19) provide a case in point.

19a) Pluto is a distant planet.
19b) 'Pluto' refers to Pluto.
19c) 'Pluto is a distant planet' is true (in English) iff Pluto is a distant planet.
19d) 'Pluto is a distant planet' expresses (in English) the proposition that Pluto is a distant planet.

I believe all these things. The reason I believe them is not that I have seen or had direct contact with Pluto. On the contrary, my only contact with the planet has been an indirect one, mediated by representations of it. In my case, the most important of these has been the name 'Pluto'.

My beliefs about Pluto are similarly mediated. I believe that Pluto is a distant planet because I have read or been told that it is. I have read or been told "Pluto is a distant planet"; I have understood the sentence; and I have accepted it. It is important to note that this understanding did not consist in associating an identifying description with the name 'Pluto', and a descriptive proposition with the entire sentence. In acquiring the belief, I may or may not have associated a description with the name, and I may or may not have come to believe descriptive propositions as a result of accepting the sentence. Still, my belief that Pluto is a distant planet cannot be identified with any such descriptive belief. Even if the description I associate with the name is inaccurate and doesn't, in fact, pick out Pluto, my belief that Pluto is a distant planet is about Pluto (though the descriptive beliefs acquired at the same time may not be). Similarly, even if the descriptive beliefs turn out to be false, my belief that Pluto is a distant planet may remain true. Finally, the proposition I express by 'Pluto is a distant planet' is the same as the proposition that others express by the sentence, even if the descriptions we associate with the name are different.

In short, the explanation of my belief that Pluto is a distant planet involves the fact that, (i) I accept the sentence 'Pluto is a distant planet'; (ii) the sentence expresses the proposition that Pluto is a distant planet; and (iii) I am a competent speaker, and thereby understand the sentence. Moreover, my understanding the sentence is not a matter of my using it to express descriptive propositions that I might have come to believe on independent grounds.

Analogous points can be made regarding other attitudes I might have taken toward the proposition. If I had come to wonder whether Pluto was a distant planet, or to doubt that it was, my having that propositional attitude would have involved my having a certain attitude toward a sentence that expressed it. In short, **the only epistemic connection I have with certain propositions is mediated through sentences that express them.**

These considerations can be extended to the other examples (19b-d). For instance, I believe the propositions expressed by (c) and (d). However, these beliefs do not **explain** my understanding of (a). I don't understand the sentence **because** I have those beliefs. If anything, it is the other way around. My belief in the **propositions** expressed by (c) and (d) is (in large part) due to my understanding and accepting **sentences** (c) and (d), and to the fact that they mean what they do. Moreover, part of what it is for me to understand these sentences is for me to understand (a), which is a constituent of both. Thus, the direction of explanation in this case is not from beliefs to competence, but from competence to beliefs.

If this is right, then a natural and seductive picture of language acquisition and linguistic competence is fundamentally mistaken. According to this picture, we have the ability, prior to the acquisition of language, to form beliefs and entertain propositions. In setting up a language, we adopt certain conventions according to which sentences come to express these antecedently apprehended propositions. Learning the language amounts to learning for each sentence, which antecedently apprehended proposition it expresses.

The most fundamental thing wrong with this picture is that in the case of many sentences, we do not grasp the propositions they express prior to understanding the sentences themselves. As a result, coming to understand these sentences does not consist in searching through our stock of propositions to find the ones assigned to them. Rather, coming to understand the sentences is a matter of satisfying conventional standards regarding their use. Just what these standards are is not well understood. However, whatever they are, once they are satisfied, one is counted not only as understanding new **sentences**, but also as grasping new **propositions**. As a result, learning a language is not just a matter of acquiring a new tool for manipulating information one already possesses; it is also a means of expanding one's cognitive reach.[7]

This point is potentially more far-reaching than the examples I have used might indicate. Although my beliefs about Pluto are linguistically mediated, they need not have been. They could, presumably, have been acquired through direct, non-linguistic contact with the planet. Many of my beliefs about individuals are like this. For example, my beliefs about Plato are linguistically mediated; but they are also dependent on the fact that others have had direct contact with the man and have passed his name down to me.

In other cases, I have linguistically mediated beliefs about objects with which no one is, or could be, in direct epistemic contact -- for example, beliefs about quarks, the addition function, and the cardinal aleph null. In my opinion, there are such objects; we do succeed in referring to them; and we acquire beliefs about them in virtue of understanding and accepting sentences about them.

How this all comes about is a large and unanswered question. Somehow, using the word *plus* in a certain way counts as referring to the addition function, despite the fact that our use is logically consistent with alternative hypotheses, as well as the fact that there is no direct apprehension of the function. (See Kripke 1982.) Certainly, we do not say to ourselves, "There is this particular arithmetical function that we have been thinking about which has so far remained nameless; let's call it 'plus'." The reason we don't is that our epistemic access to the function does not precede our ability to represent it linguistically; rather, the two are simultaneous.

These considerations dramatically undermine the "Augustinian" picture of language acquisition and linguistic competence given in (20).

20a) There are objects, properties, and propositions that we apprehend prior to understanding a language.
20b) Linguistic expressions stand for these independently apprehended objects, properties, and propositions.
20c) Understanding a language is the result of knowing which expressions stand for which objects -- e.g., of knowing that 'Pluto' refers to Pluto, that '+' stands for the addition function, that 'Quarks are subatomic particles' expresses the proposition that quarks are subatomic particles; and so on.

Clause (a) is true but incomplete, since there are objects we apprehend only through linguistic mediation. Clause (b) is false, if taken as a claim about linguistic expressions in general. However, the result of deleting the words "these independently apprehended" from it is true. Clause (c) is objectionable on two grounds. First, it has the dubious consequence that understanding an expression always coincides with knowing that the expression has certain semantic properties. Second, it wrongly suggests that semantic knowledge about what expressions stand for is conceptually prior to, and explains, semantic competence.

SEMANTICS

Where does this leave semantics? I have suggested that a semantic theory must pair sentences with the propositions they express, and derive the truth conditions of sentences from those propositions. I have also noted that the knowledge provided by such a theory is not necessary and sufficient for semantic competence. However, I have argued that this is no defect, since the attempt to explain semantic competence as arising from semantic knowledge rests on an inadequate conception of the role of language in our cognitive lives -- a conception that ignores the linguistic basis of many of our semantic and non-semantic beliefs. If this is correct, then one should not look to semantics for an account of semantic competence.

Instead, one should look to it for an explication of the representational character of language. The central semantic fact about language is that it is used to represent the world. Sentences do this by systematically encoding information that characterizes the world as being one way or another. Semantics is the study of this information, and the principles by which it is encoded.

A theory of this sort can be seen as accomplishing three main tasks. First, it tells us what sentences say relative to different contexts of utterance, and thereby provides the basis for interpreting what speakers say when they assertively utter sentences in various contexts, and what they believe when they believe that which is said by one or another assertive utterance. Second, the semantic account of truth conditions explicates a fundamental aspect of the relationship between language and the world. Third, the model-theoretic machinery in the theory provides a semantic account of meaning-determined logical properties and relations holding among sentences.

Theories of semantic competence are responsive to different concerns. Whereas semantic theories focus on the fact that sentences encode information that represents the world, theories of semantic competence focus on the fact that languages are things that people understand. This focus on understanding can be developed in two ways. On the one hand, one may ask for a conceptual analysis (in terms of social, behavioral, mental, or verificationist notions) of what it means to understand an expression, a sentence, or a language. On the other hand, one may want an empirical theory that identifies the cognitive structures and processes that are causally responsible for the linguistic understanding of a particular person or group. Both types of concern with understanding are legitimate, and deserve to be developed. However, neither is essentially semantic, in the sense I have sketched.

This does not mean that there are no interesting connections between semantic theories of information encoding and psychological, or philosophical, theories of linguistic understanding. In fact, they complement one another. Semantic theories specify contents of expressions, but say nothing about the empirical factors that are causally responsible for their coming to have these contents. For certain words, it is plausible to suppose that they got their content from a causal-historical chain connecting tokens produced by different speakers to a real-world referent. This sort of foundational view has been an important supplement to recent semantic theories, even though particular causal-historical chains have no place in semantic theories themselves.

A similar point might be made about mental representations associated with sentences by speakers. A number of cognitive scientists believe that understanding a sentence involves the recovery, manipulation, and storage of abstract representational structures. This belief has led to the attempt to develop theories about how these representational structures are connected to sentences, and how they interact with other cognitive systems. Typically these theories posit rules that take syntactic structures as input and produce different linguistic objects as output, where these latter are thought of as playing some significant role in explaining speakers' understanding, their semantic judgements, or both. If they do play such a role, then they may also be important causal factors in explaining why the natural language sentences they are associated with encode the information that they do.

It must be remembered, however, that these mental representations are not themselves semantic contents. Rather, they are things that have content. Thus, a theory of the cognitive structures associated with sentences is no substitute for a semantics. Indeed, such theories tacitly presuppose a semantics; for to say of an abstract mental structure that it represents so-and-so is to say that it bears information that characterizes things as being a certain way, and thereby imposes truth conditions that must be satisfied if things are to conform to the representation. Making this explicit is the job of semantics.

Thus, there is a sense in which theories of mental representation are incomplete without an accompanying semantics. However, there may also be a sense in which semantics is dependent on theories of mental representation. It is not just that theories of mental representation may be needed to explain how expressions come to have the contents associated with them by a correct semantic theory. Such theories may also be needed to decide what semantic content a sentence has, and hence what semantic theory is correct. The crucial point involves the introduction of structure into semantic content. I have argued, both here and on other occasions, that the semantic content of a sentence cannot be analyzed solely in terms of truth conditions, but rather must be seen as a complex with a structure that parallels that of the sentence itself. But this raises a question. What level, or levels, of sentence structure does semantic information incorporate?

In the case of the simple first order language used to illustrate my propositional semantics, the answer is obvious--surface structure, since that is all the structure there is. However, in the case of natural language the matter is more complicated. Perhaps speakers of natural languages associate sentences with psychologically real underlying representations. If they do, then perhaps the propositions expressed by these sentences encode not their surface syntax, but rather the syntax of their underlying psycho-semantic representations. I don't know whether these possibilities will be born out; but the idea behind them is not unreasonable. It may very well be that cognitive structures involved in understanding sentences are closely related to propositional structures involved in explicating attitudes like saying, asserting, and believing. If they are, then semantic theories of information and psychological theories of semantic competence may turn out to be theories which, though different, have a lot in common after all.

NOTES

1. For a more extended discussion of this point, as it applies to Davidsonian truth theories, see J.A. Foster 1976. Although Foster presses the point forcefully against Davidson, he exempts approaches based on theories of truth-with-respect-to a possible world from his criticism. This, in my opinion, is a mistake. In addition to extending to such theories, the basic argument can be made to apply to any attempt to found meaning, or knowledge of meaning, on theories of truth with respect to a circumstance--no matter how find grained we make the circumstances (provided standard recursive clauses in the truth theory are maintained).

2. I am not here suggesting that the child really must repeat or represent the latter (truthless) instruction to himself. Thus, I am not claiming that the child must have the notion assertive utterance in order to learn a language. My point is a negative one. If there is anything to the suggestion that language learners must realize that assertive utterances aim at truth, that realization need not involve possession of a concept of truth. It may be that the child ultimately must come to realize something like the following: One is to say that Mommy is working only if Mommy is working, that Daddy is asleep only if Daddy is asleep; and so on. A truth predicate comes in handy in stating such rule, for it allows one to eliminate the 'and so on' in favor of quantification

over assertions plus predications of truth. But handy or not, this logical technology is not necessary for learning.

3. A directly referential singular term is one whose semantic content (relative to a context and assignment of values to variables) is its referent (relative to the context and assignment). It is this semantic content that such a term contributes to the information encoded (proposition expressed) by a sentence containing it.

4. Although this Russellian method is, I think, essentially on the right track, it does lead to certain technical problems in special cases. For example, as Nathan Salmon has pointed out to me, Russellian propositional functions must be defined on possible, as well as actual, individuals, in order to assign correct extensions to expressions in different possible worlds. This means that these functions cannot be thought of as set theoretic constructions involving only actually existing objects. Another problem involves non-well-foundedness. As Terence Parsons has observed, in order for the self-referential, but unparadoxical, (i) and (ii) to have their intended interpretations, the propositional functions corresponding to the matrices in these examples must be defined on the propositions expressed by (i) and (ii).

(i) (x) (I assert x --> I believe x)

(ii) (x) (I assert x today --> x is expressible in English)

This is impossible, if the set theoretic conception of propositions and propositional functions is maintained.

These problems can, I believe, be avoided by taking the semantic contents of compound expressions to be complex attributes rather than propositional functions. For example, the content of ⌜[λv S]⌝, w.r.t. a context C and an assignment f, might be taken to be the property of P of being an object o such that dthat[the proposition expressed by S w.r.t. C and assignment f' that differs from f at most in assigning o to v] is true. The extension of P at a world w will then be the set of objects o such that the relevant propositions containing them are true with respect to w (provided that a proposition has the one place property of being true, at a world w, iff the two place relation of being true-with-respect-to holds between it and w).

Other ways of assigning attributes to expressions (compound predicates) may also be found. For present purposes, I will leave the final resolution of this issue open, and continue in the text to use familiar Russellian propositional functions as contents of compound predicates.

5. Salmon 1986 has suggested using this lambda construction to distinguish the propositions expressed by the complement clauses of (i-iii) from those expressed by the complements of (iv-v).

(i) Pierre says (believes) that London is both pretty and not pretty.

(ii) Pierre says (believes) that London is non-self-identical.

(iii) Pierre says (believes) that London is not identical with itself.

(iv) Pierre says (believes) that London is pretty and London is not pretty.

(v) Pierre says (believes) that London is not identical with London.

This suggestion has the important virtue of allowing us to characterize (iv-v) as true while recognizing that (i-iii) are false. See also Soames 1985a and 1987.

6. The allusion to Augustine refers to the passage quoted by Wittgenstein that opens <u>The Philosophical Investigations</u>.

> "When they (my elders) named some object, and accordingly moved towards something, I saw this and I grasped that the thing was called by the sound they uttered when they meant to point it out. Their intention was shewn by their bodily movements, as it were the natural language of all peoples: the expression of the face, the play of the eyes, the movement of other parts of the body, and the tone of voice which expresses our state of mind in seeking, having, rejecting, or avoiding something. Thus, as I heard words repeatedly used in their proper places in various sentences, I gradually learnt to understand what objects they signified; and after I had trained my mouth to form these signs, I used them to express my own desires."

The "Augustinian Picture" criticized below may be seen of as an unwarranted extension of these remarks about language acquisition to cover all aspects of language.

7. I am speaking here primarily about first language acquisition (though the point applies, with less force, to some cases of second language acquisition as well).

9

Sources and Structures of Linguistic Prominence in English

Richard T. Oehrle

English utterances can be partitioned into intonational phrases and each phrase can be analyzed into a segmental structure associated with prosodic properties involving pitch, emphasis, and timing. There are a number of reasons why the investigation of these structures may appeal to those with interests in the broad field of cognitive science. The articulation of speech offers an example of intricate and exquisitely organized patterns of physical action. At the same time, speech structures serve linguistic functions. As examples in the body of this paper amply illustrate, utterances which differ only in their prosodic properties have different appropriateness conditions, in general, and, in certain cases, may even differ in their truth conditions (Dretske 1972; Rooth 1984). While these differences are easy to apprehend subjectively, it is not easy to articulate the relations among prosodic properties, appropriateness conditions, and interpretation. In what follows, I try to show how such an integration of different structures might be achieved in certain fairly simple special cases. In particular, I suggest ways in which certain prosodic properties may be interpreted, and investigate how this interpretation depends on a variety of grammatical and pragmatic factors, including the interpretive properties of individual words, the syntactical organization of expressions within an utterance, and the communicative context in which a given utterance of an expression occurs. The linguistic details of this investigation are easily accessible. Apart from their intrinsic interest, investigations of such properties bear on such broader linguistic questions as the organization of grammatical knowledge. While I touch briefly on such issues in what follows, I have made no attempt to provide an even broader perspective in which the linguistic problems analyzed here are studied in relation to such traditional problems in the study of perception as the figure/ground distinction.

The research reported in this paper has its source in two simple observations. The first observation is that the nuclear accent of an English intonational phrase -- the last stressed syllable within the phrase -- may occur in various positions relative to a single sequence of syllables.[2] For example, using upper case letters to locate the nuclear accent, all of the following, with falling intonation, are possible assertions: *Jack hit ZACK, Jack HIT Zack,* and *JACK hit Zack.* The second observation is that variation in the location of the nuclear accent can affect the appropriateness (in a fixed context) of two otherwise equivalent sentences. Compare the following miniature dialogues in which a questioner Q poses a question and A1, A2, and so on, are judged as possible answers, with peculiar, puzzling, or inappropriate responses prefixed by an occurrence of the symbol "*".

1) Q: Who did Jack hit?

A1: Jack hit ZACK.
A2: *Jack HIT Zack.
A3: *JACK hit Zack.

2) Q: What did Jack do to Zack?

A1: *Jack hit ZACK.
A2: Jack HIT Zack.
A3: *JACK hit Zack.

3) Q: Who hit Zack?

A1: *Jack hit ZACK.
A2: *Jack HIT Zack.
A3: JACK hit Zack.

How is the location of the nuclear accent in a given grammatical structure related to its acceptability in a given discourse context?

The answer to this question that I wish to develop and defend in this paper requires two steps: first, with each well-formed expression, we associate a "focus set", which consists formally of a subset of the component parts of the expression; second, we shall assume that in a complete and appropriate answer

A to a wh-question Q, the focus set associated with A contains the component which corresponds to the questioned constituent in Q. These assumptions obviously do not provide an account of the circumstances under which an expression A constitutes a complete and appropriate answer to a question, nor of the kinds of correspondence among the components of A and Q that must pertain under such conditions. Nevertheless, relative to such intuitions, this approach to the problem provides a way of systematically studying, in a context where judgments are particularly sharp and clear, how variation in the location of the nuclear accent and other grammatical properties contribute to the appropriateness judgment.

An interesting formal aspect of this problem arises from the fact that whereas the nuclear accent of an intonational phrase falls on a single syllable, the focus set associated with the phrase consists of a set of grammatical components which cannot in general be identified with the single syllable which bears the stress. As we shall see in detail in what follows, the relation between the location of the nuclear accent in a given intonational phrase and the focus set associated with it depends on a number of factors, including the individual identity of the elementary components of the phrase, the compositional structure defined over them, and the discourse context. Investigation of this relation makes it possible to determine the role that purely linguistic properties play in this relation.

Before proceeding, it is worth examining in more detail some of the motivation for taking the focus set of an intonational phrase to be distinct from the syllable on which the nuclear accent falls. In the examples given in (1)-(3) above, syllables correspond to words one-to-one, but there are two components to the sentence which do not correspond to single syllables: the verb phrase *hit Zack* and the sentence *Jack hit Zack* as a whole. To assume that answers of questions of the form *What did x do (to y)?* and *What happened next?* require answers which have a focus which denotes an action and a focus which denotes an event (respectively) is consistent with the behavior of the sentences in (4) and (5) and the related behavior of the "pseudo-cleft" sentences in (6) and (7):

4) Q: What happened next?

A1: Jack hit ZACK.
A2: Jack HIT Zack.
[requires contextualization]
A3: JACK hit Zack.
[requires contextualization]
A4: Zack was hit by JACK.
A5: Zack was HIT by Jack.
[requires contextualization]
A6: ZACK was hit by Jack.
[requires contextualization]

5) Q: What did Jack do next?

A1: Jack hit ZACK.
A2: Jack HIT Zack.
[requires contextualization]
A3:*JACK hit Zack.
A4:*Zack was hit by JACK.
A5:*Zack was HIT by Jack.
A6:*ZACK was hit by Jack.

6a) What happened next was that Jack hit Zack.
6b) *What happened next was hit Zack.
6c) *What happened next was Zack.
6d) What happened next was the inauguration.

7a) *What Jack did next was that Jack hit Zack. [...was S]
7b) What Jack did next was hit Zack. [...was VP]
7c) What Jack did next was Zack. [...was NP]
7d) What Jack did next was the scenery for <u>Endgame</u>.

The warning "[requires contextualization]" appears after some of these examples, because while they may sound odd in isolation, they are acceptable in a broader context. Consider the question in (4) and the response (A2), as they are embedded in the following, broader, context:

.
.
.

B: Well what happened then was that Zack insulted Jack.
A: It's a dang shame that Zack insulted Jack that way.
B: I agree. But hey! Don't feel too bad for Jack.
A: Why? What happened next?
B: Jack HIT Zack. / *Jack hit ZACK. / *JACK hit Zack.

We return to the problem of contextualization shortly.

The examples in (4) and (5) contain two important contrasts, which are consistent with assuming that the component in focus in appropriate answers to (4) must be construable as representing an event, while the component in focus in appropriate answers to (5) must be construable as representing an action. The only syntactic components among the answers to (4) which meet this criterion belong to the category S. The only syntactic components among the answers to (5) which meet this criterion belong to the category (active) VP. These assumptions account for the fact that answers to the question *What happened next?* can be accented on a wider range of components than can answers to the question *What did Jack do next?*, as well as for the fact that while the question *What happened next*? can be answered by either active or passive forms (under different accentual conditions that we shall return to), the question *What did Jack do next?* can be answered only by active forms. In general, we shall describe the case in which the component that corresponds to the questioned constituent consists of the entire intonational phrase at issue by the term "wide-focus" interpretation. Equally, a "narrow-focus" interpretation characterizes the case in which the focused component is properly contained in the intonational phrase in question. While the above data are consistent with the hypothesis that the component of the utterance which corresponds in the required sense to the questioned constituent contains the nuclear accent, it is clear from the examples which require contextualization that this simple criterion is too weak to provide an adequate definition of the focus set associated with an intonational phrase, since the focus set it allows is too large in many cases. By systematically studying a larger class of examples, we may discover how this hypothesis can be improved.

SIMPLE CASES

The simplest cases involve structures in which a variety of components can be construed as prominent, and a variety of components -- in different contexts -- can contain the nuclear accent on a wide-focus interpretation. In the succeeding paragraphs of this section, we first survey cases of this kind involving one- and two-place predicates and then show how the observed behavior may be modeled.

One-place Predicates

First, simple sentences compatible with a wide-focus interpretation may differ with respect to the locus of the nuclear accent, even though the sentences in question have equivalent syntactic structures. As an example, consider the following pair:

8a) The SUN is out.
8b) The sun is GASeous.

Either sentence is compatible with a discourse context in which the only preceding remark is *Imagine the following scenario*. Thus, the following discourses make sense:

9a) Imagine the following scenario: The sun is out. (There are picnicers in Central Park, accompanied by pigeons....)
9b) Imagine the following scenario: The sun is gaseous. (Radiant energy is created at the sun's surface....)

In (9a), the nuclear accent within the occurrence of (8a) must fall on *sun*; in (9b), if the nuclear accent within the occurrence of (8b) falls on *sun*, the discourse must be considered incomplete, in the sense that we must assume the existence of previously given information in order for the structure to be cogent. Similarly, if, in (9a), the nuclear accent within the occurrence of (8a) falls on *out*, the discourse must be considered incomplete. Thus, in this context, when the two sentences (8a) and (8b) are both accented on the word *sun*, the first is compatible with a wide-focus interpretation, the second is not; and when they are both stressed on the corresponding adjectives *out* and *gaseous*, the second is compatible with a wide-focus interpretation, while the first is not. This example shows that there exist pairs of simple sentences with equivalent syntactic structures which differ in the designated wide-focus position of the nuclear accent.

Contextual Effects

Second, as already mentioned above, focus-assignment is contextually-sensitive in the sense that a single sentence with a fixed locus of the nuclear accent may have different focus-sets in different discourse contexts. Consider the following contrasts:

10a) X: After David was introduced to Max, what happened next?
Y: David inSULTed Max.
10b) X: After David was introduced to Max, what happened next?
Y: David insulted MAX.

11a) X: After David was introduced to Fred, what happened next?
Y: David inSULTed Max.
11b) X: After David was introduced to Fred, what happened next?
Y: David insulted MAX.

The point of the comparison is this: in (10a), Y's response is cogent with no further assumptions, but in (10b), Y's response makes sense only relative to some previous assumption that what happened is distinct from David insulting Max; in (11), however, these judgments of cogency are reversed: it is (11b) in which Y's response is cogent with no further assumptions and (11a) in which Y's response requires further discourse presumptions. In all four cases, in order for the discourse to make sense, the response to X's remark must be consistent with a wide focus interpretation, since Y must provide an answer to the question *what happened next?*. What the above examples demonstrate is that what counts as wide focus in one context need not count as wide-focus in another, a point ably argued by Ladd 1980. This means that the focus-set assigned to an expression depends on both its component parts (as argued in the preceding section) and the context-sensitive values of its constituent sub-expressions.

Deaccentuation and Wide-Focus

Third, two sentences may share a common syntactic structure and share in addition the favored locus for marking wide focus, yet differ in how the wide focus is marked when this favored locus is contextually deaccented. For example, in contexts in which no mention has been made of the Greeks or the Persians, the accentual locus compatible with a wide-focus interpretation of *The Greeks defeated the Persians* is on the strongest syllable of *Persians*. If *Persians* is contextually deaccented, as it might be following the question *What happened to the Persians?*, the accentual locus compatible with a wide-focus interpretation shifts to the strongest syllable of *defeated*.

In contrast, it seems that similar deaccentuation with respect to the sentence *Your cousin passed the elevator* causes the accentual locus compatible with a wide-focus interpretation to shift from *elevator* to *cousin*. In this case, we cannot use the contextual shift from *what happened?* to *what happened to the elevator?*, since *Your cousin passed the elevator* is difficult to construe as having the sort of consequences for the elevator that the second question presumes. But we can compare the accentuation of this sentence in two different narratives, where there is no reason to suspect that a narrow-focus interpretation would be appropriate. Suppose first that a detective who has been shadowing my cousin delivers the following oral report to me:

12) I picked up your cousin as he walked into the hotel. Your cousin passed the elevator. Then he headed straight across the lobby toward the cigarette counter....

In this context, the nuclear accent on the occurrence of the sentence *Your cousin passed the elevator* must be on the strongest syllable of *elevator*. But if *elevator* is deaccented, the accent shifts, not to the verb *passed* (as our previous example would suggest), but rather to the strongest syllable in *your cousin*. A plausible example of the required context is given in (13):

13) An interesting thing happened to me this morning when I rode down to the lobby. Just as the car reached the ground floor and the doors opened, your cousin passed the elevator.

If we assume that *the car* and *the elevator* agree in reference and that this justifies the deaccentuation of *elevator*, it is natural to suppose that the accent shifts to *cousin*. It is possible, of course, to construct a context in which the accent would fall on *passed*, but to do so requires that we shape the narrative so that the relationship between cousin and elevator is of interest.

Compositionality

Fourth, focus-assignment has a compositional character. To see this, one need only embed simple sentences which are similar in their syntactic structure, yet differ in the relation between the locus of the nuclear acent and induced focus-set (for corresponding contexts). For example, expressions of the form *x claimed that S* mark wide focus by assigning the nuclear accent to the syllable within S compatible with a wide-focus interpretation for S:

14) Q: What happened next?

A1: John claimed that the SUN was out.
A2: John claimed that the sun was OUT.
A3: John claimed that the SUN was gaseous.
A4: John claimed that the sun was GASeous.

Just as (8a) and (8b) differ in the relation between accent locus and induced focus set, in spite of other similarities, so in these cases, we find that while A1 and A4 are straightforward answers to Q, the acceptability of A2 and A3 depends on the accessibility of further contextual assumptions. The parallelism between these cases and those in (8a,b) follows at once from the assumption that focus assignment has certain compositionally-specifiable properties. But the compositional properties of focus-assignment will come as no surprise to those familiar with the tradition of compositional stress-assignment exemplified by Chomsky, Halle, and Lukoff 1956, Chomsky and Halle 1968, Bresnan 1971, Halle and Keyser 1971, Jackendoff 1972, Liberman and Prince 1977, and Culicover and Rochemont 1983.

AN ACCOUNT

We infer from these examples the following basic properties: first, that in some structures (such as the structure **NP is Adj**), the locus of the nuclear accent compatible with a wide-focus interpretation is not determinable on the basis of syntactical properties defined in terms of category and linear order; second, that contextual deaccentuation of the component which normally contains the nuclear accent on a wide-focus interpretation can make available other loci for the nuclear accent which preserve the possibility of a wide-focus interpretation; third, that in certain structures (such as the structure **NP V NP**), while the second NP contains the nuclear accent in the cases we have examined (when it is not contextually deaccented), deaccentuation of the second NP may yield different "fall-back" positions for the nuclear accent; and fourth, that the association of a fixed syllabic location with a set of components as possible foci is compositional.

It is not too difficult to see that the compositional aspect of this problem can be satisfactorily resolved relative to assumptions about the contribution of lexical distinctions, on the one hand, and the action of contextual deaccentuation, on the other. The solution developed below is compatible with a variety of different approaches to grammatical analysis, though particularly congenial to members of the family of categorial grammars.[3]

First, we assume that any good expression is either simple (so that its properties are assumed to be given) or can be partitioned into a set of immediate sub-expressions in such a way that the (compositional) properties of the expression as a whole can be be expressed as a function of the corresponding properties of these component parts. We call this Ajdukiewicz's Principle (cf. Ajdukiewicz 1935). If the component parts of an expression are complex, Ajdukiewicz's Principle applies to them as well. Successive application of this procedure on successively smaller components leads to successively finer partitions of the original expression until a point is reached when all the elements of the partition are simple.

In order to define a prosodic calculus which will associate any locus of the nuclear accent within a well-formed expression with a set of candidate foci in a way consistent with the behavior observed earlier, we need to specify three things: 1) the contribution of lexical elements and compositional structures; 2) the role of contextual information; and 3) a function which maps two arguments associated with an analyzed expression -- the first, a locus of the nuclear accent and an abstract structure which reflects the contributions of lexical elements and compositional structures; and the second, contextual information -- to a set of components of the expression which can be construed as focused when the nuclear accent falls in the given position.

With regard to the first of these tasks, assume that the contribution of lexical elements and compositional structures to the abstract prosodic structure associated with a given expression is to assign to the immediate components of each complex compositional domain a linear order.[4] Assuming as well that the standard position for word-stress in simple forms (e.g., words) can be fixed and constitutes a maximal element in each word-domain, we then have at our disposal a maximal element in every compositional domain. It is convenient to represent each such linear ordering by associating the components of a compositional domain with a set of positive integers in the obvious way: if C and D are components of a given compositional domain and C < D, then the integer associated with C is less than the integer associated with D.

Ignoring for the moment cases in which the nuclear accent falls on some non-maximal syllable within a word, these assumptions allow us to state the following fundamental rule, which we call the Focus Recursion Law:[5]

15) The Focus Recursion Law

> The focus set of an expression E, foc(E), is characterized by the following two requirements:
> 1) s ∈ foc(E), where s is the syllable of E bearing the nuclear accent;
> 2) for every component c of E, c ∈ foc(E) <---> the maximal element in the linear ordering associated with c belongs to foc(E).

Given this rule, we can characterize the contrast between *The sun is out* and *The sun is gaseous* by assigning the structures **NP is out** and **NP is gaseous** different linear orders: in the first case, the sequence of constituents **NP is AP** is associated with the ordering indicated by the corresponding sequence **3-1-2**, in which the subject NP is maximal; in the second case, the sequence of constituents **NP is AP** is associated with the ordering **2-1-3**, in which the AP *gaseous* is maximal.[6]

Now, if we make the further assumption that the "contextual deaccentuation" of a component means that the component is removed from the compositionally-based linear ordering (which we may indicate schematically by associating it with the integer 0), then the Focus Recursion Law makes two predictions when the deaccented component is a proper part of the evaluated expression: first, if there is a locus of the nuclear accent compatible with a wide-focus interpretation, that locus is not contained within the contextually-deaccented component, since an unordered component can never be maximal in the associated linear ordering; second, if a contextually-deaccented component contains the nuclear accent, the deaccented component acts as an upper bound on the focus set assigned to the evaluated expression, in the sense that the components of the deaccented component which contain the nuclear accent (including the deaccented component as a whole) belong to the focus set assigned to the evaluated expression, but no components of the expression which properly contain the deaccented component are possible foci.

It is the first of these two properties which is relevant to the contrast between *The Greeks defeated the Persians* and *Your cousin passed the elevator*. The differences we observed in these cases with respect to the location of nuclear accent on a wide-focus interpretation when the NP following the verb is deaccented can be characterized by assuming that the syntactic structure **NP V NP** which the two sentences share is associated with two different linear orderings: **1-2-3** (in the case of *The Greeks defeated the Persians*) and **2-1-3** (in the case of *Your cousin passed the elevator*). In both cases, the final NP is maximal (i.e., associated with the highest integer), but the orderings differ with respect to the next highest value. And thus, in a context in which the final NP is deaccented, the resulting structures are converted to **1-2-0** and **2-1-0**, respectively. In such contexts, then, a wide-focus interpretation requires (by the Focus Recursion Law) that the accent fall on the verb in the first case and on the strongest accent within the subject NP in the second, which is what was observed earlier.

The second consequence of the Focus Recursion Law is supported by contrasts such as the following:

16) Q: What did J do when Max came in?
A: J insulted DAVE. [focus = insult Dave]

17) Q: What did J do when Max came in?
A: J inSULTed Max. [focus = insult Max]

18) Q: Who did J insult when Max came in?
A: J insulted DAVE. [focus = Dave]

19) Q: Who did J insult when Max came in?
A: J insulted MAX. [focus = Max]

Example (16) shows that the normal way of indicating focus on a

VP of the form **insulted NP** is to place the nuclear accent on the maximal element within **NP**. When this NP is contextually deaccented (as in (17)), the locus of the accent compatible with a VP focus is the maximal syllable in *insulted*. The contrast between (18) and (19) shows that a deaccented component can nevertheless be stressed and focused. The fact that the answer to (19) cannot be appropriately used as a response to a question that requires a VP or sentential focus and serves as an environment for the deaccentuation of Max is compatible with the treatment advocated here.

Finally, it is easy to see how this model deals with the compositional properties observed above: assume that **NP claimed S'** is associated with the ordering **1-2-3**, that S' is expanded as **that S** with S maximal, and that the ordering within S depends on its internal properties. These assumptions yield the facts already observed, though they do not as yet provide a satisfactory account of the result of letting the accent fall on the complementizer *that* which directly follows *claimed*.

Given the Focus Recursion Law, then, the nesting of linearly-ordered components that we have assumed serves a variety of purposes. First, relative to any component C of an expression, it requires that the maximal component within C contain the nuclear accent if C as a whole is to be construed as prominent. Second, by the same token, if the nuclear accent falls within a non-maximal component of C, then the focus set associated with C cannot contain C itself; nor can any more inclusive component be taken to belong to the focus set. These two properties alone are compatible with a weaker formal structure than we have assumed -- namely, one in which a designated element is picked out in each domain. The stronger assumption of a linear ordering is justified by the shift of accent observed in contexts in which the maximal element in one or another domain can be reasonably construed as deaccented.

The examples in the section on Deaccentuation and Wide-Focus show that such shifts in the accent position compatible with a wide-focus interpretation can be independent of surface syntactic form. Thus, with respect to the examples already discussed, it seems that the removal of any single assumption will lessen the adequacy of the system as a whole. In particular, any weaker theory formulated within this general framework is less adequate than the theory based on the assumptions advocated here. By this criterion, the account offered here is preferable to many current alternative formulations of rules for the assignment or interpretation of the nuclear accent in English. In the next section, we shall take up examples in which the properties of focus interpretation are more constrained than they are in the examples already discussed.

ELABORATIONS

The account just sketched of the interpretation of the nuclear accent position is more constrained than an account which defines the focus set of a sentence as the set of components which contain the nuclear accent. But the sole constraint imposed derives from the context-dependence of the interpretive procedure. That is, the account sketched above is compatible with the view that for a given analysis A of an expression E, a fixed locus L within it of the nuclear accent (maximal within some word domain), and a chosen component C whose phonological projection contains L, there is a context in which C belongs to the focus set associated with A. While this flexible and efficient relation between context and focus assignment is characteristic of many English sentences, interpretation of the prosodic system of English in fact requires subtler and more complex means. In this section, we examine first some expressions with special focal properties: some cannot be identified with the focus (on the requisite interpretation) and others must be. We then consider some particularly dramatic ways in which syntactic variation can affect focus-interpretation. The emphasis in this discussion is descriptive. Finally, we take up the question of how the facts described here can be integrated with the theoretical account offered of focus assignment offered earlier.

Special Focal Properties: Unstressable

"Epithets" -- definite NP's with affective content used anaphorically -- offer a good illustration of a type of expression which cannot belong to the focus of a larger expression of which they form a proper component. In the following examples, the behavior of the epithet *the bastard* differs from the behavior of the pronoun *him*, although both can be taken throughout to refer to Miller. (In the examples below, square brackets are used to enclose alternatives, which are separated by slashes.)

20) I'm sorry I ever MET Miller: I can't STAND [him/the bastard].

21) I hope you didn't invite the Millers: Mrs Miller is allright, but I can't stand [HIM / *the BAStard].

22) Q: What happened after you were informed of Miller's illness?

A1: After I realized how SICK Miller was, I called him UP.
A2: After I realized how SICK Miller was, I called the bastard UP.
A3:*After I realized how SICK Miller was, I called HIM up.
A4:*After I realized how SICK Miller was, I called the BAStard up.

A3 and A4 are both strange here, because the normal way to indicate wide-focus in the structure **call NP up** when **NP** is contextually deaccented is by placing the accent on *up*, as in A1 and A2. The more telling case arises when we seek a narrow-focus interpretation on the anaphoric expression:

23) Q: After you realized how SICK Miller was, who did you call UP?

A1:*After I realized how SICK Miller was, I called him UP.
A2:*After I realized how SICK Miller was, I called the bastard UP.
A3: After I realized how SICK Miller was, I called HIM up.
A4:*After I realized how SICK Miller was, I called the BAStard up.

We may assume that A1 and A2 are inappropriate answers because their focus sets do not contain an expression which matches the wh-word *who* in the question. A3 overcomes this deficiency, but A4 is unable to. One way to account for this (relative to the Focus Recursion Law) is to assume that epithets simply cannot belong to the focus-set of a structure which contains them. This hypothesis is inconsistent with epithets being stressed qua epithets. And indeed, while the phonological form of an epithet can be stressed in metalinguistic uses (such as the director of a play using A4 to correct an actor who had mistakenly uttered *After I realized how SICK Miller was, I called the buster UP* instead of A2 in a context like that of (22) in which A2 is appropriate), it makes sense to say that in such contexts, the use of *the BAStard* is one which refers to the phonological form of the epithet -- not one in which it refers to Miller.

Special Focal Properties: Obligatory Stress

If epithets illustrate a class of expressions which cannot be stressed, there is a converse set of expressions which must be stressed if the segmental sequence in which they occur is to be construed non-metalinguistically. A nice example of this class is the emphatic form *too* used in denials of denials:

24) X: He doesn't.
    Y: He does TOO.

Even in longer sentences in which it occurs following a tensed aux-element, *too* always carries the accent.

Special Focal Properties: Fixed Stress and Focus

In addition to particular expressions which either must or cannot be identified with the focus component of a phrase, there are a variety of syntactic constructions which have less flexible focus properties than the cases examined earlier in section 1. Consider the two constructions with the respective forms **PP NP V** and **PP V NP**, exemplified by *Into the elevator Fred walked* and *Into the elevator walked Fred*. In each case, the accent falls on the final component of the form (in accordance with the Focus Recursion Law, of course). If the accent is shifted away from the final component (as in *Into the elevator FRED walked*,[7] *Into the ELevator walked Fred*, *Into the elevator WALKED Fred*, or *Into the ELevator walked Fred*), the resulting sentence can be used metalinguistically as a correction (we might correct *Into the escalator walked FRED* with *Into the ELevator walked Fred*), but cannot be used, as can the related sentence *Fred WALKED into the elevator*, as an appropriate answer to the question *How did Fred get into the elevator?*, regardless of where the accent is placed. The rigidity of the accent is matched by a corresponding rigidity of focus interpretation. On the view that any component containing the nuclear accent in an expression can be the focus, we would expect there to be at least two members of the focus set assigned to a sentence like *In walked FRED*, namely, the noun phrase *Fred* and the sentence as a whole. Yet while judgments in this case seem less certain than in earlier discussion, utterances of this type seem more appropriate as answers to questions compatible with a propositional focus than they are as answers to questions compatible with an NP focus:

25) Q: What happened then?

A1: In walked FRED.
A2: FRED walked in.

26) Q: Who just came in?

A1:?In walked FRED?
A2: FRED walked in.

If these judgments are correct, then it would seem that not only is the stress fixed in this structure, but the focus is fixed as well. This constitutes a double difference from cases of the sort first discussed and obviously requires an extension of the formal structure proposed there, which is incapable of expressing either rigidity of accent or rigidity of focus.

Globally-induced Constraints

We have thus far added to the set of examples in which we find limits placed on the assignment of focus -- limits which arise either from the contribution of proper parts of an expression (such as lexical elements like emphatic *too* or definite descriptions used as epithets) or from the (global) analysis of the expression itself. The hallmark of all these cases is the existence within the expression of a proper part which can be highlighted prosodically only under a metalinguistic interpretation -- that is, under a different linguistic analysis. The local cases involving epithets and such forms as emphatic *too* exhaust the simplest possible specifications with respect to the focus-set of the expressions they appear in: they either must or cannot belong to the focus-set in question. As a result, they either must (in the case of *too*) or cannot (in the case of epithets) contain the stress. And it seems that all the local cases are of this simple kind.

Globally-induced constraints on focus-interpretation offer a wider range of options. In contrast to the construction discussed in the immediately preceding section, consider the sentences in (27) and (28):

27) Scott is the author of Waverley.

28) The author of Waverley is Scott.

We wish to construe these sentences in the following way, using the terminology of Higgins (1973): (27) is a predicational sentence, in which *Scott* is a referring expression, but *the author of Waverley* is not; (28) is a specificational sentence, in which the arguments to the copula in (27) are simply inverted. Thus, the interpretation of (28) we wish to discuss is compatible with the tagged sentence (29) below, but not with (30):

29) The author of Waverley is Scott, isn't it.

30) The author of Waverley is Scott, isn't he.

Now, on the interpretation we have in mind, (27) and (28) have the same truth conditions. If every component of every sentence were a potential member of the focus set assigned to that sentence, then we would expect that the two sentences would be appropriate in exactly the same contexts, although it might be possible to indicate a wide-focus interpretation differently in the two cases. But this is incorrect. Consider the following examples (which in some cases involve the modal *could* to distinguish interrogative and declarative forms):

31) Q: What did you find out?

A1: Scott is the author of WAVerley.
A2: The author of Waverley is SCOTT.

32) Q: Who could be the author of Waverley?

A1: SCOTT is the author of Waverley.
A2: The author of Waverley is SCOTT.

33) Q: Who could Scott be?

A1: Scott is the author of WAVerley.
A2:*The author of WAVerley is Scott.

34) Q: Who could be Scott?

A1: The author of WAVerley is Scott (*isn't it).
A2: Scott is the author of WAVerley.

The most striking fact here is the infelicity of (33A2): while (33A1) is appropriate, and it seems reasonable that (33A2) should be compatible with an interpretation of the accent in which the focus is *the author of Waverley*, this simple extrapolation is impossible. In fact, the sentence *The author of WAVerley is Scott* can only be used metalinguistically as a correction (on the interpretation we have imposed on its components).

A reasonable theoretical interpretation of this particular paradigm is that in the inverted structure *The author of Waverley is Scott*, the initial NP *the author of Waverley* must be construed as not belonging to the focus set. Yet this is not because the focus of this construction is fixed, for it is possible to stress the copula if one wishes to emphasize the polarity or tense of the sentence, or to insert emphatic *too*, as in *The author of Waverley is TOO Scott.*

Intermediate Cases

We have considered cases in which the focus set of a given construction is fixed and case in which a particular constituent in a given construction cannot belong to the focus set. There is an important intermediate case, in which an expression E can belong to the focus set associated with it only if the nuclear accent falls within a particular constituent C (typically, the final major constituent in E); yet the nuclear accent can occur outside C without forcing a metalinguistic interpretation of E. We will consider a number of examples of this type.

Active and passive. Earlier, we noticed that the focus structure of sentences of the form **NP defeated NP** may be represented in neutral contexts as **1-2-3**. What is the focus structure associated with the corresponding passive sentence?

In neutral wide-focus contexts, either active or passive is acceptable. Thus, in (35), both A1 and A2 are possible responses to Q:

35) Q: What happened next?

A1: The greeks defeated the PERsians.
A2: The persians were defeated by the GREEKS.

We can introduce a contextual bias in such contexts by extending Q to a form of the type *what happened to x*, a form which still requires a wide-focus response. Consider (36):

36) Q: What happened to the persians?

A1: The greeks defeated the PERsians.
A2: The PERsians were defeated by the greeks.
A3: The greeks deFEATed the persians.
A4: The GREEKS defeated the persians.
A5: The persians were defeated by the GREEKS.
A6: The persians were deFEATed by the greeks.

A1 and A2 are both impossible here, apparently as a result of placing the accent on a component whose discourse deaccentuation in this environment is obligatory. According to the focus structure associated with *the greeks defeated the persians*, however, A3 is compatible with a wide-focus interpretation in contexts in which *the persians* is deaccented, and hence ((36,Q),(36,A3)) is a coherent dialogue. Unless we make further presumptions about the discourse, A4 is aberrant here, a fact consistent with the associated focus structure (since *defeated* outranks *the greeks* in this structure). We have already seen that A5 has a wide focus interpretation (cf. (35,A2), a fact compatible with its felicity here. But A6 is odd in this context; evidently, then, it lacks a wide-focus interpretation.

We now consider this same set of responses to a similar question about the greeks.

37) Q: What happened to the greeks?

A1: The greeks defeated the PERsians.
A2: The PERsians were defeated by the greeks.
A3: The greeks deFEATed the persians.
A4: The GREEKS defeated the persians.
A5: The persians were defeated by the GREEKS.
A6: The persians were deFEATed by the greeks.

Corresponding to the impossibility of A1 and A2 as responses to (36,Q) above, A4 and A5 are impossible here, presumably for the same reason. Yet, there is no problem with A1 and A3 is possible if we extend the discourse context appropriately. But A2 and A6 are odd. Why?

Before turning to further evidence on this question, let us consider two basic strategies for accounting for the aberrance of (37,A2) and (37,A6). To be felicitous in this context, a sentence must be compatible with a wide focus interpretation and an occurrence of *the greeks* must be deaccented. One way to treat the infelicity of (37,A2) and (37,A6) is to assign a focus structure to the sentence as a whole which makes these two conditions not jointly satisfiable. An alternative is to block deaccentuation from applying to material in the *by*-phrase.

It is easy to find further evidence which bears on the choice between these alternatives. Consider narrow-focus contexts in which both active and passive are possible:

38) Q: Who defeated the persians?

A1: The GREEKS defeated the persians.
A2: The persians were defeated by the GREEKS.

39) Q: Who did the greeks defeat?

A1: The greeks defeated the PERsians.
A2: The PERsians were defeated by the greeks.

Here, the decisive example against a proposal to restrict the by-phrase of a passive to non-deaccented expressions is (39,A2). But taken together, (38) and (39) show that both active and passive are compatible with narrow focus on either NP.

Other narrow-focus contexts are constructible:

40) Q: What took place between the greeks and the persians.

A1: The greeks deFEATed the persians.
A2: The persians were deFEATed by the greeks.

At the same time, since active and passive make available different sets of components, not every possible focus of an active sentence is a possible focus in the corresponding passive sentence:

41) Q: What did the greeks do next?

A1: The greeks defeated the PERsians.
A2: the persians were defeated by the greeks.

Here, while A1 is felicitous, no locus of the nuclear accent makes A2 good. If the focus required in response to (41,Q) is VP (as is consistent with the pseudo-cleft construction **what x did to y was VP**), we account for this fact on the grounds that while it is possible to analyze the active sentence (41,A1) as containing a VP component *defeat the persians*, no such analysis is possible for the corresponding passive form. In fact, any component of (41,A2) which contains *the persians* and *defeated* must also contain *the greeks*, for *defeated by the greeks* is a component of (41,A2). To see why, consider the interesting fact that when *defeated by the greeks* can be taken to be contextually deaccented, locating the accent on the maximal element of *the persians* is compatible with a wide-focus interpretation:

42) Q: After the mixolydians were defeated by the greeks, as you have so vividly described, what happened next?

A: The PERsians were defeated by the greeks.

We can summarize all these observations as follows: both active and passive are compatible with wide-focus interpretations, but they behave differently when the maximal element of S is contextually deaccented; in the active sentence *the greeks defeated the persians*, the three major components are linearly ordered in the associated focus structure; the corresponding components in the passive sentence *the persians were defeated by the greeks* cannot be linearly ordered in the same way, for although there is a maximal element in this sentence, when it alone is deaccented, no wide-focus interpretation is possible.

To account for the properties of focus-assignment in this passive example, we shall associate it with a focus structure compatible with the following diagram:

43)

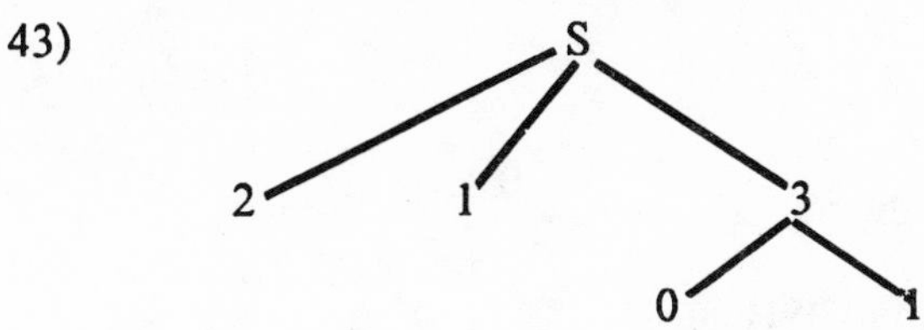

the persians were defeated by the greeks

When *the greeks* alone is deaccented, then the component *defeated by the greeks* has no maximal element, and hence the sentence as a whole has no maximal element, and hence only narrow-focus interpretations are possible (cf. 37); somewhat surprisingly, however, when *defeated by the greeks* as a whole is deaccented (cf. 41), wide-focus compatibility is restored.

The theoretical interest of this example resides in the fact that constituents of rank 0, which behave exactly as if they had been deaccented, can be introduced on syntactic grounds alone.

Particles. Exactly this property can be found with regard to other forms of variation in the English verb phrase, for example, in the variation in the position of the class of post-verbal "particles", exemplified by the pair of sentences *The waiter brought the fish in* (...V NP PRT) and *The waiter brought in the fish* (...V PRT NP). Permutation of NP and PRT affects focus assignment. In wide focus environments in which NP is not contextually deaccented (and thus not of rank 0) either construction is possible and the nuclear accent falls on the syllable within NP which marks wide focus within NP:

44) Q: What happened then?

A1: The waiter brought the FISH in.
A2: The waiter brought in the FISH.

When the NP of this construction is contextually deaccented, however, it is odd for the NP to precede the PRT. Consider:

45) Q: What happened to the fish you caught?

A1: The waiter brought the fish IN.
A2: ?The waiter brought IN the fish.

When the NP is itself the desired focus, it may occupy either position:

46) Q: What did Jack bring in?

A1: He brought the FISH in.
A2: He brought in the FISH.

If the particle is construed as a locative or directional focus, however, only the outside position is possible:

47) Q: Where did Jack put the fish?

A1: He brought the fish IN.
A2: ?He brought IN the fish.

While (47,A2) is odd as a response to (47,Q), it nevertheless has its uses. In particular, consider a case where we wish to deny one relation between the waiter and the fish and assert another:

48) The waiter didn't SERVE the fish; he only brought IN the fish.

On empirical grounds, then, we find that **bring NP in** is associated with a linear ordering with NP ranked maximally, and <u>in</u> ranked positively; the ordering associated with **bring in NP** again ranks NP maximally, but must treat the construction as containing a component **bring in** of rank 0 in the larger phrase **bring in NP.**[8]

Ditransitives. There are other types of verb phrases which have the properties found in the examples of the two immediately preceding subsections: a designated position is compatible with a wide-focus position, and all other positions give rise to focus-sets which contain only narrow-focus interpretations. For example, the double NP construction **V NP NP**, associated with the focus-structure **0-0-1**, is of this type, in contrast to the prepositional construction **V NP PP**, which has the linearly-ordered focus-structure **1-2-3** (leaving aside details about **P** in **PP** which deserve further investigation). Thus, pairs of sentences such as *The lawyer* *sent the letter to Fred*) and *The lawyer sent Fred the letter* which seem to be similar, if not identical, in their truth-conditions, have different focus-structures. The argument is by now familiar.

Sentences of either kind can be used appropriately in neutral contexts as an answer to a question which requires a wide-focus answer:

49) Q: What happened next?

A1: The lawyer sent the letter to FRED.
A2: The lawyer sent Fred the LETter.

In contexts in which *Fred* is contextually deaccented, there are wide-focus interpretations of either sentence:

50) Q: After learning of Fred's request, what did the lawyer do next?

A1: He sent the LETter to Fred, just as Fred had requested.
A2: He sent Fred the LETter, just as Fred had requested.

In contexts in which *the letter* is contextually deaccented, however, we find that the prepositional structure and the double NP structure behave differently. Both allow a narrow-focus interpretation when the accent falls on *Fred*:

51) Q: Who has the letter now?

A1: The lawyer sent the letter to FRED.
A2: The lawyer sent FRED the letter.

But in contexts which demand a wider focus, placing the nuclear accent on the first NP in the double NP construction is odd. In particular, (51,A2) is inappropriate:

52) Q: After he read the letter, what did the lawyer do next?

A1: The lawyer sent the letter to FRED.
A2: The lawyer sent FRED the letter.

While subtle, the judgment that (52,A2) is strange in this context is still palpable.

EXTENDING THE SYSTEM

The system of ranking components in any given compositional domain introduced above accounts well for the location and contextually-induced shifts of the nuclear accent observed in sentences with particularly simple structure. But this system, which takes every compositional domain to have a linearly-ordered focus-structure, cannot treat adequately the more complicated examples just considered. There are two simple reasons for this: first, it presumes that every component can be accented; second, it presumes that every component can be de-accented. The examples immediately preceding section show that these two premises, while often satisfied, do not hold in general, sometimes because of the intrinsic properties of components sometimes because of the global properties of particular syntactic constructions. Nevertheless, there are strong reasons to maintain the properties of this system of ranking: as argued earlier, without them, we won't be able to account adequately for the simple examples. In this section, I show how it is possible to extend this system to cover the phenomenal properties of tahe more complicated examples. In the following section, we shall consider the extent to which the observed properties of focus-structure correlate with other grammatical structures.

Formally, we now extend the focus structure associated with an expression E to an ordered pair <A,B>, where A is a prosodic calculus of exactly the sort characterized for the simple cases, consisting of the application of the Focus Recursion Law to a linear ordering of a subset of the components of the structure, adjusted to meet the current discourse conditions and placement of the nuclear accent, and B is a set of components which are taken to be syntactically eligible members of the focus set associated with E. In any given context, the focus set of E consists of the intersection of A and B.

The simple cases, all of the relevant components of the examples discussed are possible foci under appropriate prosodic conditions. In each case, then, we take B to contain every component. The intersection of A and B is thus equal to A by itself. In the more complicated cases, it is necessary to either require that a given component C belong to B or exclude C from B.

Epithets are to be excluded from B. Hence, they are never in the intersection of A and B. Hence, they never belong to the focus set of the expression in which they occur. An alternative is to exclude them from A by requiring that they be unaccentable. But this approach belies the fact that we know perfectly well where the accent would fall were it to fall on them. Moreover, we shall see shortly that an account of epithets on purely phonological grounds is untenable.

The emphatic *too* is the sole member of B in non-metalinguistic interpretations of the expressions it occurs in. (More generally, whenever the intersection of the sets A and B is empty, a metalinguistic interpretation of the component is forced.)

The constructions **PP NP V** and **PP V NP** involving "directional adverb preposing" both may be associated with pairs <A,B> where in each case A is the trivial ordering consisting of just the last component and the first two components are unordered (**0-0-1**) and B is the expression as a whole. These assumptions have a number of consequences. First, placing the nuclear accent on either of the first two components in either structure will give rise only to a metalinguistic interpretation. Second, placing the accent on the last component is compatible with a wide-focus interpretation, but only (third) when the last component is not contextually-deaccented (which would locally convert the positive ranking of the last component to 0). The examples (27) and (28) are more delicate. It is clear, first of all that under the relevant interpretation of *The author of Waverley is Scott*, the initial NP *the author of Waverley* must be excluded from the focus set. This is easily accomplished by excluding it from B. So B cannot contain every component. Moreover, it apparently cannot contain only *Scott*, since we can have *The author of Waverley is TOO Scott*. On these grounds, however, we ought to be able to replace *Scott* with an epithet or a stressless pronoun. But examples such as *The author of Waverley is Scott and the author of Ivanhoe is the bastard*, where *Scott* and *the bastard* are taken to refer to the same person, are odd, regardless of where the accent falls in the second conjunct. At first glance, this set of examples seems to show that the plausible accounts of epithets, *too*, and the whole prosodic calculus developed for the simple cases are mutually inconsistent. But if we sharpen the interpretation of these accounts, they already contain the solution to this problem. We need to assume first of all that the components of *the author of Waverley is Scott* are the aux-element *is* and the pair <*the author of Waverley, Scott*>. In the focus-structure associated with the sentence as a whole, the pair outranks *is*. Internally, the focus-structure of the pair must be taken to be such that *Scott* is necessarily the focus. With regard to the prosodic calculus A associated with this structure, we are free to make any assumption we like. But structure B will consist only of *Scott*. Substituting an epithet for *Scott* would result in the epithet being counted the focus of the pair. But this is inconsistent with our assumption that an epithet cannot belong to B, as long as we interpret this requirement to hold of each component in such a way that the component in question has a consistent focus-structure. (An inconsistent focus-structure forces a metalinguistic interpretation, but in a case of this kind, the metalinguistic interpretation has no uses, except as an example of a structure of the ill-formed sort that it represents.) Thus substituting an epithet for *Scott* in this case leaves the pair with no consistent focus-interpretation. Under the less constrained conditions of the examples in (21) through (23), removing the epithet from B leaves B non-empty, and a choice of possible focus-interpretations remains. If this proposal is correct, it provides further support for the view advanced above that the distribution of epithets is not to be attributed to purely phonological properties. In particular, as we see from the examples on which this discussion is based, it is not in general true that an epithet can occur in any unstressed NP position.

Finally, since the final set of complicated examples differ from the simple cases only in that they contain components of rank 0 whose rank is assigned on lexical grounds rather than as the result of contextual de-accentuation, it is obvious that they can be accommodated directly within the account of simple cases, and hence in any extension of that account, such as that developed here.

POSSIBLE CORRELATIONS

This account of focus-assignment is one that emphasizes the compositional properties of focus-assignment and its dependency on lexical properties, the properties of particular syntactic domains, and assumptions about context. The formal properties of this account are flexible enough to accommodate the variety of examples discussed earlier. Many alternative theories are either inconsistent with this observed variety or so incomplete that it is difficult to tell whether any extension of them consistent with this variety is possible. These uncertainties flow from a number of independent assumptions (all rejected here): first, that the location of the nuclear accent under "normal" conditions is predictable from the order and accentual properties of the elements in any given phonological domain; second, that the location of the nuclear accent when the "normal" location is unavailable is predictable from the order and accentual properties of the remaining elements in any given phonological domain; third, that any component of an expression E is a possible member of the focus set associated with E. While there are restricted domains in which all of these assumptions hold, none of them holds of the full range of cases observed here. This provides strong motivation for accepting the framework advocated here: it provides an adequate characterization of a wide range of examples.

Yet the framework developed here in fact accommodates a great deal more: the observed range of cases is actually a small fraction of the possible modes of focus-interpretation which can be formulated within this framework. This fact suggests that it might prove useful to investigate whether there is any correlation between the focus-structure associated with a given expression and its other grammatical properties.

As a first step, we classify the observed range of simple focus-structures into three groups. The first consists of cases in which all the immediate sub-components of an expression are positively ranked in the linear ordering associated with it. We will refer to this class as the class of maximally-ordered focus-structures. Maximally-ordered focus-structures are never syntactically restricted -- that is, in such cases, the set B of the last section contains all the ordered components. The second group consists of cases in which a single component is positively ranked and all other components are unordered (that is, of rank 0), and every component belongs to B. We will refer to this class as the class of minimally-ordered, syntactically-unrestricted focus-structures. The third set is the class of syntactically-restricted focus-structures (all of which are associated with minimal orderings). The central cases considered here involve tensed verbs with one or more NP or PP arguments. There is a strong correlation between the relative order of tensed verb and arguments, on the one hand, and the nature of the associated focus-structure.

In particular, we shall call such a structure "canonical" when it has the form **NP V (NP) (PP)***, that is, when it consists of a "subject" NP, followed by the tensed verb, followed optionally by a single noun phrase and zero or more PP arguments. Canonical structures are apparently always associated with maximal focus-structures. Thus, the syntactic structure **NP-V** can be associated either with the ordering **1-2** (associated with structures of the form **NP wept**, for example) or with the ordering **2-1** (as is the case with structures of the form **NP** arrived). And we have seen examples in which the structure **NP-V-NP** is associated either with the ordering **1-2-3** (e.g. structures of the form **NP destroyed NP**) or with the ordering **2-1-3** (e.g. structures of the form **NP passed NP**). Which of these orderings is consistent with a given structure depends on its interpretation, though in many cases the decisive factor seems to be rather subtle. Exactly how the interpretive properties of the predicate (individuated in some frameworks by the "thematic roles" assigned to arguments by the predicate) influence which ordering is chosen is too complicated to discuss here, but nevertheless appears to be a problem amenable to further analysis. Non-canonical structures (of the sort which involve only NP and PP arguments to a verb) always are associated with minimal focus-structures. When the structure in question is non-canonical only with respect to material to the right of the tensed element, the associated focus structure is minimal, but not syntactically restricted. This is the case with the double NP construction (e.g. *The lawyer gave Fred the letter*), those "verb-particle" constructions in which the particle does not occur to the right of the first and only NP (e.g. *The waiter brought in the fish* or *The waiter brought Max in the fish*), and cases in which an NP argument appears to the right of a PP argument. With the exception of the last, these are the cases discussed at the end of the preceding section.

When the structure in question deviates from the canonical form in ways that involve (in declarative sentences) the ordering relations of the tensed element, the resulting structure is both minimally-ordered and syntactically-restricted. It is less easy to see how to determine which element will be taken to be maximal, without listing cases. A single intonational phrase which contains an additional argument to the left of the tensed element will be syntactically focused (cf. Ellen Prince's example *MacaDAMia nuts we call these things* (with no intonation break following *nuts*)). Similarly, inverting "subject" and "predicate" in specificational sentences such as *the author of Waverley is Scott* leaves *Scott* the only focus element. But the directional-adverb preposing cases seem to have a propositional focus, rather than a focus on one or another argument. The criterion stated here requires that such cases be syntactically restricted. Whether the syntactically-designated focus is predictable on general syntactic grounds which do not refer to particular cases remains an open problem.

The passive construction stands outside this classification. If we consider the passive *by*-phrase to be a PP and the passive participle to be analogous to a verb, then the structure of a passive is canonical -- even though it has a minimal focus structure. On the other hand, if we consider the fact that the NP subject of the corresponding active appears to the right of the participle, it has obvious affinities with the more radically-structured cases discussed in the previous paragraph. Perhaps a deeper analysis of focus-interpretation will provide a more inclusive classification in which the passive finds a proper place. A promising line of inquiry, which cannot be pursued here, would be to integrate the approach advanced here with the pragmatic approach beautifully expressed and applied in Atlas and Levinson 1981.

CONCLUSION

It is clear from the examples in this paper that the full range of focus properties are not predictable from properties of order and category alone, nor from semantic properties alone, nor from pragmatic properties of discourse context alone. The focus-structures developed here offer a way to mediate the sometimes conflicting demands that these systems make on focus-interpretation.

Given a conception of focus-structure of the sort developed and defended here, it is possible that properties of focus-structure interact with other grammatical properties. It is well-known, for example, that in English there are interesting constraints on the operation of the relation referred to, for traditional reasons, as wh-movement. If we require that wh-movement is applicable only to arguments of positive rank, we may deduce immediately a number of striking properties. First, wh-movement is inapplicable to the first of two NP arguments to the right of V (since this is not a canonical structure). (Cf. ??*Who did John give 0 the book*, where the symbol "0" indicates that the question involves the argument to *give* which is also satisfiable by the occurrence of an NP in the syntactic position of "0"). Second, wh-movement is inapplicable to any element which occurs between V and a shifted NP. (Cf. ??*Which table did John put on 0 the book you lent me*.)

Third, sentences with syntactically-restricted foci are incompatible with (non-echo) questions, even if there is no movement. (Cf. as non-echo questions: **Into which room walked Jack*, **John did too see who(m)*, **Who(m) did too John see*, **Who(m) did John too see* (on the relevant interpretation, not directly related to *John too saw Zack*).) Since structures with maximally-ordered focus-structures tolerate unmoved question constituents with no difficulty, the oddness of these cases is not easy to explain on standard assumptions. This suggests that the investigation of prominence and the abstract structures which give rise to it may have wider grammatical interest.[9]

NOTES

1. Earlier versions of this paper were presented at SUNY Stony Brook and the University of Pennsylvania in the spring of 1982, at the University of Arizona in the fall of 1982, and at the Instituut voor Algemene Taalwetenschap, Rijksuniversiteit Groningen, in the winter of 1983, where I was supported by a visiting fellowship from ZWO and where the first draft of this paper was written. I am grateful to ZWO and to the members and staff of the ATW in Groningen for material and intellectual support. I would also like to thank Mark Aronoff, Mark Baltin, Jeannette Gundel, Ray Jackendoff, Ellen Prince, and Jack Hoeksema, and especially Crit Cremers and Frans Zwarts, for comments and conversations on the topics covered here. Throughout my research in this area, Susan Steele has been a constant source of encouragement and useful criticism for which I am most grateful.

2. Much more detailed analyses of English intonational phenomena can be found in the works of Liberman and Pierrehumbert cited in the references.

3. Cf. Oehrle, Bach, and Wheeler 1988.

4. Formally, a linear ordering is a relation "<" on the set of components which satisfies the following requirements for any choice of three (not necessarily distinct) components A, B, and C: 1) Trichotomy: A < B or B < A or A=B; 2) Irreflexivity: A < A is impossible; 3) Transitivity: A < B and B < C imply A < C.

5. While the compositional nature of accentuation has been a central problem within the generative tradition from its very beginnings in Chomsky, Halle & Lukoff 1956, the rule suggested for the relation between accent and focus formulated by Ray Jackendoff 1972: 237) is particularly close in spirit to the prin-

ciples adopted here. This rule reads: "If a phrase P is chosen as the focus of a sentence S, the highest stress in S will be on the syllable of P that is assigned highest stress by the regular stress rules." The primary difference between Jackendoff's approach and the approach advocated here is that Jackendoff's "regular stress rules" are replaced by abstract structures, typically partial orderings. Other differences will emerge as we investigate more complex cases.

6. Oehrle 1983 contains a formal account of how this can be achieved.

7. This is to be construed as consisting of a single intonational phrase, exactly like the sentence *In Fred walked*, and distinct from *Into the elevator, Fred walked*, construed as a sequence of two intonational phrases.

8. This analysis is not complete: why is it possible to let the accent fall on *in* in (47), without the possibility of a narrow focus interpretation on *in* (cf. the judgement associated with (46,A2) as a response to (46,Q). There are a number of ways of resolving this problem, but it is impossible to do justice to them all within the scope of this paper.

9. See Erteschik-Shir 1986 and the earlier work of hers cited there for a similar view, based on somewhat different empirical assumptions.

References

Ajdukiewicz, K. (1935). "Syntactic connexion", in S. McCall, (ed.), Polish Logic, 1967, 207-231. Oxford: Oxford University Press. English translation of "Die Syntaktische Konnexitat", Studia Philosophica, Vol. 1, 1-27.

Armstrong, S.L., L.R. Gleitman, and H. Gleitman (1983). "What some concepts might not be". Cognition 17: 263-308.

Atlas, J., and S. Levinson (1981). "It-clefts, informativeness and logical form: radical pragmatics (revised standard version)", in P. Cole (ed.), Radical Pragmatics, 1-61, New York: Academic Press.

Ballard, D and Brown, C. (1982). Computer vision. New Jersey: Prentice-Hall.

Bennett, B., Hoffman, D. and Prakash, C. (1987). "Perception and computation". Proc. IEEEE First International Conf. Computer Vis. 356-364.

Bennett, B., Hoffman, D. and Prakash, C. (1988). Observer mechanics, under review.

Bennett, J. (1976). Linguistic behavior. Cambridge, England: CambridgeUniversity Press.

Berwick, R. (1985). The Acquisition of syntactic knowledge. Cambridge, Massachusetts: MIT Press.

Billingsley, P. (1979). Probability and measure. New York: Wiley & Sons.

Borer, H., and K. Wexler (to appear). "The maturation of syntax", in T. Roeper and E.S. Williams (eds.), Parameter-Setting. Dordrecht: Reidel.

Bransford, J.D., and J.J. Franks (1971). "The abstraction of linguistic ideas". Cognitive Psychology 2: 331-350.

Breiman, L. (1969). Probability and stochastic processes. Boston: Houghton Mifflin.

Bresnan, J.W. (1971). "Sentence stress and syntactic transformations". Language 47: 257-281.

Bryant, P.E., and T. Trabasso (1971). "Transitive inferences and memory in young children". Nature 232: 456-458.

Bullock, M., R. Gelman, and R. Baillargeon (1982). "What some concepts might not be". Cognition 13: 263-308.

Carey, S. (1985). "Cognitive development: The descriptive problem",in M. Gazzaniga (ed.), Handbook for Cognitive Neurology. Hillsdale, NJ: Erlbaum.

Carey, S. (1985a). "Are children fundamentally different thinkers than adults?", in S. Chipman, J. Segal, and R. Glaser (eds.), Thinking and Learning Skills 2: 485-518. Hillsdale, NJ: Erlbaum.

Carey, S. (1985b). Conceptual changes in childhood. Cambridge, Massachusetts: MIT Press.

Chi, M.T.H., R. Glaser, and E. Rees (1982). "Expertise in problem solving", in R.J. Sternberg (ed.), Advances in the Psychology of Human Intelligence, Volume I. Hillsdale, NJ: Erlbaum.

Chomsky, N., M. Halle, and F. Lukoff (1956). "On accent and juncture in English", in For Roman Jakobson, 65-80. The Hague: Mouton.

Chomsky, N. (1965) Aspects of the theory of syntax. Cambridge, Massachusetts: MIT Press.

Chomsky, N., and M. Halle (1968). The sound pattern of English. New York: Harper & Row.

Chomsky, N., and H. Lasnik (1977). "Filters and control". Linguistic Inquiry, 8: .

Chomsky, N. (1986). Barriers. Cambridge, Massachusetts: MIT Press.

Chung, K. (1974). A course in probability theory. New York: Academic Press.

Cohen, B., and G.L. Murphy (1984). "Models of concepts". Cognitive Science 8: 27-60.

Cooper, L.A. (1976). "Individual differences in visual comparison processes". Perception and Psychophysics 19: 433-444.

Cooper, L.A., and P. Podgorny (1976). "Mental transformations and visual comparison processes: Effects of complexity and similarity". Journal of Experimental Psychology: Human Perception and Performance 2: 503-514.

Cooper, L.A. (1980a). "Recent themes in visual information processing: A selected overview", in R.E. Nickerson (ed.), Attention and Performance, Volume VIII, Hillsdale, NJ: Erlbaum.

Cooper, L.A. (1980b). "Spatial information processing: Strategies for research", in R. Snow, P.A. Federico, and W.E. Montague (eds.), Aptitude, Learning, and Instruction: Cognitive Process Analyses. Hillsdale, NJ: Erlbaum.

Cooper, L.A. (1982). "Strategies for visual comparison and representation: Individual differences", in R.J. Sternberg (ed.), Advances in the Psychology of Human Intelligence, Volume I. Hillsdale, NJ: Erlbaum.

Cooper, L.A., and D.T. Regan (1983). "Attention, perception, and intelligence", in R.J. Sternberg (ed.), Handbook of Human Intelligence. New York: Cambridge University Press.

Cooper, L.A., and R.J. Mumaw (1985). "Human spatial aptitude", in R. Dillon and R. Schmitt (eds.), Individual Differences in Cognitive Processes. New York: Academic Press.

Crider, C. (1981). "Children's conceptions of the body interior", in R. Bibace and M. Walsh (eds.), Children's Conceptions of Health, Illness, and Bodily Functions. San Francisco: Jossey-Bass.

Culicover, P., and M. Rochemont (1983). "Stress and focus in English". Language 59: 123-165.

Cunningham, J.P., L.A. Cooper, and C.C. Reaves (1982). "Visual comparison processes: Identity and similarity decisions". Perception and Psychophysics 32: 50-60.

Dennett, D.C. (1969). Content and consciousness. London: Routledge.

Dretske, F. (1972). "Contrastive statements". Philosophical Review 411- 437.

Dretske, F. (1981). Knowledge and the flow of information. Cambridge, Massachusetts: MIT Press.

Erteschik-Shir, N. (1986). "Wh-Questions and focus". Linguistics and Philosophy 9: 117-150.

Field, H. (1977). "Logic, meaning and conceptual role". Journal of Philosophy 74: 379-409.

Flavell, J., E. Flavell, and F. Green (1983). "Development of the appearance reality distinction". Cognitive Psychology 15: 95-1220.

Fodor, J.A. (1968). Psychological explanation: An introduction to the philosophy of psychology. New York: Random House.

Fodor, J.A. (1980). "Methodological solipsism as a reseach strategy in psychology". Behavioral and Brain Sciences, 3. Reprinted in J.A. Fodor, Representations. Cambridge, Massachusetts: Bradford Books/MIT Press. 1981.

Fodor, J.A. (1983). The modularity of mind. Cambridge, Massachusetts: MIT Press.

Fodor, J.A. (1984). "Semantics, Wisconsin style". Synthese 59: 231-250.

Fodor, J.A. (to appear a). "Narrow content and meaning holism".

Fodor, J.A. (to appear b). "Psychosemantics, or Where do truth conditions come from"?

Foster, J.A. (1976). "Meaning and truth theory", in G. Evans and J.McDowell (eds.), Truth and meaning. Oxford: Oxford University Press.

Gibson, J.J. (1979). The ecological approach to visual perception. Boston: Houghton Mifflin Co.

Grimson, W.E.L. (1980). "A computer implementation of a theory of human stereo vision". Phil. Trans. R. Soc. Lond. B292: 217-253.

Gueron, J.S. (1978). "The grammar of PP extraposition". ms, University of Paris VIII.

Halle, M., and S.J. Keyser (1971). English stress: Its form, its growth, and its role in verse. New York: Harper and Row.

Harman, G. (1987). "(Nonsolipsistic) conceptual role semantics", in E. LePore (ed.), New directions in semantics. London: Academic Press.

Harman, G. (1973). Thought. Princeton, NJ: Princeton University Press.

Higgins, F.R. (1973). The English pseudo-cleft construction, Ph.D. dissertation, MIT.

Hildreth, E. (1984). The measurement of visual motion, Cambridge: MIT Press.

Hoffman, D. (1983). "The interpretation of visual illusions". Scientific American 249: 154-162.

Hoffman, D. and B. Flinchbaugh (1982). "The interpretation of biological motion". Biol. Cybernet 42: 195-204.

Hoffman, D. and Bennett, B. (1985). "Inferring the relative three dimensional positions of two moving points". J. Opt. Soc. Am. 2: 350-353.

Hoffman, D., and B. Bennett (1985). "The computation of structure from fixed-axis motion: rigid structures". Biol. Cyb. 54: 71-83.

Horn, B. (1974). "Determining lightness from an image". Comp. Graph. Im. Proc. 3: 277-299.

Horn, B. (1975). "Obtaining shape from shading information", in P. Winston (ed.), The psychology of computer vision, 115-155, New York: McGraw-Hill.

Horn, B. (1985). Robot vision. Cambridge, Massachusetts: MIT Press.

Horn, B. and Schunck, B. (1981). "Determining optical flow". Artif. Intell. 17: 185-203.

Hunt, E., C. Lunneborg, and J. Lewis (1975). "What does it mean to be high verbal?". Cognitive Psychology 7: 194-227.

Hyams, N. (to appear). The acquisition of parameterized grammars. Dordrecht: Riedel.

Ikeuchi, K. and Horn, B. (1981). "Numerical shape from shading and occluding boundaries". Artif. Intell, 17: 141-184.

Jackendoff, R. (1972). Semantic interpretation in generative grammar. Cambridge, Massachusetts: MIT Press

Jacubowicz, C. (1984). "On markedness and binding principles", in C. Jones and P. Sells (eds.), NELS 14. Amherst: University of Massachusetts Graduate Linguistic Student Association.

Johansson, G. (1973). "Visual perception of biological motion and a model for its analysis". Perception & Psychophysics 14: 201-211.

Johansson, G. (1975). "Visual motion perception," Scientific-American 232. 6: 76-88.

Jones, G.V. (1982). "Stacks not fuzzy sets: An ordinal basis for prototype theory of concepts". Cognition 12: 281-290.

Just, M.A., and P.A. Carpenter (1985). "Cognitive coordinate systems: Accounts of mental rotation and individual differences in spatial ability". Psychological Review 92: 137-171.

Kaplan, D. (1979). "On the logic of demonstratives". Journal of Philosophical Logic 8: 81-98. Reprinted in N. Salmon and S. Soames eds.), Propositions and attitudes. Oxford University Press, 1988.

Keil, F.C. (1986). "The acquisition of natural kinds and artifact terms", in A. Marras and W. Demopopoulos (eds.), Language learning and concept acquisition: Foundational Issues. Norwood, NJ: Ablex.

Klein, S. (1982). Syntactic theory and developing grammars. Ph.D. dissertation, UCLA.

Koenderink, J. and van Doorn, A. (1975). "Invariant properties of the motion parallax field due to the movement of rigid bodies relative to an observer". Opt. Acta. 22: 773-791.

Koenderink, J. and van Doorn, A. (1976). "Geometry of binocular vision and a model for stereopsis". Biol. Cyb. 21: 29-35.

Koenderink, J. and van Doorn, A. (1976). "Local structure of movement parallax of the plane". J. Opt. Soc. Am. 66: 717-723.

Koenderink, J. and van Doorn, A. (1980). Photometric invariants related to solid shape," Opt. Acta 22: 773-791.

Koenderink, J. and van Doorn, A. (1981). "Exterospecific component of the motion parallax field." J. Opt. Soc. Am. 71: 953-957.

Koenderink, J. and van Doorn, A. (1986). "Depth and shape from differential perspective in the presence of bending deformations". J. Opt. Soc. Am. A 3: 242-249.

Kosslyn, S.M. (1980). Image and mind. Cambridge, Massachusetts: Harvard University Press.

Kripke, S. (1982). Wittgenstein on rules and private language, Cambridge, Massachusetts: Harvard University Press.

Ladd, D.R. (1980). The structure of intonational meaning, Bloomington: Indiana University Press.

Land, E. and McCann, J. (1971). "Lightness theory". J. Opt. Soc. Am. 61: 1-11.

Lasnik, H. (1985). Presentation at BU Language Acquisition Conference.

Laurendeau, M., and A. Pinard (1962). Causal thinking in the child: A genetic and experimental approach. New York: International Universities Press.

Liberman, M. (1975). The intonational system of English. Ph.D.-dissertation, MIT.

Liberman, M., and J. Pierrehumbert (1984). "Intonational invariance under changes in pitch range and length", in M. Aronoff and R.T. Oehrle (eds.), Language Sound Structure, 157-233. Cambridge, Massachusetts: MIT Press.

Liberman, M., and A. Prince (1977). "On stress and linguistic rhythm". Linguistic Inquiry 8: 249-336.

Lightfoot, D. (1982). The Language lottery. Cambridge, Massachusetts: MIT Press.

Loar, B. (1981). Mind and meaning. Cambridge, England:-Cambridge University Press.

Longuet-Higgins, H. C. (1982). "The role of the vertical dimension in stereoscopic vision". Perception 11: 377-386.

Longuet-Higgins, H. C. and Prazdny, K. (1980). "The interpretation of moving retinal images". Proc. R. Soc. Lond. B208: 385-397.

Lust, B. (to appear). Studies in the acquisition of anaphors: defining the constraints. Dordrecht: Reidel.

Lycan, W.G. (1984). Logical form in natural language. Cambridge, Massachusetts: Bradford Books/MIT Press.

Maloney, L. (1985) Computational approaches to color constancy. Ph.D. dissertation, Stanford.

Marr, D. (1982). Vision. San Francisco: W.H. Freeman Co.

Marr, D. and Poggio, T. (1979) "A computational theory of human-stereo vision". Proc. R. Soc. B204: 301-328.

Marr, D. and Ullman, S. (1981). "Directional selectivity and its use in early visual processing". Proc. R. Soc. Lond. B211: 151-180.

Matthei, E. (1981). "Children's interpretation of sentences containing reciprocals", in S. Tavakolian (ed.) Language acquisition and linguistic theory Cambridge, Massachusetts: MIT Press.

Matthews, R. (to appear). "Formal learning approach to linguistic theory", in R. Matthews, R.W. Demopoulos, and R. May (eds.), Learnability and linguistic theory. Dordrecht: Reidel.

Mayhew, J. (1982). "The interpretation of stereo-disparity information: the computation of surface orientation and depth". Perception 11: 387-403.

Medin, D.L., and M.M. Schaffer (1978). "Context theory of classification learning". Psychological Review 85: 207-238.

Mervis, C.B., and E. Rosch (1981). "Categorization of natural objects". Annual Review Psychology 32: 89-115.

Morris, C. (1946). Signs, language, and behavior. New York.

Nisigauchi, T. and T. Roeper (to appear). "Deductive parameters and the growth of empty categories", in T. Roeper and E.S. Williams (eds.), Parameter-setting. Dordrecht: Reidel.

Oehrle, R.T. (1983). "Focus assignment...". ms., Instituut voor Algemene Taalwetenschap, Rijksuniversiteit Groningen.

Oehrle, R.T., E. Bach, and D. Wheeler (1988). Categorial Grammars and Natural Language Structures. Dordrecht: Reidel.

Osherson, D.N., and E.E. Smith (1981). "On the adequacy of prototype theory as a theory of concepts". Cognition 9: 263-289.

Osherson, D.N., and E.E. Smith (1982). "Gradedness and conceptual combination". Cognition 12: 299-318.

Otsu, Y. (1981). Universal grammar and syntactic development in children. Ph.D. dissertation, MIT.

Papineau, D. (1985). Journal of Philosophy 82: 57-74.

Pellegrino, J.W., and R. Glaser (1979). "Cognitive correlates and components in the analysis of individual differences". Intelligence 3: 187-214.

Pentland, A. P. (1984). "Local shading analysis". IEEE Trans. Patt. Anal. Mach. Intell. PAMI-6: 170-187.

Piaget, J. (1929). The child's conception of the world. London: Routledge and Kegan Paul.

Piaget, J., and B. Inhelder (1941). Le developpement des quantites chez l'enfant. Neuchatel: Delachaux et Niestle.

Pierrehumbert, J. (1980). The phonology and phonetics of English intonation. Ph.D. dissertation, MIT.

Pinker, S. (1984). Language learnability and language development. Cambridge, Massachusetts: Harvard University Press.

Place, U.T. (1956). "Is consciousness a brain process". British Journal of Psychology 47: 44-50.

Poggio, T. Torre, V., and Koch, C. (1985). "Computational vision and regularization theory". Nature 317: 314-319.

Posner, M.I., and S.W. Keele (1968). "On the genesis of abstract ideas". Journal of Experimental Psychology 77: 353-363.

Putnam, H. (1960). "Minds and machines", in Sidney Hook (ed.), Dimensions of mind. New York: NYU Press.

Putnam, H. (1964). "Robots: Machines or artificially created life?". Journal of Philosophy 61: 668-691.

Putnam, H. (1967a). "The mental life of some machines", in H. Castaneda (ed.), Intentionality, minds and perception. Detroit: Wayne University Press.

Putnam, H. (1967b). "Psychological predicates", in Capitan and Merrill (eds.), Art, mind and religion. Pittsburgh: University of Pittsburgh Press.

Putnam, H. (1975). Mind, language and reality: Philosophical papers, Volume 2, 429-440. Cambridge: Cambridge University Press.

Quine, W.V. (1960). Word and object. Cambridge, Massachusetts: MIT Press.

Randall, J. (1985). "Retreat strategies". Presented at Boston University Conferences.

Revuz, D. (1984). Markov chains. Amsterdam: North-Holland.

Richards, W. (1983). "Structure from stereo and motion," Artif. Intell. Lab. Memo 731. Cambridge: MIT.

Rips, L.J. (1988). "Similarity, typicality and categorization", in S. Voisniadou and A. Ortonyl (eds.), Similarity, analogy, and thought. New York: Cambridge University Press.

Rizzi, L. (to appear). "Null objects in Italian and the theory of pro". Linguistic inquiry.

Roeper, T. (1982). "The role of universals in the acquisition of gerunds". in E. Wanner and L. Gleitman (eds.), Language acquisition: The state of the art. Cambridge: Cambridge University Press.

Roeper, T. (1981). "Core grammar and acquisition theory: Connecting triggers and primitives". ms, University of Massachusetts.

Roeper, T., and E.S. Williams (to appear). Parameter-setting. Dordrecht: Reidel.

Roeper, T, M. Rooth, L. Mallis, and S. Akiyama (1985). "On the problem of empty categories in language acquisition". ms, University of Massachusetts.

Rooth, Mats (1984). Association with focus. Ph.D. dissertation, University of Massachusetts at Amherst.

Rubin, J. and Richards, W. (1987). "Spectral categorization of materials", in W. Richards and S. Ullman (eds.), Image Understanding 1985-1986, 20-44. New York: Ablex.

Salmon, N. (1986). "Reflexivity". Notre Dame Journal of Formal Logic 27. Reprinted in N. Salmon and S. Soames (eds.), Propositions and attitudes. Oxford: Oxford University Press. 1988.

Schiffer, S. (1981). "Truth and the theory of content", in H. Parret and J. Bouveresse (eds.), Meaning and understanding, 204-222. Berlin: W. De Gruyter.

Sellars, W. (1954). "Some reflections on language games". Philosophy of Science, 21, 204-228. A revised version appears in Sellars W. (1963). Science, perception, and reality, 321-358. London: Routledge.

Shepard, R.N. (1978). "Externalization of mental image and the act of creation", in B.S. Randhawa and W.E. Coffman (eds.), Visual learning, thinking, and communication. New York: Academic Press.

Shepard, R.N., and L.A. Cooper (1982). Mental images and their transformations. Cambridge, Massachusetts: MIT Press.

Shultz, T.R. (1982). "Rules of causal attribution", in Monographs of the Society for Research in Child Development. Chicago: University of Chicago Press.

Smart, J.J.C. (1968). Between science and philosophy: An Introduction to the philosophy of science. New York: Random House.

Smith, C., S. Carey, and M. Wiser (1985). "On differentiation: A case study of the development of the concepts of size, weight, and density". Cognition 21: 177-237.

Smith, E.E., and D.L. Medin (1981). Categories and concepts. Cambridge, Massachusetts: Harvard University Press.

Smith, E.E., and D.N. Osherson (1984). "Conceptual combination with prototype concepts". Cognitive Science 8: 337-361.

Smith, E.E., D.N. Osherson, L.J. Rips, and M. Keane (1988). "Combining prototypes: A selective modification model". Cognitive Science (in press).

Smith, E.E., E.J. Shoben and L.J. Rips (1974). "Structure and process in semantic memory: A featural model for semantic decisions". Psychological Review 81: 214-241.

Snow, R.E., and D.F. Lohman (1984). "Toward a theory of cognitive aptitude for learning from instruction". Journal of Educational Psychology 76: 347-376.

Soames, S. (1984). "Linguistics and psychology". Linguistics and Philosophy 7: 155-179.

Soames, S. (1985a). "Lost Innocence". Linguistics and Philosophy 8: 59-71.

Soames, S. (1985b). "Semantics and psychology", in J.J. Katz (ed.), The philosophy of linguistics, 204-226. Oxford: Oxford University Press.

Soames, S. (1987). "Direct reference, propositional attitudes, and semantic content". Philosophical Topics 15. Reprinted in N. Salmon and S. Soames (eds.), Propositions and attitudes. Oxford: Oxford University Press. 1988.

Soames, S. (1988). "Direct reference and propositional attitudes", in J. Almog, J. Perry, and H. Wettstein (eds.), Themes from David Kaplan. Oxford: Oxford University Press.

Solan, L. (1983). Pronominal reference: The acquisition of anaphora. Dordrecht: Reidel.

Spearman, C. (1927). The abilities of man. New York: Macmillan.

Stalnaker, R. (1984). Inquiry. Cambridge, Massachusetts: MIT Press.

Stampe, D. (1977). "Toward a causal thoery of linguistic representation". Midwest Studies in Philosophy 2: 42-43.

Sternberg, R.J. (1977). Intelligence, Information Processing and Analogical Reasoning: The Componential Analysis of Human Abilities. Hillsdale, NJ: Erlbaum.

Sternberg, R.J., and E.M. Weil (1980). "An aptitude x strategy interaction in linear syllogistic reasoning". Journal of Educational Psychology 72: 226-236.

Tavakolian, S. (1981). Language acquisition and linguistic theory. Cambridge, Massachusetts: MIT Press.

Taylor, C. (1964). The explanation of behavior. London: Routledge.

Thagard, P. (1984). "Conceptual combination and scientific-discovery", in P. Asquith and P. Kitcher (eds.), PSA, 1. East Lansing: Philosophy of Science Association.

Thurstone, L.L. (1938). "Primary mental abilities". Psychometric Monographs 1.

Tversky, A. (1977). "Features of similarity". Psychological Review 84:327-352.

Ullman, S. (1979). The interpretation of visual motion. Cambridge: MIT Press.

Ullman, S. (1981). "Analysis of visual motion by biological and computer systems". IEEE Computer 14: 57-69.

Ullman, S. (1984). "Maximizing Rigidity: The incremental recovery of 3-D structure from rigid and robbery motion". Perception 13: 255-274.

Waxman, A. and Wohn, K. (1987). "Contour evolution, neighborhood deformation, and image flow; textured surfaces in motion", in W. Richards and S. Ullman (eds.), Image Understanding 1985-86, 72-98. New Jersey: Ablex.

Webb, J. and Aggarwal, J. (1981). "Visually interpreting the motion of objects in space". IEEE Computer 14: 40-46.

Wexler, and R. Manzini (to appear). "Parameters and Learnability", in T. Roeper and E. S. Williams (eds.), Parameter-setting. Dordrecht: Reidel.

Williams, E.S. (1981). "X-bar features and acquisition". in S. Tavakolian (eds.), Language acquisition and linguistic theory. Cambridge, Massachusetts: MIT Press.

Williams, E.S. (to appear). "Introduction", in T. Roeper and E.S. Williams (eds.), Parameter-setting. Dordrecht: Reidel.

Zadeh, L. (1965). "Fuzzy sets". Information and Control 8: 338-353.

Zadeh, L. (1982). "A note on prototype theory and fuzzy sets." Cognition 12: 291-297.